5-2-73

Atencingo

Atencingo

The Politics of Agrarian Struggle in a Mexican Ejido

David Ronfeldt

Stanford University Press, Stanford, California 1973

Stanford University Press
Stanford, California
© 1973 by the Board of Trustees of the
Leland Stanford Junior University
Printed in the United States of America
ISBN 0-8047-0820-7
LC 74-190528

1748438

Dedicated here to
my father and mother,
my brother and his family,
and my sister and her family

Dedicated there to
the peasants of Atencingo and annexes

Preface

The materials for this study were gathered in Mexico during 1968 and 1969, specifically in Mexico City, in the state capital of Puebla, and in the region of Atencingo. They principally include informal tape-recorded interviews and conversations with various peasants and peasant leaders in the Atencingo region; petitions and documents composed by peasants during their various struggles; numerous government documents, letters, and reports, mostly from the Archives of the Department of Agrarian Affairs and Colonization (DAAC) and from the National Peasants' Confederation (CNC); periodical clippings; informal interviews and conversations with a few government functionaries, newspaper reporters, certain friends in the Atencingo region, and former managers of the ejidal cooperative society; and letters and documents from the archives of the leftist Independent Peasants' Confederation (CCI).

In collecting the DAAC material I tape-recorded extensive field notes and quotations from the DAAC archives and then transcribed them into "Field Notes on the DAAC Archives," cited here as FNDA with the page number the material in question appears on. Other archival materials have been arranged as follows: "Materials from the Archives of Pedro Bueno and Alfredo Carranza" (MAPBAC), provided by two peasant leaders of the opposition in the Ejido of Atencingo and Annexes; "Materials from the Archives of Esteban Martínez" (MAEM), containing some important historical memoranda and observations written by an outsider; "Materials from an Archive on a CNC Investigation" (MACNCI); "Field Notes on 1969 General Assemblies" (FNGA), taken by me at four different assemblies; and "Field Notes on the CCI Archives" (FNCCI).

As a rule interviewees and persons whose archives I consulted are cited in the Notes by false names to preserve their anonymity. The exceptions are those whose identity is obvious from the text. They are cited by their real names, denoted by the addition of "Sr." at the first mention. Correct names are used in the citations to all books, all petitions, all letters, and most personal memoranda. Scholars who undertake further research in the area may consult me about the identity of persons whose names I have altered.

Professor Richard Fagen and Professor Robert Packenham provided valuable commentary and hearty support. Parker Palmer, Kathy Robinson, John Shelton, Linda Stevens, and Aunt Connie Zetterberg gave technical and secretarial assistance I greatly needed and appreciated during an earlier stage of this work. Ellen Hershey made numerous excellent improvements in the manuscript as the editor for Stanford University Press. Each deserves a special word of thanks. I also want to thank Stanford University's Committee on International Studies and the Ford Foundation for their financial support. Finally, I am exceedingly grateful to my Mexican friends, who treated me superbly during my stay in their country. Their help was indispensable; yet I alone am directly responsible for the contents of this book.

D.R.

Contents

Atencingo

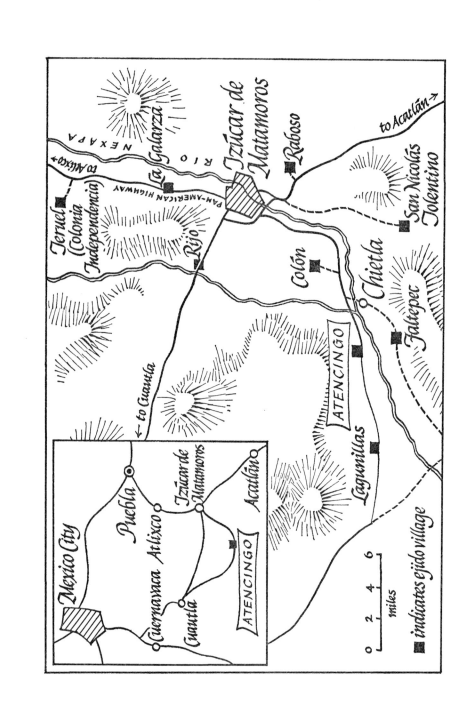

CHAPTER ONE

Introduction

The geographic focus of our attention is the warm, fertile, river-laced valley of Matamoros and its large municipalities, Matamoros and Chietla, in the state of Puebla, Mexico.* The valley lies directly southeast of Mexico City, on the opposite side of a volcanic mountain range. It extends some 30 to 35 miles roughly northeast to southwest, and its width averages some four miles. Both the old Mexico City–Cuautla–Puebla railroad line and the important Pan-American highway pass through the valley. The southwestern end forms the boundary with the state of Morelos, Mexico's historic heartland of cane agriculture, sugar industry, and Zapatismo,† while the northeastern end approaches the city of Atlixco, renowned for its textile mills and for violent labor union agitation during the 1920's and 1930's.

Seventy to eighty thousand people live in the valley, mostly in villages but also in the large towns of Matamoros, Chietla, and Atencingo. Agricultural occupations predominate. The principal cash crop is sugar cane, and the cane harvest brings the fullest employment for field laborers. The major industrial establishment in the region is the privately owned sugar mill at Atencingo, which employs a number of men living in Atencingo and in the village of Lagunillas. In addi-

---

* The municipality is the smallest autonomous political and administrative unit in the Mexican federation.

† The great agrarian revolutionary Emiliano Zapata was born in Morelos in 1879 and died there in 1919. His land reform movement was initially based among the peasants and Indians of the state's cane growing regions, spreading later to other states.

tion the Bacardi Company operates in La Galarza a small but important fermentation plant for its famous rum, using the alcoholic by-
products of the Atencingo sugar mill. A few residents of La Galarza
work there. Several small gypsum and limestone plants dot the area,
but they employ very few people (though they produce excellent
profits for their owners). The biggest local nonindustrial business, in
terms of the quantities of money and people involved, is the credit
society of the cane producing Ejido of Atencingo and Annexes—the
ejido focused on in this study.* Together the fertile cane lands, the
huge ejido, its credit society, and the sugar mill constitute the most
important agricultural-industrial complex in the state of Puebla and
one of the most valuable sugar production centers in Mexico.

Situated in the heart of the valley is Izúcar de Matamoros (or just
Matamoros), with a population of about twenty thousand. It is the
political center of the municipality of Matamoros, and the area's largest
and most modern town, currently featuring among other things a
well-kept *zócalo* (central town square), a well-built marketplace, a
number of recently constructed buildings, paved roads throughout, a
wide variety of shops and businesses, several bus terminals, the valley's
major secondary school, and a complex telephone installation.

Some twelve miles west along a paved road linked to the Pan-
American highway one descends to the smaller, poorer, tree-sheltered
town of Chietla, lying slightly off the main route. A town of about
six thousand people, Chietla is the political center of the municipality
of Chietla. It has no paved roads, few recently constructed homes or
other buildings, and no secondary school. Here one sees fewer signs
than in Matamoros of middle-class well-being, economic enterprise,
and progress, and many more signs of poverty.

---

* An ejido is a tract of land controlled by a group of peasants as the result of a
Mexican land reform process in which the title to certain agricultural property is
granted by the government to the peasants' village or other residential unit. Depending
on the ejido, the land may be farmed collectively or distributed as individual or family
plots. Locally, ejidal affairs are regulated by a three-man ejidal commissariat elected
by the member ejidatarios. The granting of ejidos by the government, the rights of the
ejidatarios, and the conduct of ejidal affairs are subject to the federal Agrarian Code.
For a basic discussion see François Chevalier, "The *Ejido* and Political Stability in
Mexico," in Claudio Veliz, ed., *The Politics of Conformity in Latin America* (London,
1967), pp. 158–91. For the Agrarian Code, see *Código agrario de los Estados Unidos
Mexicanos* (Mexico City, 1968); it is not available in translation.

Another mile along the road one encounters Atencingo, where some 7,500 people live. Atencingo seems more like an unnatural population center than like a real town or community. It has no zócalo. It has instead its semitropical heat, the fortresslike sugar mill with three stacks, the offices of the mill workers' union, some political and police offices, the offices and buildings and auditorium of the local ejidal credit society of the Ejido of Atencingo and Annexes, lots of the credit society's trucks and tractors and other machinery parked or moving about, one smallish cathedral, some cloth awnings demarcating a market zone, a few businesses and shops, numerous small one-story adobe dwellings, and constant reminders of poverty. All is scattered spaciously alongside the railroad tracks and the single paved road that jab through the locality. Whereas Matamoros seemed to bustle and Chietla to brood, Atencingo seems to vibrate softly and tensely: the mill rattles and churns, off-duty workers enjoy a noisy basketball game, adolescents veer their rackety motorcycles along the road, fancy cars occasionally pass by on officious missions, state police eye the situation, soldiers guard the gate to the mill, and peasants roam about on errands or simply sit watching and whispering. Atencingo used to be a hacienda; it was never intended to be a large Mexican town.

Elsewhere about the valley numerous small villages and hamlets continue their decades and even centuries of impoverished existence, though in general their residents enjoy a higher standard of living than the averages for the state and nation. Eight of these villages belong to the Atencingo ejidal system, in addition to Atencingo itself. They are Lagunillas and Jaltepec, which like Atencingo are in the municipality of Chietla; Rijo, in the small municipality of Tilapa; Colón, originally in the municipality of Tilapa but designated part of the municipality of Matamoros during a redistricting in the 1940's; San Nicolás Tolentino, Raboso, and La Galarza, all in the municipality of Matamoros; and Colonia Independencia, a community established by government authorization in the late 1940's and populated by former residents of the village of Teruel, in the small municipality of Tepeojuma. None of these communities are nearly as large as Atencingo; they range in population from about seven hundred up to

TABLE I

Population and Number of Ejidal Rights Granted
in Villages of the Atencingo Ejido

Village	Population			Ejidal rights		
	1940	1950	1960	1938	1954	1969
Atencingo	2,390	4,456	6,330	264	349	320
Lagunillas	421	832	1,781	377	400	480
Jaltepec	174	257	155	319	332	330
Raboso	1,239	1,321	1,726	238	246	246
La Galarza	736	972	1,543	233	292	290
San Nicolás Tolentino	770	1,057	1,302	222	247	235
Colón	550	604	898	134	166	148
Rijo	325	302	701	87	126	108
Teruel (Colonia Independencia)	165	429	789	169	171	172
TOTAL	6,770	10,230	15,225	2,043	2,329	2,329

SOURCES: For the population figures, Dirección General de Estadística, *Censo general de la población, resumen 1940, 1950, 1960*. The ejidal rights figures for 1938 are from an official file supplied by Gabriel Cardoso Leyva in the offices of the Agrarian Delegation in Puebla; for 1954, from an undated [1968?] DAAC memorandum by Jesús Miranda, FNDA, p. 338; for 1969, from data provided by Augustín Vazquez, comptroller of the local ejidal credit society, except for the Raboso and Teruel figures, which were estimated from comments made by ejidatarios and are accurate within plus or minus three.

NOTE: The figures for ejidal rights include the one right granted to the primary school in each village. Although the total number of rights remained the same in 1969 as in 1954, the number in each village changed owing to a reallocation of rights that required some families to move from one village to another.

about two thousand. Table 1 shows population figures for the Atencingo ejidal villages and the number of memberships in the ejido, or ejidal rights, granted to heads of households or other eligible persons during the past three decades.

Politically speaking, the peasants in these villages have undergone a long series of struggles for control of the area's land, labor, and production. This intriguing history of struggle extends from before the Mexican Revolution began in 1910 to the present day; indeed, when I was in Mexico collecting information during 1968 and 1969, Atencingo was still one of the most serious agrarian trouble spots in the country. The struggles have involved Mexico's most powerful political and economic elites as well as the humblest peasants. The major institutions and organizations that have taken part are the privately owned Atencingo sugar mill; the Atencingo ejido, which by law must be worked collectively and supply cane to the mill; the cooperative and subsequently the credit society that have administered the agricultural and financial operations of the ejido; and the state and federal governments with their party organs. In addition, certain leftist peasant defense organizations have played a lesser role. The principal individual and group participants have been the peasants in the Atencingo ejido and its cooperative (or credit) society; neighboring peasants, many of them landless and land-hungry; private landowners, particularly those whose properties were expropriated to form the ejido; the capitalist entrepreneurs and administrators of the sugar mill; and numerous government officials and authorities. Others are the mill workers and the leaders of independent leftist peasant defense organizations.

Historically, the peasants have been pitted successively against the landowners, against the mill administration, against the state and federal authorities (though government has sometimes been an ally), and even against each other, with control of the ejido as the lucrative prize. The various struggles have developed from fundamental conflicts of interest and opinion about such issues as agrarian reform, agricultural development, and the exercise of political and economic influence. Confrontations between the adversaries have often led to violence.

This study's purpose is to analyze the causes and consequences of political struggle in the revealing Atencingo case. Unfortunately, the evidence is far from complete. For example, material on the role of the Agrarian Department (later to become the Department of Agrarian Affairs and Colonization, or DAAC) in Atencingo is plentiful, the DAAC archives having supplied some of the most interesting and revealing sources used in the study, but relatively little is available about the roles of other government agencies. Partly because of this gap in the evidence, the narrative concentrates heavily on the Agrarian Department. My experience in the field similarly left some ground uncovered. I had considerable contact with the Atencingo

peasants, but only limited contact with government and party officials, and no contact with the administrators of the sugar mill, who
did not wish to be interviewed. As a result the peasants' point of view
is reflected here perhaps more than it ideally should be. But if some
gaps remain, the history of the Atencingo case can nonetheless be
reconstructed, much as an ancient mosaic can be visualized even
though many of its pieces have been lost. The investigator must work
with what he has at hand; if he can locate enough pieces from enough
important areas of the original picture, he may be able to see fairly
well what it once showed.

As the evidence is assembled, and as the central theme—the politics
of agrarian struggle in Atencingo—takes shape, a number of important subthemes begin to emerge. These include the conflicts between the official criteria for national economic development and the
peasants' conceptions of economic and political liberation; the effectiveness of forceful—but respectful—direct actions by the peasants in
conjunction with regular bureaucratic politicking; the critical role of
the peasants' middle- and high-level political allies; the efforts of the
state and federal governments to control and coopt the peasants; the
transformation of struggles for policy change into struggles for power;
and the attraction of independent leftist organizations as allies to the
peasants. As these and other subthemes become clear, they are high-
lighted in the concluding sections that end each chapter.

Ultimately the analysis turns on questions of political strategy. The
final chapter offers a comprehensive interpretation of the politics of
agrarian struggle in terms of strategy and tactics. It covers the determinative nature of the political and strategic context in which agrarian struggles develop; the particular strategy and tactics most effective for peasants in opposition; the counterstrategy and countertactics
most effective for the dominant elites; and the historical consequences
of the interactions between the groups.

CHAPTER TWO

Revolution and Agrarian Reform, 1910-1938

The early history of the valley of Matamoros followed closely the pattern for the rest of Mexico. Though the valley now shows little evidence of Indian cultural traditions, the Indians were its first residents and landowners. Like most Indians in that part of Mexico, they organized their economy and society according to a communal system called the ejido. Later, after Cortés, the Spanish conquerors, colonizers, and missionaries descended on the area. Enterprising Spaniards brought in sugar cane, tested its production for profit, and reaped bountiful success. The first mill in the future state of Puebla was constructed in the valley, and it was eventually followed by a number of others. Indian labor was exploited, initially through the encomienda system and later through the hacienda system.

During the nineteenth century the valley of Matamoros became one of Mexico's important sugar producing regions. In order to acquire the extensive land tracts needed for profitable cane agriculture, the Spanish (and some French) hacendados deprived the peasant villagers of their holdings. The Ley Lerdo, promulgated during the presidency of Benito Juárez, allowed the distribution of communal lands that had traditionally belonged to Indian and peasant villages. The hacendados acquired these lands particularly during the Porfiriato. In addition they bought or seized private lands that belonged to individual Indian and mestizo peasants.

To process the cane on his property, almost every hacendado constructed his own small sugar mill. The largest in the valley was at Atencingo. For decades these mills were quite crude, but during the rapid modernizing period of the Porfiriato, the hacendados began to industrialize their operations by introducing water power, electricity, and new machinery. As a private labor force, each owner acquired a group of peons who were obligated to live and work on the hacienda. They were kept in virtual servitude, being forced to work long hours and to abide by certain customs, such as singing a devotional song for the hacendado's particular saint before they started the day's work. Unruly and rebellious peons were immediately consigned to the army or to hard construction labor for the government in Valle Nacional. The hacendados could depend on the support of the central government against any serious disruptions within their domains. Indeed, virtually all had important economic influence in the state, and some held high political posts as well.[1]

Thus by the onset of the Revolution in 1910, the haciendas in the valley had become agricultural and industrial enterprises that nourished the wealth, status, and power of the hacendado and his peers by authoritarian and exploitative means. Meanwhile, in the surrounding villages, impoverished farmers and now-landless peasants turned envious, calculating thoughts toward the hacendados' lands.

A Capitalist Entrepreneur

During the violence of the Revolution, local insurgents and Zapatista forces—some of them from neighboring Morelos—burned the small sugar mills, vandalized the haciendas, and chased away the landowners. Cane cultivation halted until the early 1920's, and no mill was rebuilt until 1921. In the interim work patterns changed dramatically, as peasants from the villages invaded the haciendas and cultivated subsistence crops of corn and beans on the former cane lands, which still legally belonged to the hacendados.[2]

Eventually the hacendados ventured a return to their properties. But in trying to rebuild their agricultural enterprises, they were beset not only by a multitude of hostile peasants under Zapatista leadership but by a former American consul, William Jenkins. The hacendados were no match either for the turbulent revolutionary situation or for

Jenkins. In the ensuing struggle over their lands, it was Jenkins, not the Mexican revolutionaries, who emerged the victor. As a result the semifeudal capitalism that had characterized the valley's prerevolutionary economy was superseded by a capitalistic monopoly.

As consul, Jenkins had already gained considerable wealth and political influence, and he had already demonstrated his administrative craft. In 1919, while he was stationed in Puebla, the capital of the state of Puebla, Jenkins had been kidnapped by two Zapatista generals. He was freed only after an international crisis, during which the United States government paid a sizable ransom and entertained the idea of intervening to halt the Mexican Revolution.[3] Supposedly it was thus that Jenkins began to amass his fortune, for he is said to have engineered the kidnapping, splitting the ransom with his captors. He also augmented his wealth by means of some nonagricultural business investments. But what turned him into one of Mexico's most wealthy and powerful men was his subsequent exploits in Puebla's fertile valley of Matamoros.[4]

Jenkins started his empire in the valley in 1921, when he purchased the mill and lands of the hacienda of Atencingo, owned by the Díaz Rubín family. Manuel Díaz Rubín, a former millionaire, had been one of the first hacendados to return after the Constitutionalist Army began to pacify the region in 1916 and 1917. He planned to rebuild his mill and to renew cane agriculture in his fields. The events of the Revolution had depleted his funds, however, and lacking the investment capital necessary to carry out his plans on a large scale, he was forced to settle for a limited agricultural operation. Then Jenkins appeared and proffered a loan. Díaz Rubín accepted, putting up his property as collateral. Instead of enjoying renewed prosperity, however, he was soon faced with financial ruin. Jenkins, seeing his opportunity, foreclosed on the loan and became the owner of the valuable property.

Next Jenkins turned his attention to the other deteriorated haciendas and mills in the valley. In order to force the owners to sell, he brought off a series of similar financial power plays. Moreover, he took advantage of renewed agitation for agrarian reform among the Zapatista villagers during the early 1920's. Apparently Jenkins not

only convinced the local insurgents temporarily to leave him unmolested, but also encouraged them to put pressure on the remaining
hacendados in the region. When a hacendado was at the point of
ruin, Jenkins appeared as a financial rescuer. Cooperation with him,
Jenkins told the hacendados, would bring the same tranquility that
reigned on his own hacienda and among his own workers; moreover,
he said, owing to his excellent relationship with the government, he
did not expect to be affected by the agrarian reform laws. The hacendados succumbed. Soon Jenkins secured direct ownership or indirect
control of all the cane haciendas and mills in the valley.

Within only a few years during the early 1920's, then, Jenkins successfully formed and centralized the vast Atencingo system, the greatest concentration of land under a single owner in the history of
Puebla. The system comprised the lands of eleven haciendas, other
smaller properties, and all but one of the small mills.* Altogether
Jenkins's properties spread over some 123,000 hectares; they not only
included most of the valley's cultivable lands but included all of its
best crop lands (about 15,000 hectares). To organize and centralize
the system with himself at the apex, Jenkins meanwhile established
his Civil and Industrial Company of Atencingo. He also began to
reconstruct the Atencingo mill so that it could serve as the one central
mill for the entire region. The other mills were stripped, and their
equipment removed to Atencingo.[5]

Jenkins next moved to make the system productive. The key problem was to find a knowledgeable cane agriculturalist who could also
manage the enterprise ably. Jenkins's first and second choices proved
inadequate to the job. Finally he turned to Manuel Pérez, a Spaniard
who was reputed to be Mexico's best cane agronomist but who had
managed his own properties badly. Pérez accepted Jenkins's offer and
at Atencingo displayed such admirable administrative capacity that
he continued to manage the mill until his fatal illness some twenty
years later.

Pérez dedicated himself eagerly to the problem of productivity—

---

* Jenkins did not actually hold the title to the small mill at Raboso until the middle
of the 1930's; before then it was operated by the original hacendado (collective interview with ejidatarios of Raboso, May 23, 1969).

no mean task, for the lands and mill had lain virtually idle from 1910 to 1922. First, he undertook the arduous labor of preparing the fields for cultivation without tractors and other machinery, which had not yet appeared on the market. Second, he imported and planted for the first time in Mexico new and superior varieties of cane that had been developed abroad. Third, he built a private railroad network linking the extensive fields to the mill and connecting with the Mexico City–Cuautla–Puebla railroad line. Fourth, he totally reconstructed and enlarged the Atencingo mill, once burned and destroyed by the Zapatistas. Finally, he installed a vast irrigation system (including canals, aqueducts, and small dams), supplied by various rivers and wells, to serve the fertile heartlands of the haciendas.

These improvements required years of labor, but Pérez was eminently successful. Naturally productivity was low at first. Before the Revolution the fields had produced an average of 64 tons of cane per hectare. Returned to cultivation after the revolutionary anarchy, they yielded 78 tons per hectare in 1924 and 85 in 1927. By the early 1930's, however, as a result of Pérez's astute guidance, Jenkins's enterprise was flourishing. Some 120 tons per hectare were harvested in 1931, and 161 in 1934. The mill was said to have become the most productive in Mexico, and the fields to have produced the highest yield in all Latin America. Furthermore, Jenkins's income from sugar was greatly enhanced by illicit sales in the United States of contraband alcohol produced at Atencingo as a by-product. Now a millionaire, he also enjoyed the friendship and support of powerful political elites.[6]

Pressures for Land Reform

Meanwhile, during the 1920's and 1930's, popular pressures for land reform mounted. The targets, of course, were the valley's haciendas and the men who controlled them—first the weakened hacendados and subsequently Jenkins and Pérez. In the surrounding villages Zapatista leaders agitated and organized among a multitude of landless, restless peasants. Many of them (or their fathers) had once cultivated plots seized years before by the hacendados. Others had lost their property as a result of having fled the area during the early violence of the Revolution.[7] Having lost their former means of support, most of them had turned to Jenkins's company for occasional employment as wage laborers at the mill or in the fields. Now by the hundreds, and later by the thousands, they rallied and organized to press for land reform and ejidal grants.

Of course, Jenkins and Pérez resisted. In general, they exercised stringent control over their principal labor forces, the peons on the haciendas and the permanent mill workers. These groups remained relatively quiescent until the early 1930's. In fact, for many years the peons attached to the haciendas had little reason to join the land reformers in the villages, for until the mid-1930's they were not legally permitted, as were the villagers, to petition for ejidal grants. Allied with Puebla's political leaders, Jenkins and Pérez also wielded forceful political and economic influence in the villages,[8] though they were not influential enough to crush the Zapatista organizers there.

The principal leaders of the land-hungry villagers were Celestino Espinosa Flores and his wife, Dolores Campos, the famed "Doña Lola." Celestino was the son of a livestock rancher who lived near Chietla. Doña Lola had been born in 1878 to peasants living in a settlement on the hacienda of San Nicolás Tolentino, where they sustained themselves by subsistence farming and by raising a few livestock. Through her own determination, she had learned reading, writing, and simple arithmetic from a lady who taught her in exchange for Doña Lola's service in her household. She thus became useful to her father in his business as a renter of horses, and traveled with him throughout the villages and work centers. She also learned how to shoot a gun, as protection against bandits and ruffians on the roads.

Doña Lola and Celestino Espinosa were married in 1895. During the peaceful years of the late Porfiriato, they prospered as farmers and livestock ranchers. Then the Revolution arrived in 1910. The newly installed president, Francisco I. Madero, was murdered, and unfortunately Gen. Victoriano Huerta seized power. This reactionary dictator imposed an unpopular levy and ordered the burning of settlements and crops in retaliation against the Zapatista insurgents. Having suffered some losses, Celestino and Doña Lola, like other small ranchers, moved their livestock into the hills, where it helped sustain the

Zapatista forces. Meanwhile, the couple continued to reside at their house in Chietla.

Celestino had numerous friends among the Zapatistas, and even became acquainted with General Zapata himself. Sympathizing with Zapata's ideals, Celestino and Doña Lola and their son Rafael (born in 1896) soon became fiercely loyal partisans, supporting the agrarian movement politically and economically despite the retaliations of Huertista officials. In later years, even after the assassination of Zapata in 1919, the family continued to supply provisions to the dwindling revolutionary forces. Moreover, Doña Lola, serving as secretary for her illiterate husband, addressed inspirational letters to them.

Finally, in 1920, Gen. Alvaro Obregón began his term as president (1920–24), and soon thereafter new agrarian laws were enacted that won the support of many Zapatistas. In 1922 Celestino received instructions from a Zapatista leader, Antonio Díaz Soto y Gama, to organize peasants in the nearby villages and settlements to press for the redistribution of land in accordance with the new laws. In some villages Celestino's efforts were well received, but in others they encountered marked hostility. In general, only those peasants who had fought in the Revolution offered support. Finally, after great difficulty, Celestino, his wife, and his small coterie succeeded in organizing groups in some twenty villages and settlements.

Once organized, Celestino's groups drew up petitions for ejidal grants of hacienda lands and submitted them to the state governor. Not surprisingly, a legal battle ensued as the landlords sought to defend their holdings. They argued that residents of settlements located within the haciendas had no right to demand land grants, since by law petitions for such grants had to be made in the name of a village that constituted a legal political entity. Doña Lola accordingly studied the laws and drew up documents to solicit from the state governor a ruling that would recognize the independent political status of the hacienda settlements. With one exception, she won her case. Nevertheless, time passed and the grants were not given.

As a next step, the majority of the impoverished towns, villages, and settlements agreed to name Celestino Espinosa their general representative to lobby in Puebla for a satisfactory response to their petitions. His house in Chietla became a busy headquarters. Neither he nor Doña Lola asked for financial compensation for their services, and they had to sell some of their property in order to survive. In late 1923 Celestino and about three hundred men left the area for some months to help put down the rebellion of Don Adolfo de la Huerta against President Obregón. Soon after their return Celestino and his companions renewed their local campaign for land. At last they were rewarded with several ejidal grants by the federal government, which ordered the expropriation of certain hacienda lands.

The irate administrators retaliated by obtaining protective amparos* and by trying to bribe the authorities. Some yielded to temptation, with the result that alterations were made in the boundaries of the new ejidos. Still, the peasants could claim a partial victory. As they continued their petitioning, however, a wave of terror swept their communities, bringing the deaths of several agrarian officials and constant threats to Celestino and Doña Lola.

Celestino died from an illness in late 1924, and his peasant followers named his son Rafael his successor. Soon afterward the hacendados unsuccessfully sought to intimidate Rafael with death threats. Next Pérez tried to bribe him and his mother, Doña Lola, with large sums of money, but they spurned the offer. Finally Pérez hired an assassin to kill Rafael, but Rafael killed the assassin instead. The peasants continued to voice their demands, with the result that Rafael was put in jail. While he was in jail and the peasants were trying to secure his release, Doña Lola became very ill. Pérez offered her money for medicine and the freedom of her son as a bribe. She scorned the temptation, saying she would rather die than accept Pérez's money and that her son would one day be free. Eventually his followers did obtain his freedom.

Later Pérez sent some of his workers to invade the lands of the Chietla ejido, held by Rafael and his followers. Planting a flag on the ejidal lands, Rafael and a number of peasant defenders turned back

---

* The amparo, a very important legal device in the Mexican system, is "a writ calling for a stay of government action"; it resembles the writ of injunction and the writ of habeas corpus in Anglo-Saxon law. L. Vincent Padgett, *The Mexican Political System* (Boston, 1966), pp. 148–49.

the tractors and the scared drivers sent by the mill administration. But soon after, during early 1929, Pérez finally won a round: the obstinate Rafael was murdered in the streets of Chietla by paid assassins, who also managed to wound Doña Lola.

Undaunted, Doña Lola assumed the task of leadership, along with her socialist daughter, and pressed the struggle against Jenkins's and Pérez's monopoly. On one front, during the early 1930's, she and her peasant allies helped sympathetic mill workers (many of whom were villagers) organize an independent underground labor union, the Karl Marx Syndicate, some of whose leaders and members were affiliated with the Regional Confederation of Mexican Workers (CROM). Apparently the impetus for the unionization effort came not only from opposition to Jenkins and Pérez but also from efforts by the large and nationally powerful CROM to penetrate the Atencingo region. The new syndicate survived only about a year, for Pérez managed to undermine and coopt it. Nevertheless, Doña Lola's temporary success infuriated Pérez, who now regarded her and her daughter as mortal enemies.

Elsewhere in the region Doña Lola also counted the primary school teachers among her allies. She had been instrumental in securing the appointment of a brigade of teachers for the area, though the school buildings were actually constructed with money provided by the mill administration. Apparently because of their support for Doña Lola's movement, the teachers received death threats and warnings to abandon their schools. Doña Lola countered by assigning small groups of peasants to guard them.

On the main front, meanwhile, she guided efforts by the remaining landless villages and peasants to petition for their own ejidos from the lands of Jenkins's company. Finally, during the presidency of Gen. Abelardo Rodríguez (1932–34), the political climate in Puebla changed, perhaps because future president Lázaro Cárdenas was military zone commander and thus available as a political broker. Villages' petitions were attended to, and new ejidal grants from additional sections of Jenkins's holdings were made by presidential decree. Even so, several thousand landless peasants still remained in the villages.[9]

Confrontation and Climax

By the mid-1930's, then, Jenkins had reportedly been divested of more than 90 percent (115,068 hectares) of his total holdings (123,401 hectares). The lands had been expropriated at the behest of Doña Lola and her allies in order to grant ejidos to forty villages and hamlets that had filed petitions.[10] Nevertheless, Jenkins's wealth remained virtually intact in the form of the irrigated cane growing heartlands of nine haciendas plus the central mill, altogether regarded as the single most important agricultural and industrial unit in the state of Puebla, and the most productive sugar enterprise in Mexico. In other words, the expropriations had affected only Jenkins's less desirable holdings—his hills and his less fertile or unirrigated lands.

While thus holding the villagers at bay, Jenkins and Pérez also kept tight control over their principal labor force in the fields and the mill, namely the wage-earning peons and workers who resided on the haciendas. In 1934 President Rodríguez promulgated a law extending to resident peons the right to petition for lands just as the villagers did. But no peons filed petitions in the Atencingo region, whether from ignorance or from fear. Certainly Doña Lola found very few adherents among the peons,[11] though she had support among the mill workers. Jenkins and Pérez, moreover, were able through their employment practices to obstruct land-hungry outsiders from establishing themselves as resident peons eligible to petition for a land grant. During seasons when the resident labor force was insufficient, the mill employees were dispatched to the villages to recruit temporary work gangs. These wage-labor fieldworkers were rotated every two weeks or so from hacienda to hacienda, so that they did not spend enough time in any given place to establish themselves legally as customary or resident users of the land. Owing to a labor surplus in the region, Pérez could readily recruit temporary outside laborers, locate replacements for unsatisfactory ones, and subject those already employed to working conditions they might otherwise have objected to.[12]

Jenkins and Pérez even controlled the local labor organization. Instead of completely eliminating the original labor syndicate at the mill, Pérez coopted it, maintaining his control in succeeding years under various guises. All the resident mill workers and peons, and the many men who alternated between the two roles, were regarded as members of the syndicate, whose leaders collaborated closely with the mill administrators. Dissidents and agitators were either expelled or murdered, and organizers from established labor unions and confederations had limited success in the region. Nevertheless, Jenkins and Pérez apparently permitted at least a semblance of affiliation with the government-favored Regional Federation of Workers and Peasants (FROC) at the state level, and through it, the new semiofficial Mexican Workers' Confederation (CTM) at the national level.*

In 1937, however, pressures from above and below mounted against the powerful millionaire. On the one hand, President Cárdenas was preparing a sweeping national land reform program; on the other, the several thousand landless village peasants who remained in the Atencingo region were demonstrating increasing impatience, militance, and strength. Since most of these landless peasants lived in villages that had already been granted ejidos, the local ejidal authorities now petitioned for the enlargement of existing ejidos or the formation of new ones to accommodate them.

At first Doña Lola and her forces seemed to triumph. Sometime after President Cárdenas assumed office in 1934, an ally and active supporter of Doña Lola, Gil Vega, became head of the municipal council of Chietla after a turbulent electoral campaign during which state officials intervened to maintain order. Gil Vega's assumption of office was a marked setback for Jenkins and Pérez, for in the ensuing months the open support of the municipal government for the villagers' petitions commanded the attention of state and federal authorities. Eventually Doña Lola and her followers secured an audience

---

* Interview with Juan Gómez, a former ejidatario, 31.vii.69; interview with Francisco Aguilar, ejidatario, 28.vii.69. My data on this subject are sparse and somewhat indefinite. Apparently there were some serious disturbances within the local union in 1935, in part because of rivalries involving a FROC organizer, who was eventually murdered, and in part because of agitation by allies of Doña Lola. The local agitation may have been caused not only by local unrest but by severe competition between the CROM and the FROC throughout Puebla. The FROC was the state-level affiliate of the CTM, and the CTM was formed and led by the prestigious Marxist and former CROM member Vicente Lombardo Toledano.

with President Cárdenas. Sympathizing with their plight, he agreed that they—the only petitioners to that date—should indeed receive the lands. Sometime during the middle of 1937 (apparently in June), he ordered the Agrarian Department to attend to the expropriation and allotment of Jenkins's holdings. The joyful villagers thought they had finally won their struggle.[13]

Jenkins recognized that the political and insurgent pressures against him had at last become uncontainable. Yet if he was bound to lose legal title to his enterprise, he still hoped to retain practical control by having his hacienda lands granted as ejidos to his own force of resident peons and workers. Thus he cleverly maneuvered to turn to his own advantage the 1934 agrarian laws, which had given hacienda residents the right to petition for land. Even peons who occasionally worked in the mill could qualify as peasants, unlike the permanent industrial mill workers.

Jenkins first enlisted the help of his formidable ally and compadre, Gen. Maximino Avila Camacho, the state governor. The governor accordingly prepared a study in which he concluded that resident peons and workers should have first claim to hacienda lands. The residents had no land at all, he reasoned, and already occupied the land in question, whereas the villagers already had ejidos and only sought enlargements. The governor then used the study to intervene with President Cárdenas on Jenkins's behalf, and by early July secured from the president a temporary suspension of his original distribution order, which otherwise would have been executed very soon by agrarian engineers.[14]

Meanwhile, Jenkins turned his attention to rallying his workers and peons, organized into the Atencingo Workers' and Peasants' Syndicate. As an assistant he recruited the state's important FROC leader, Blas Chumacero. From the surprised labor force of the Atencingo complex, commissions were elected to represent the nine haciendas in their forthcoming petitions. The peasants were encouraged, furthermore, to defend their territory from aggression by the Zapatistas.

On learning of all this activity, a horde of Zapatista villagers from the ranks of Doña Lola, led in part by Deputy Gen. Emilio N. Acosta, decided to invade and seize the hacienda lands without delay. The result was a shoot-out in front of the hacienda of Lagunillas, where the insurgents were blocked by mill administrators and workers, Pérez's *pistoleros* (gunmen), state police led by the chief of police from Puebla, federal soldiers, firemen, and a few resident peons. Several men were killed on both sides. The state police apprehended some four hundred insurgents and hauled them to Puebla, where they were reprimanded by Governor Avila Camacho and freed. The invasion had failed.[15]

In the bureaucratic and executive arenas, meanwhile, Jenkins and the state governor moved ahead with their efforts to convince President Cárdenas that the resident laborers of the Atencingo complex should have first claim to the property. Conveniently enough, not only for Jenkins but for many other owners of industrialized haciendas and plantations in Mexico, President Cárdenas on August 9, 1937, promulgated from Yucatan new laws confirming and clarifying the rights of resident peons to the lands they worked. As the president boated up from Yucatan after announcing his impressive land reforms there, Governor Avila Camacho, certain agrarian officials, and a commission of peons and workers escorted by Blas Chumacero all rushed to Veracruz to intercept him. During an interview on August 26, 1937, they convinced him of their right to Jenkins's property. Moreover, to make the deal more attractive, in a show of generosity Jenkins offered to present the lands to his peons and workers, and to the president, as a gift.[16] As a result the president telegraphed the agrarian engineer already in Chietla, ordering him to refrain from executing the original distribution order pending further developments.

The several thousand Zapatista villagers congregated in Chietla greeted the official pronouncement with outraged cries of protest. Another shoot-out seemed imminent, but none occurred. Probably the Zapatistas were discouraged from taking any violent steps this time by intervening authorities and by the superior size of the opposing forces. Instead they indulged in a day of record alcohol consumption. Jenkins had won, and the Zapatistas had lost.[17]

Through the Bureaucracy

During the ensuing months yet another struggle was fought over the official terms of the grant. This issue had already been discussed during the Veracruz interview with President Cárdenas, and the informal position he had accepted then closely resembled the grant's final wording. Specifically, the grant authorized the formation of an ejido dedicated to cane cultivation, to be worked collectively and administered by a cooperative society, with credit and financing supplied by the mill company.[18]

This design represented something of a compromise for at least two parties to the undertaking, namely Jenkins and the state governor on the one hand, and the top leadership of the CTM, led by its secretary-general, Vicente Lombardo Toledano, on the other. Lombardo Toledano was a very close adviser to President Cárdenas and a major proponent of his cooperative-based agrarian reform program. Though he was not present at the Veracruz meeting, Lombardo Toledano had earlier informed the president of his opinions and policy viewpoint.

Both sides agreed that the integrity of the Atencingo agricultural and industrial complex should be conserved for the sake of the national and state economies. Moreover, both agreed that in major respects the existing system of extensive cane agriculture ought to be maintained. Hence the lands should go to the resident peons and workers, and cane agriculture should be obligatory. All work should be done collectively, since this system was the most economical; the ejidal lands should not be divided into individual parcels even if the peasants preferred them.[19] All the leaders agreed on these principles, notwithstanding what the peasants may have thought.

Beyond these fundamental similarities, however, there were some marked differences of opinion. In particular, Lombardo Toledano, in accordance with his well-known views, advocated the expropriation of Jenkins's entire company, or at least the irrigation and transportation systems, along with the lands. The entire system, he felt, should then be administered by the recipients through a cooperative society to be established by the government.[20] He must have known, however, that such an expropriation might cost the government a lot of money, for Jenkins would never give his industry to the government without financial compensation.

As noted previously, at the Veracruz interview President Cárdenas had explicitly prescribed the formation of a cooperative society for the ejido, while acknowledging that the peasants would receive at least the hacienda lands. To that extent the president agreed with Lombardo. Although one obvious source of future credit for the cooperative would be the National Ejidal Credit Bank, Blas Chumacero, the FROC (and CTM) representative, argued that the mill company should become the ejido's credit source, with the cane crop serving as its collateral for credit extended. Such an arrangement would further oblige the ejidatarios to produce cane, as the ejidal grant stipulated. Evidently Jenkins and Governor Avila Camacho favored Blas Chumacero's idea, and it was also acceptable to the president.[21] Of course, the arrangement meant in effect that Jenkins's mill would remain under private ownership.

Only after all this high-level activity did peasant representatives of the peons and workers of the Atencingo complex finally file official petitions for ejidal grants. Ordinarily such petitions preceded or even initiated elite action rather than following it; but in the case of Atencingo the elites were the initiators and the peons only their pawns. The petitions were presented to the state governor on August 27, 1937, one day after the Veracruz interview with the president. In effect they offered him two options. The first was represented by nine separate petitions, each from peons (but not mill workers) living on one of Jenkins's nine haciendas—Atencingo, San Nicolás Tolentino, Colón, Rijo, Teruel, Jaltepec, Raboso, Lagunillas, and La Galarza— and each soliciting a separate ejido for the village where the peons lived. In other words, this option called for the granting of nine ejidos.

The second option was represented by a single petition, signed by a multitude of peons and workers both. This petition, arguing that the Atencingo system constituted a harmonious agricultural-industrial complex, requested that the lands of the nine haciendas be granted collectively as one giant ejido for the peons and the workers of all the haciendas.[22] On September 9 a second joint petition was submitted, again signed by a multitude. Its tone revealed that it was inspired and sponsored by the FROC and the National Committee of the CTM. In contrast to its brief and simple predecessor, this petition not only requested a collective ejidal grant but specified the form the grant should take. Using the wording of a letter written by Lombardo Toledano and reported to have won the approval of President Cárdenas at Veracruz, the new petition observed: "The distribution of individual parcels is impossible, and the lands must be utilized by means of a cooperative and a collectivization of all the work. If parcellation were carried out, each ejidatario would get a very small portion of land, and there would not be sufficient water for everybody." Therefore, in order to preserve the agricultural and industrial productiveness of the Atencingo complex, the petition proposed

> first, that the whole enterprise, that is, the fields, the means of transport, and the factory, be delivered to the workers, who will manage it in a cooperative form, for which the government will seek the most adequate procedure. Second, in case it is not possible to achieve this, that all the lands, systems of irrigation, agricultural equipment, means of transport, and so on be delivered to a cooperative that the workers will form. . . . The cooperative should rely on the support of the government, so that it can be readily financed.[23]

Such radical ideas, of course, went far beyond Jenkins's intentions and threatened his core industrial interests.

Once the August petitions were filed, normal bureaucratic procedures could take over, first at the state and subsequently at the federal level. In the regular procedure the original petition is filed with the state governor and with state agrarian officials. The governor orders the state's Mixed Agrarian Commission to study the matter and design a proposal. In particular, the commission must take a census to determine the number of peasants who would legally qualify for an ejidal grant. It must determine the location, the size, and other characteristics of the property to be transferred. And it must recommend to the governor the actual form of the proposed ejidal grant. Taking this proposal into consideration, but not necessarily following it to the letter, the governor formulates his decision on the matter and signs the appropriate orders, which are then turned back to the

Mixed Agrarian Commission to be carried out. The implementation, however, remains provisional until the later concurrence of the federal authorities. The commission must submit the relevant documents to the Agrarian Department, which then examines the matter, hears any protests from the landowners involved, draws up its investigative report, and tenders its proposals to the president. The president, taking into account the results of all the preceding efforts, publishes his decision in a presidential decree. Finally, the stipulations of the grant are carried out by the Agrarian Department and termed definitive.

In other words, the process produces five successive documents proposing a course of action: the original petition, the Mixed Agrarian Commission's proposal, the governor's decision, the Agrarian Department's report, and the president's decree. Each document is ordinarily submitted before the next stage of the process is undertaken; and each takes into account its predecessors, though it may reach different conclusions. Moreover, each document must be published in the official organ of the state or federal government, depending on the procedural level. In practice, of course, federal and state authorities, peasant representatives, or other interested parties may be informally involved at any stage of the formal process.[24]

In the Atencingo case the petitions for nine separate ejidos were the first to receive official acknowledgment, being published in the state's official periodical on September 10, 1937. Subsequently, however, they languished without official attention, until they were formally denied in the early 1940's by the governor and the president. Meanwhile, owing to the impetus of the September 9 collective petition as well as to Jenkins's own preferences, the government concentrated on the petitions for a single giant ejidal grant to all the nine villages collectively. The August 27 petition was published alone on October 1, 1937. The September 9 version, treated as an adjunct to the original, was never published. On October 5 the state's Mixed Agrarian Commission submitted its report to Governor Avila Camacho. The governor followed the commission's proposals almost to the letter. "With incredible rapidity," as an official later noted,[25] he ordered that same day the concession of a single giant ejidal grant to the peons and workers of the Atencingo complex. The governor's decision was published on October 19, and provisional possession of the ejido was awarded in a ceremony on December 20, 1937.

The governor's decision and the Mixed Agrarian Commission's study were duly forwarded to the Agrarian Department and the president, and on March 30, 1938, President Cárdenas, confirming the governor's resolution in most respects, signed a decree establishing the ejidal grant. On April 4 the secretary of national economy, following the recommendation of President Cárdenas and the CTM, authorized the organization of the ejidatarios into the Ejidal Cooperative Society of Atencingo and Annexes.[26] The presidential decree was published in the federal government's official bulletin on April 21, 1938,[27] and definitive possession of the property was officially granted just two months later, on June 18.

The Decree

The lengthy presidential decree not only sets forth the terms of the ejidal grant but offers considerable information about the process leading to the grant. It has three parts. The first contains excerpts from the Mixed Agrarian Commission's report and the governor's decision, and summarizes the position advocated by the CTM in its lobbying; the second presents the proposals made by the Agrarian Department; and the third contains the actual text of the presidential decree.

According to the Mixed Agrarian Commission's report, as quoted in the decree, the joint petitions deserved preference over the nine separate petitions because the joint petitions had been signed by all the peons and workers together. Moreover, since Atencingo constituted a unique industrial center, its unity should be preserved, and the lands granted collectively, in the interest of maintaining high productivity. A census of the population of the Atencingo region taken in late September of 1937 had disclosed a total of 6,995 inhabitants, of whom 1,675 were heads of families and 2,365 were deemed legally eligible to receive land. The report noted that the census had been carried out by representatives of the Mixed Agrarian Commission and one representative of the peons and workers; Jenkins's Civil and Industrial Company had not designated a representative.

In reality, the census procedures had not been so straightforward. The census taker thought to be the elected representative of the petitioners was actually a trusted associate of Jenkins and Pérez (and today is one of the most influential and wealthy residents in the town of Matamoros).[28] According to one eyewitness the peons were called together by Pérez during the census and told to sign their names; most signed without understanding what Pérez and Jenkins wanted their signatures for.[29] Many other peons, according to another ejidatario, were not counted in the census, for despite efforts to mobilize them they did not go down to sign at the tables in front of the mill: "That ejidal census was not completed with the people from the annexes, because they were afraid, mistrustful. They did not know what was planned for those signatures." At the same time the census figures included many persons from distant towns in Puebla and Morelos who had come to work in the Atencingo complex.[30] Even so, the total number considered eligible for ejidal rights, 2,365, was considerably smaller than preliminary estimates that some four or five thousand peasants in the area might qualify.[31]

Although Jenkins's lands were in fact suited to growing a variety of crops,[32] the commission wrote that they were "destined exclusively for the sowing of sugar cane that is processed in the mill, . . . rice being cultivated secondarily with the exclusive object of benefiting the lands at rest, in the understanding that all the cane cultivations are irrigated." This statement has been interpreted to mean that legally the ejidatarios were required to restrict themselves to a rotational agriculture of cane and rice on the irrigated lands. The commission further declared that the region's cane agriculture "requires a process of industrialization as well as operating procedures that should be organized in collective form." Actually, the commission had earlier made a much blunter and more revealing statement:

> It is vitally important to the interests of the petitioners, the state, and the nation to conserve the center of work and industry established at the mill. . . . The operation of the ejidos should be organized in collec-

tive form, so that the beneficiaries cannot divide them into individual parcels, because cane growing requires a process of industrialization and demands investments greater than the individual capacities of the ejidatarios.[33]

The arguments for collectivization and cane cultivation were bolstered further by the CTM's opinion, at least as it was described in the decree: "The totality of the crop lands embraced by the system should be delivered to the workers and resident peons of said property, in the form in which it has been worked, on the basis of cooperativism." The decree made no mention, however, of the radical CTM proposals for the expropriation of the mill and its equipment.

The figures recorded by the commission for the size and quality of the transferable lands were as follows:

Hacienda or annex	Irrigated land (hectares)	Seasonal land (hectares)	Hacienda or annex	Irrigated land (hectares)	Seasonal land (hectares)
Atencingo	1,056	0	San Nicolás		
Lagunillas	1,509	0	Tolentino	887	0
Jaltepec	1,277	0	Colón	468	132
Raboso	921	60	Rijo	349	0
La Galarza	932	0	Teruel	677	0

These figures included some valuable lands that had already been granted to two neighboring ejidos: 64 irrigated hectares to be reallocated from San Juan Tilapa to Colón, and 20 irrigated hectares to be reallocated from Matzaco to San Nicolás Tolentino. In both cases the commission considered the original grants to have been excessive. Not surprisingly, however, the effort to reallocate the lands would generate considerable conflict in the future among the ejidos involved. The commission's figures excluded the maximum private property Jenkins was legally allowed to retain, 150 hectares in Atencingo. They also excluded some 2,585 hectares the commission had located that were occupied by buildings or unfit for cultivation.

On the basis of this survey, then, the Mixed Agrarian Commission proposed "a grant to the workers and resident peons of the mill of Atencingo and annexes of 8,268 hectares, of which 8,076 are irrigated and 192 seasonally cultivable, forming 2,043 parcels, the irrigated ones being four hectares each, and the seasonal ones being eight hectares each." Thus 2,043 of the eligible peasants counted in the census could be granted rights as ejidatarios, leaving several hundred peasants with what could be called rain-check rights.* Moreover, the commission concluded that the company's rightful "zone of protection" included the buildings on the properties, and it discounted from the ejidal grants the "areas occupied by dams, canals, roads, railway tracks, and so on."

In reality, as we shall learn later, the Mixed Agrarian Commission had flagrantly and perhaps deliberately undervalued the size and quality of Jenkins's holdings. Nonetheless, its figures and proposals became the basis for the terms of the actual grant. The state governor largely followed the commission's recommendations in authorizing the collective grant, departing from them only to affirm that rights to the river waters should be assigned to the new ejido and apparently to add the dams and canals to the grant. Still excluded from the grant were the former hacienda's buildings, the roadways, a strip twelve meters on either side of the private railroad lines, the 150 hectares in Atencingo reserved for Jenkins, and the industrial rights to certain river waters.

Next the Agrarian Department, after generally validating the commission's field data, passed along the proposals of the governor and his commission with only a few limited changes. The 322 peasants left with rain-check rights were empowered to petition for the creation of a new agricultural center in another area. Also, it was stated that the uncultivable lands possessed by the company would be allocated as enlargements for other ejidos in the region.

Finally came the president's authorization and the actual stipulations of the grant. Confirming the governor's October 5 decision, President Cárdenas granted to Atencingo and its eight annexes "a total of 8,268 hectares, of which 8,076 will be irrigated and 192 seasonally cultivable, which will be taken from the holdings of the Civil and

* The number of parcels was calculated in accordance with the existing laws, which stipulated that an ejidal grant must allot at least four hectares of irrigated land, or eight hectares of seasonally cultivable land, for each ejidatario, and of course that the former property owner had the right to retain 150 irrigated hectares.

Industrial Company of Atencingo." The decree specified the size and location of the lands expropriated from each hacienda, as well as the disposition of the water rights, and sanctioned the reallocation of the so-called excess grants from the two neighboring ejidos—all in accordance with the recommendations submitted to the president. One important clause asserted that all work must be organized collectively. Furthermore, the decree provided for future government control and intervention; the ejidatarios, it said, would be obligated to "subject themselves to the dispositions that the federal government dictates over ejidal administration and economic, agricultural, and social organization." Those, then, were the major points. The final decree was signed by President Cárdenas and by the chief of the Agrarian Department, Gabino Vázquez.

A few days after the signing of the decree, as we have seen, the secretary of national economy authorized the formation of the ejidal cooperative society of Atencingo and annexes. The society was designed to be the economic and administrative organ of the ejido, with broad powers over work schedules, wages, annual planning and investment, and the delivery and sale of the harvest to the mill. It was charged with overseeing the collective farming of the lands. Funds for the sugar and rice crops were to be provided on credit (with interest) to the cooperative by the mill administration rather than by any government agency, such as the National Ejidal Credit Bank. The cooperative's associated membership was to consist only of the 2,043 ejidatarios whose names appeared in the census lists. In the case of Atencingo the manager of the mill, namely Pérez, was empowered to select and appoint the manager of the cooperative. In another critical clause, moreover, the mill was allowed to retain all of its "technical personnel," that is, its administrators and supervisory employees, in the various annexes.[34]

In sum, the president's decree had formed a single giant ejido from the widely dispersed lands of the nine haciendas. All lands were to be worked collectively; no individual parcels were allocated. Sugar cane and rice were the only crops permitted by law. And only the former peons and workers of the haciendas were supposed to qualify as ejidatarios. Managing the ejido's financial and agricultural affairs was the new cooperative society. While only ejidatarios were supposed to be admitted as associate members, the manager of the mill, Pérez, was extended considerable power over its operation.

In theory the president's decree was an instrument of agrarian reform in keeping with the aims of the Mexican Revolution. In practice, of course, it mean that Jenkins had won another round against the Zapatista villagers, this time with the blessing of the president. The creation of the ejido and the installation of the cooperative actually obstructed the transfer of Jenkins's lands to the villagers. The stipulations about the ejido's workings, moreover, signified the continuation of established agricultural and financial practices, and the structure of the cooperative assured Jenkins and Pérez of a strong and legalized influence over the management of the ejido. Thus Jenkins's enterprise could remain much the same; as he later remarked to a friend, "I came out on top."[35]

President Cárdenas and the CTM secretary-general, Lombardo Toledano, had come out on top too: another agrarian reform had been authorized for the peasants; a vital industry had been protected; the principles of collective agriculture and cooperative organization had been confirmed; the FROC was still the dominant workers' confederation in the Atencingo region; and the government had not had to pay the former owner any compensation for the expropriated lands.

Conclusions

Before the Mexican Revolution the struggle for land was waged between two parties, the hacendados and the villagers; the hacendados won. During the Revolution the situation altered in favor of the villagers, who again moved to regain control of their former plots. Now, however, this classic peasant-landlord confrontation was complicated by the entrance of a third actor—William Jenkins, a North American capitalist entrepreneur with considerable political influence. As a result the old hacendados were caught between the Zapatista villagers and Jenkins, and a three-way struggle ensued. Jenkins managed to defeat the hacendados by taking advantage of their financial debility and by inciting the villagers against them. Thus in the Mexican revolutionary context and in an area of high agricultural productivity, the classic village-hacienda confrontation redounded to the benefit of a capitalist entrepreneur. In this sense revolution fostered capitalism.

With the hacendados eliminated, the struggle continued between the villagers and Jenkins. While Jenkins developed and consolidated his political and economic domain, the Zapatista villagers organized and mobilized. Both sides turned to violent methods, but neither had much success in undermining the other's position. The struggle in the valley having reached a stalemate, its outcome came to depend largely on the position taken by the president in Mexico City, and hence on the capacities of the contestants to gain favorable bureaucratic representation there.

As a result of expropriations authorized by presidents Obregón and Rodríguez, the Zapatistas did acquire ejidal grants for some forty villages. Yet the heartlands of Jenkins's enterprise remained untouched—primarily because of their economic importance and Jenkins's attendant political influence. The accession of General Cárdenas to the presidency, however, resulted in an agrarian reform policy that would affect valuable productive land throughout Mexico. In the Atencingo region the change in the presidency was accompanied by the election of municipal candidates who supported such reforms, and they brought the local Zapatistas and their leader, Dolores Campos de Espinosa, greater influence at the federal level. As a result the president decided to grant Jenkins's heartlands to the only peasants who had filed petitions up to that time—the villagers.

Seeing that he could not avoid losing title to his lands, Jenkins maneuvered to keep indirect control by having them granted to an obedient group of subordinates, his peons and mill workers. Although his counterthrust came almost too late, his influence in official circles ensured the success of his plans. With the formation of the new ejido and cooperative, Jenkins was assured of continuing to rule his agricultural domain and reap its benefits.

The only popular pressures for land reform in the Atencingo region had come from the Zapatista villagers; only they had fought for the Revolution and the return of the lands they had formerly owned, and only they had actively sought reform by political means. But determined as they were, and though they had some successes, the villagers

lost the decisive battle to Jenkins. At his behest, the least revolutionary, least mobilized peasants in the valley were granted the best lands.
Certainly the peons of the old haciendas were not fully aware of
the nature of the land struggle. Certainly, too, their late entrance into
the dispute as rival petitioners for the ejidal grant was essentially the
work of the mill administration.

All things considered, then, Jenkins had arranged quite a good deal,
even though he had ostensibly lost title to all but 150 hectares of his
former lands. Most of his lands had been handed over to peasants in a
number of villages, but the irrigated heartlands essentially remained
subject to his control. The new ejidatarios were obligated by law to
produce sugar cane and sell it only to Jenkins's mill, thus guarantee-
ing it a continuing supply. The stipulation that the ejido would be
owned and worked collectively and the establishment of the cooperative enabled Jenkins and Pérez to continue operating on a huge scale,
and to avoid the conflicts and inefficiencies that might have resulted
if the peasants had been granted their own individual parcels. The
majority of the peons were uneducated, politically unmobilized, and
accustomed to taking orders; they made docile, cooperative ejidatarios.
In practice, as the next chapter shows, Jenkins and Pérez directly controlled the recruitment to all posts in both the ejido and the cooperative. Through the cooperative, moreover, they were able to make
sure that the established work patterns were maintained. Indeed, the
cooperative was little more than an appendage of the mill. Ultimately
one might say that the primary function of the cooperative and the
ejido was to block, politically and legally, any further encroachment
by the Zapatista villagers on the sources of Jenkins's wealth, thus preserving the Atencingo complex as Jenkins's untrammeled domain.

Of course, good economic arguments can be mustered in defense of
this outcome. Jenkins and Pérez had transformed the old, technologi-
cally mediocre, decentralized system of haciendas and mills into a
smoothly functioning, industrialized, centralized, capitalistic unit of
very high productivity. The Atencingo complex was a critical component in the national and state economies, both as producer and as
employer. Officials at both levels of government knew that their interests lay in preserving its integrity and productivity. Thus the lands

were granted as a unit with the stipulation that only cane and rice could be cultivated. At the time, moreover, only the mill's former administrators had the financial, technical, and administrative expertise necessary to make the system function efficiently; the peasant beneficiaries of the grant certainly could not be expected to assume control without incurring considerable losses in production. Apparently because of this consideration, the government allowed the manager of the mill both to appoint the manager of the cooperative and to exercise wide-ranging influence over its operations. Finally, the collective organization of the agricultural work clearly favored the interests of the mill economy over the peasants' likely preference for individual parcels.

The political reasons for the outcome are just as evident as the economic ones. As we have seen, the battle over Jenkins's core interests was fought at the local, the state, and the national level, with its resolution depending ultimately on the will of the president. At the local level the adversaries essentially reached a stalemate; despite constant pressure from the insurgents, Jenkins and his forces remained in possession of his holdings. In middle-level bureaucratic circles the villagers lacked political influence and allies, whereas Jenkins's influence was considerable. More important, he was closely allied with the most powerful political figure in the state, Governor Avila Camacho. The FROC and the CTM, concerned about national productivity, also lined up in support of Jenkins's proposals for a collective ejidal grant to his peons. Finally, a law put into effect by the president not long before gave resident peons and workers precedence over villagers for grants of hacienda lands. Given all these conditions, it is no wonder that the president was persuaded to grant the ejido to Jenkins's peons and workers rather than to the Zapatista villagers.

CHAPTER THREE

Peasants Against the Mill Administration, 1938-1947

The first phase in the history of the Atencingo ejido and cooperative extended from their founding in 1937–38 until 1947. Its definitive characteristic was direct control by the mill administration over the operation of the entire Atencingo complex. In response to the mill administration's exploitative rule, what amounted in many ways to a classic peasant movement was organized among the ejidatarios. Allied with a similar movement among the industrial mill workers, it waged a struggle that culminated in the crisis of 1946–47, when the rebellious ejidatarios and their leaders, supported by federal authorities, captured full control of the ejido and the cooperative.

Possession in Dispute

Under the terms of the Atencingo ejidal grant, as we have seen, the villagers had in effect lost an important round in the struggle for control of Jenkins's heartlands. To many of them the grant appeared inequitable and unjust, if not illegal.[1] For one thing, it required ejidatarios in a few neighboring villages to turn over parts of their so-called excess lands to the Atencingo ejido.[2] For another, in part because of the location of disputed plots, it jeopardized the access of some villages to the river waters.[3] Worst of all, it failed to take into account large tracts apparently still owned by Jenkins. Now these tracts were being concealed as part of the new ejido, when they might have been used to form or enlarge other ejidos.[4] In general, the villagers blamed not only Jenkins but also the state government for the grant's unfavorable outcome.

The villagers did not let possession of the new ejido go unchallenged. First, in late 1938 they sought to block physically the transfer of their own ejidal properties in Chietla, Tilapa, and Matzaco to the Atencingo ejido. They apparently failed, however. The new ejidal commissariat and cooperative representatives for Atencingo blamed the "invasion of our lands" on agitators supported by "some elements" in the Agrarian Department.[5] Governor Avila Camacho protested to the Agrarian Department chief, arguing that the Atencingo ejidal grant had authorized the subtractions from the neighboring villages' previous grants and that for economic reasons the new ejido must be kept intact.[6] Moreover, sharing the governor's view, the state's agrarian delegate,* Aarón Merino Fernández, directed the villagers to halt their opposition.[7]

Later, for a few days in April and May 1939, the challenge assumed far greater proportions as hundreds of men and women from numerous villages, joined by some landless residents of Atencingo and its annexes, mounted major invasions in most of the lands of the Atencingo complex. According to reports by Merino Fernández (who years later became governor), the invaders in La Galarza claimed a presidential order as their authorization for taking possession of the invaded lands. But, they further claimed, the order had been filed with the state government, which had refused to carry it out. "Because of this they had decided to take matters into their own hands (being tired of promises) and thus oblige the federal government to intervene in their favor."[8] Moreover, in Raboso a spokesman for the invaders had informed the agrarian delegate: "They pursue this conflict so that the higher authorities will intervene in the resolution of their problems.... They are tired of so much waiting and ... are not

---

* The agrarian delegate may be regarded as the state-level counterpart of the Agrarian Department chief, though the chief's post is provided for by Mexico's constitution, whereas the agrarian delegate's post is not. The agrarian delegate is appointed by the chief, and may be removed from office at any time the chief orders. But though he is formally responsible primarily to the Agrarian Department, in practice the agrarian delegate has closer dealings with the state governor, tends to be politically more subject to the governor's wishes than to the chief's, and indeed is probably the governor's personal nominee for the office.

disposed to continue being the victims of the politicians and of the elements surrounding the president, because while the president helps the people, the others in the government are a bunch of bandits."[9] Clearly the invading villagers—or at least their leaders and spokesmen—perceived their strategy as being aimed against political unresponsiveness at the state and federal levels of government.

Indeed, one account held that the invasions were precipitated by preparations for the forthcoming presidential election. Apparently peasants from the fifty or so villages and hamlets where Doña Lola had supporters had decided at an assembly held sometime in 1938 that they would not campaign publicly for any of the presidential candidates until the candidates' various programs were well defined. Sometime afterward, nevertheless, the supporters of a minor candidate, Gen. Rafael Sánchez Tapia, incited the peasants to invade by convincing them that the general would support their claim to the lands. According to the account Doña Lola opposed the invasion, but taken by surprise in the middle of 1939, she was unable to halt most of the invaders, who were led by a schoolteacher from Matzaco.[10]

From a different perspective Merino Fernández reported to his superiors: "The agitation was politically motivated, with the parties involved trying to provoke bloody clashes between the peasants—who serve as their unwitting instruments—and the police in order to create a pretext for attacking the higher authorities." He further mentioned that Deputy Gen. Emilio N. Acosta, as well as "a rural schoolteacher" and Doña Lola, had taken a very active part in these unpropitious events. Thus as far as the agrarian delegate was concerned, outside agitators had been the principal cause of the local insurgency.[11]

Meanwhile, the various invasions were soon repulsed by state police and federal soldiers stationed in the area. As a result of confrontations in several of the ejido's villages, two men were killed on each side. The few peasants who carried weapons were disarmed. A great number of the invaders were arrested and jailed in the penitentiary in Puebla, including the principal leader, the schoolteacher from Matzaco. Apparently all but he were soon freed, while the blame for the incident was directed at him, Doña Lola, and Acosta.[12]

Sometime later an order was issued for the apprehension of Doña

Lola, now 61 years old. She obtained an amparo against the order, but in August she was seized at her home by soldiers and imprisoned in Puebla. After some difficulty her daughter obtained her release. Soon afterward Doña Lola took refuge in the neighboring state of Morelos, under the protection of Zapatista generals and even President Cárdenas himself.[13] She was certain to have found friends there, for Morelos was becoming the principal refugee center for alienated and endangered peasants and workers from the Atencingo region.[14]

What did these events signify? First, Jenkins and the governor had fought off a major challenge to Jenkins's control of the valuable ejidal lands. Not only was the local insurgency stopped, but it had brought no major interference from federal authorities. With the protection of the powerful governor, Jenkins and Pérez were clearly the masters of the region. Their security was further enhanced in 1940 and again in 1944, first by Governor Avila Camacho and then by his successor, Governor Gonzalo Bautista, another close ally of Jenkins. Both governors officially denied the August 27, 1937, petitions for nine individual ejidal grants on the grounds that the petitioners of Atencingo and annexes had been satisfied by the 1937 provisional grant, and moreover that no transferable land remained.[15] Now it was unlikely that the ejido would be divided, at least in the near future.

Second, the various boundary disputes and irregularities made it virtually impossible for the government to grant the ejidatarios of Atencingo and annexes definitive possession of their ejidal lands. In December 1937 the provisional grant had been extended by state authorities: all papers and procedures were held to be complete, including the survey and mapping of the boundaries.[16] In June 1938, at the ceremonies for the definitive transfer of the lands, everything again appeared to be in order. The engineer commissioned by the Agrarian Department declared that the ejido had been dutifully surveyed and mapped.[17] As higher authorities in the Agrarian Department soon realized, however, the survey and maps were inaccurate and subject to dispute. This state of affairs was already reflected in boundary disputes with neighboring ejidatarios, who resisted having to relinquish certain plots as the presidential decree had ordained. Probably the mapping issue was also complicated by hushed awareness among government officials that Jenkins was illegally concealing certain property—tracts that had been ignored by the engineers in their 1937 labors—as part of the ejido.[18] In any case, because of the legal and administrative confusion, the Agrarian Department did not authorize definitive possession, despite occasional pressure from the agrarian delegate and the Atencingo grantees.[19] Possession of the new ejido was deemed "virtual" rather than "definitive." Moreover, though orders to make an accurate survey were sent down the line by Agrarian Department officials, the endeavors ultimately miscarried, producing no precise results from the field.[20]

For the time being the uncertain status of the ejidal grant did not mean much to the ejidatarios. Nor did it have any noticeable effect on Jenkins's and Pérez's agricultural operations, especially since their underlings had repulsed the villagers and taken physical possession of the disputed lands anyway. Nevertheless, the problematic existence of the ejido as a legal entity was to have great importance some years later—as it still does today.

The Structure of the New Regime

Within the ejido and cooperative, Jenkins's victory was far more complete than the formal documents indicated. Practically speaking, the federal government could exercise little control in the valley of Matamoros; hence the Atencingo complex could remain under the power of Jenkins and Pérez, who in turn enjoyed the protection of Governor Avila Camacho. Thus the prescribed reforms were manipulated to suit the interests of Jenkins and Pérez, with the acquiescence, if not the complicity, of some middle- and lower-level government functionaries of the Agrarian Department and the Secretariat of National Economy. As a result neither the cooperative nor the ejido functioned as it was intended to; the cooperative was a simulated "paper cooperative," as many ejidatarios have said. To direct the ejido's affairs, the mill administration fashioned a strict apparatus of control over the ejidatarios and cooperative members. All leadership posts, whether elective or appointive, were filled by cronies of the mill administration. Recruitment was tightly controlled, with very little circulation of the ejidal and cooperative elites. Strong pressures—

including physical force—were applied to make the ejidatarios work hard and obey their masters.

Since the entire Atencingo complex formed one ejido, a single ejidal commissariat was authorized to take charge of all nine sections. As specified by the Agrarian Code, it consisted of six members: a president, a secretary, and a treasurer, and alternates for each office.[21] In addition, there was a vigilance council, also composed of six members: a president, a secretary, and a spokesman, and alternates for each. According to the law both ejidal bodies were supposed to be elected jointly every three years during a general assembly of the ejidatarios. Two slates of six candidates were to be proposed and voted on, with the winning slate becoming the commissariat and the losing slate becoming the vigilance council. Except for the general assembly of the ejidatarios, the ejidal commissariat was to be the highest authority of the ejido, especially in regard to dealings with government authorities. The vigilance council would perform a watchdog function below that of the commissariat.[22]

In the case of Atencingo, leaders favored by Pérez were elected to form the new ejidal commissariat at a general assembly at the time of the governor's provisional grant in December 1937. Rufino Mejía, a prominent mill worker affiliated with the FROC, became president. He remained entrenched in office for the next seven years, and continued to subordinate the ejido's management to the policies of Jenkins and Pérez.[23] Moreover, appointments to the lesser ejidal offices were evidently made without calling general assemblies.[24]

The leadership structure for the cooperative society, prescribed by the General Law of Cooperative Societies, was somewhat more complex, consisting of both elective and appointive posts. In a design similar to that of the ejido, the highest authority by law was the general assembly of the society's associates. The top elective posts were those of the administration council: a president, a secretary, and a treasurer, and an alternate for each. Below the administration council stood the vigilance council, with a president, a secretary, and a spokesman, and their respective alternates. These councils were supposed to be elected every two years. The real administrative chief, however, was the manager of the cooperative. Under the law he would normally be named by the administration council, subject to the veto of the vigilance council. In the case of Atencingo, though, the secretary of national economy, who was responsible for cooperative affairs, had specially authorized the manager of the mill, Pérez, to appoint the manager of the cooperative. Finally, in each of the ejido's nine member villages the cooperative had field staff officers, the *capitanes* and the *mayordomos*, who directed and reported on the actual work in the fields. These officers were appointed directly by the manager of the cooperative and received their orders from him.*

In the case of Atencingo apparently no general assembly was called for the election of the councils in 1938 or during the succeeding eight or nine years. Instead the councils were selected covertly by mill employees and subsequently registered with the Secretariat of National Economy's Bureau of Cooperative Development in Mexico City. Pérez, of course, used his special prerogatives to appoint his minions, often mill workers who supposedly were also ejidatarios, to the cooperative's other central posts. Within the ejido villages, peasant ejidatarios were named to the field staff.[25]

Actually, within each village the top leaders were not the staff attached to the cooperative but the so-called technical personnel carried over from the old hacienda-style operation under the authority of the cooperative's charter. More an administrative than a technical staff, this group consisted of trusted employees of the mill, including for each village an administrator, his second-in-command, a timekeeper to keep track of the workers' hours, and a bursar. The power structure in the villages also included overseers and pistoleros whose strong-arm methods served to ensure obedience and hard labor from

---

* The term "administration" as used in this book in references to the Atencingo ejido's local government denotes primarily the political and economic management of the cooperative society (or its successor, the credit society): the cooperative manager (or the credit society delegate); the administration council; and the field staff, consisting of the mayordomos, the capitanes, and the supervisors added during the Jaramillo administration. "Regime" is used in a broader, more political sense that embraces the entire local system of rule, which in practice was largely an authoritarian, hierarchical, closed system over the years. It thus refers to all those directly involved in the local power structure, whether or not their function was primarily administrative: the ejidal commissariat; the cooperative society management; mill employees who sometimes functioned as advisers or overseers; and even the pistoleros who during some periods were an important adjunct to the system.

the ejidatarios. In the fields the ejidatarios were constantly prodded by gun-toting mill employees on horseback. A crew of pistoleros was kept on call to serve the staffs of both the cooperative and the mill. Usually they were stationed either in Raboso or in Lagunillas, which were located at opposite ends of the ejidal complex, and one of which was usually administered by Pérez's feared son. Often a pistolero who murdered someone at one end of the ejidal complex would be sent subsequently to work at the other end.[26]

To round out the apparatus of exploitation and cooptation, Jenkins and Pérez ignored the legal requirement that associates of the cooperative be ejidatarios. They stacked the cooperative with illegal associates, apparently using membership as a reward for their friends and allies. Thus hundreds of mill workers, administrative employees, and special confidential personnel were put on the cooperative's payroll, becoming eligible to receive annual dividends even though they were not ejidatarios. Some of these persons did not even live in the area. Naturally, to conceal these facts, certain irregularities accompanied the registration procedures.[27]

The Ejidatarios Under the New Regime

How did the ejidatarios react to these conditions? In general they were an obedient lot, unprepared to oppose Jenkins and Pérez, and inclined to go along with what they understood. According to one ejidatario leader from that period, in fact, the former peons at first either did not believe or did not comprehend that they were now ejidatarios, even though they had been informed of the fact by Pérez and others. They remained virtually unaware of their new status and rights, and persisted in regarding themselves as peons. Moreover, they did not understand that under the new system they could earn annual profit dividends as associates of the cooperative. Those who received extra money after the harvests generally believed they had been given gifts from the mill for working hard.[28] That the ejidatarios failed to understand the significance of the new ejido and cooperative cannot be put down solely to ignorance, however. There had been few changes in their daily existence to convince them of any significant changes in other spheres.

Revealing testimony about the new ejido came from one observant witness who visited the Atencingo complex in May 1939, about two weeks after the land invasions. He was Rubén Jaramillo, a great agrarian radical and organizer from the cane region in Morelos who was eventually assassinated in 1962 by army troops. As he reported in a letter to President Cárdenas, Jaramillo discovered that the Atencingo ejidatarios knew little or nothing about the ejido's affairs. When he had asked an old man with years of experience working at Atencingo how the ejidal cooperative was organized, the old man had replied that "he knew nothing about that cooperative."[29] Jaramillo had then approached a number of other ejidatarios, including "one of the oldest peons of Atencingo, a man who is surely the master general of the carpenters," with further basic questions. When had the lands of Atencingo been distributed, and how many hectares were in the cooperative? Who financed the cane cultivation? How many tons of cane did one hectare yield, and what was the total production? How much did it cost to cut the cane and haul it from the field to the factory? Where were the receipts for the cane delivered to the mill? How much did the ejidatarios receive in profit dividends? How many kilograms of sugar did one ton of cane produce, and at what price was the sugar sold by the mill? How much did the ejidatarios pay in taxes to the state government? Did they have documents showing they were associates of the cooperative? How many members of the cooperative's administration council were mill workers? Did the ejido have an efficient medical service, and schools for the children? Such issues were totally foreign to the ejidatarios. They had answered "that there was nothing like this in Atencingo.... They only know that they receive their salary, which they earn as peons of the enterprise, and that their work day is up to twelve hours."

Dismayed by these findings, Jaramillo concluded that in effect there had been no land distribution in Atencingo; "neither is there any cooperative or anything that looks like one. During my stay in that place I did realize, though, that there are many cantinas and games of chance where the master's [*patrón's*] exploited wretches lose all hope of progress and happiness, as much for themselves as for their children." Moreover, though the ejidal commissariat of Atencingo claimed that 2,043 men had been granted parcels of four hectares each, and that they were working their lands cooperatively,

> the sad existence I was able to observe among the workers of that place convinces me that such is not the case, and that the commissariat is nothing but a blind minion of the hacendado, Jenkins, who treats them [the workers] like little children. Experience has taught us that only when we see them enjoy a more comfortable life can we be sure that the workers of the countryside are indeed receiving benefits. But so long as a land distribution such as that in Morelos is not made in Atencingo, it cannot be said that those of Atencingo have a satisfactory life economically. It can only be said that in Atencingo one man exploits the rest.

Then, addressing the president directly, he made an eloquent plea on behalf of the Atencingo ejidatarios:

> I must tell you, Mr. President, with all due respect, that in Atencingo your noble wishes have not been fulfilled, since the land is monopolized by a single individual who has submerged our compañeros in economic misery.... I implore you, Mr. President, to intervene in the affair of our Atencingo compañeros, so that some day not far off they may enjoy the fruits of the Revolution, as other areas of the Republic have done.

His plea had little effect, however. President Cárdenas and his fellow leaders either could or would do nothing to remedy the situation.

Meanwhile, the ejidatarios in the Atencingo region worked on under tight control. Regular work was evidently plentiful in the fields, where mechanization had not yet been introduced. As fieldworkers the ejidatarios were paid low daily wages by the mill (through the cooperative): in the late 1930's the typical remuneration for a day's work was 1.25 or 1.50 pesos. Yet the cost of living was so low that this meager amount was enough to live on. The ejidatarios could even afford to buy some chocolate, milk, or meat each week—luxury items by their standards.[30] By 1946 the typical wage increased to 2.50 and 3.00 pesos a day.[31] Of course, many ejidatarios did not even receive this much, while a privileged few earned considerably more because they were field staff officers or had other well-paying jobs. Wages were disbursed weekly according to records kept by the field staffs of the mill and the cooperative. In brief, the ejidatarios were treated as common landless wage laborers.

As associates of the cooperative the ejidatarios were supposed to receive whatever profit dividends remained after the delivery and sale of the cane harvest to the mill. The dividends were supposed to be prorated according to the number of days a man had worked during the season. But the ejidatarios, failing to understand what these dividends were or how they were calculated, regarded what they received as gifts or bonuses for working hard.[32] During the first two years of the cooperative's operation, the dividends given most ejidatarios ranged from 120 to 300 pesos apiece. Yet some of the ejidatarios received less, and others received nothing.[33] Some money, moreover, was given to fieldworkers who had been brought in from the outside and were not ejidatarios at all. In general the mill administration apparently distributed the dividends in an irregular, inequitable, and illegal fashion, so as to reward their friends and very favored laborers.[34] Then, after the first two years, no further dividends were announced, at least not to the ejidatarios.[35]

The apparatus of control enforced harsh measures against those who did not work hard and conform to the established work and pay schedules. According to a local observer, an ejidatario who did not want to work as he was ordered to might well expect to be told by the administrator: "If you do not want to work, move out of your house and get going. Go somewhere else." Thus he would have to "grab together his family and things, and leave." One who requested additional work, however, would often be told harshly: "There is no money. There is no more work."[36] An ejidatario who fell out of favor with a mill employee or field staff officer during one harvest might suddenly be informed at the beginning of the next harvest: "Your work papers did not come. You are not an associate anymore." Or he might even be forced to leave, fearing for his life. In general, according to the ejidatarios, "There was lots of work, because you went to the fields and no other crop was to be seen but pure cane and fields in preparation for cane.... [But] from 1938 on they gave you crumbs. The mill gave you just what it wanted to." Thus when the mill said it was going to pay an ejidatario a certain wage or dividend, no one complained about the amount being offered. "Who said anything? You had to take it, or else you died—and so everybody went to work.

Life was just like that until 1945."³⁷ Meanwhile the displaced ejidatarios were replaced by outsiders hired as wage-labor fieldhands.³⁸
Indeed, this replacement of the founding ejidatarios with landless
day laborers became quite marked by the mid-1940's.

If individual complaints about working conditions were forcibly
suppressed, any efforts toward collective protest and organization
were even more violently put down. The ejidatarios could not exercise their legal right to have a voice in the operation of the cooperative
or the ejido, to hold general assemblies with popular voting on issues,
to elect popular candidates to the ejidal commissariat or to the cooperative posts, or to seek a legal remedy for their grievances against
mill administrators and henchmen. Ejidatarios and cooperative associates who tried to organize were often deprived of their rights,
forced to flee, beaten, or murdered, as the following testimonies reveal:

> In the days of the Pérezes, terrorism and hired guns were clearly there.
> Anyone they did not want around disappeared overnight. Those who
> took their turn at defending the rights of the rest of the peasants were
> chased away or killed. Nobody could say anything about the boss, or
> raise his voice to protest the wages or ask for more work, because there
> was no liberty.³⁹

> The peasants did not have the right to claim their rights. Anyone who
> did was murdered and thrown in the canebrake. Others were thrown
> out of work. Reprisals and crimes broke out, especially against anyone
> who showed a willingness to become a leader.⁴⁰

> From [the mill's] founding in 1938 until 1947, the renowned multi-
> millionaire William Jenkins, then owner of the mill, contrived by means
> of his official influence to manage the cooperative, and consequently
> the ejido, as he pleased. The methods used by this gentleman were the
> bribe, the payoff, intimidation, and terror by gunmen. In the sad history
> of the Atencingo mill there is a list of our murdered companions, crimes
> that have never been punished by justice, since the influential multi-
> millionaire Jenkins, just as he used to manage the cooperative and mill
> of Atencingo, managed justice by way of the local judges, who held
> their posts by virtue of his influence, and by way of politicians that he
> subsidized and for whom he has always held open his pocket to help
> them in their electoral campaigns, and who obeyed him in everything.⁴¹

> Jenkins ... managed our affairs according to his caprice, fancy, and will,

removing and imposing the representatives of our cooperative and ejidal commissariat as best served his interests. For nine years he sustained this situation with the support of the municipal and state authorities and moreover with a band of pistoleros and salaried bullies who terrorized us all during that time, leaving many widows and orphans.[42]

So successful was this system of subjugation and exploitation, in short, that no serious opposition to it could be mounted until the mid-1940's, when certain circumstances altered the situation.

Quite clearly, then, the agrarian reform prescribed on paper for Atencingo was in practice nonexistent. The former peons and workers of the Atencingo complex were not ejidatarios but wage laborers who could be hired, suspended, fired, or replaced almost at will. They were not associates of a cooperative who collected dividends but wage laborers who sometimes received gifts or bonuses. They had no electoral rights: their general assemblies were not convened, and their officers were imposed on them rather than elected by them. They had no means of seeking redress for crimes committed against them. Those who protested were pressured, threatened, beaten, chased, and murdered. For them the ejido was a figment and the cooperative a fraud. For them Jenkins and Pérez were the overlords, and the federal authorities in Mexico City hardly existed.

Even so, there were a number of conditions favoring the ejidatarios. The reform measures of 1937 and 1938 had provided the legal and institutional basis for the ejidatarios to assert themselves one day. It only remained for a majority of them to understand their status and rights, and to gain the motivation and capacity for collective political action. Moreover, under Jenkins and Pérez the so-called cooperative wielded such enormous financial power that it would almost inevitably become a focus for instability and struggle. Finally, all these factors were at work in a region with an already long history of revolutionary struggle and direct political action.

Collective Protest and Organized Struggle

Jenkins's system functioned quite well—at least until 1945 and 1946. Economically and agriculturally his enterprise continued to be productive, as Table 2 shows. Politically his interests remained reason-

TABLE 2

Sugar Cane Produced and Processed by the Atencingo
Cooperative and Mill, 1937–1947

		Mill	
Harvest	Cooperative: Total delivered to mill (tons)	Total milled from all sources (tons)	Av. yield of all sources (tons/ha.)
1937–38	—[a]	353,154	118.7
1938–39	—	301,215	116.6
1939–40	—	330,350	123.2
1940–41	—	348,852	110.0
1941–42	—	420,570	136.1
1942–43	—	416,045	129.4
1943–44	—	366,201	118.0
1944–45	304,430	334,673	119.8
1945–46	307,275	316,315	102.0
1946–47	294,500	330,570	100.8

SOURCES: For the cooperative, memorandum of the local ejidal credit society of Atencingo and annexes, July 12, 1967, MAEM. For the mill for 1937–42, Banco Nacional de México, *Industria azucarera de México* (Mexico City, 1954), Vol. III, Pt. 2; and for 1942–47, Unión Nacional de Productores de Azúcar, *Estadísticas azucareras* (Mexico City, 1965), pp. 44–45.
[a] Figures for 1937–44 are not available.

ably secure, both from outside interference and from local unrest. Even after the expiration in 1943 of the five-year contract between the cooperative and the mill, no crisis developed.

But sturdy as it seemed, Jenkins's system of control and exploitation depended on a complex set of outside circumstances. It depended very much on the protection and cooperation of the state government, and specifically the governor. It depended on the noninterference of federal authorities and other outsiders with reformist intent. It depended on the suppressed and disorganized condition of the peasants, and especially of the ejidatarios. It depended on the cooptation and control of the mill workers and the cooperative associates. And it depended on Pérez.

There was nothing inherently durable about any of these circumstances. Indeed, in a sense, their very complexity made for a certain fragility, as witnessed by Jenkins's reliance on coercion and repression to make his system work. Thus when over the years a multitude of developments combined to alter the situation, Jenkins's system became very fragile indeed. The result was a fierce and in many ways classic struggle for control of the cooperative and ejido. Here we shall concentrate on examining some prominent political developments that energized the struggle and spurred the ejidatarios to triumph.

At first, to be sure, the ejidatarios as a body were ignorant, subdued, and disorganized. Yet individually they were not all resigned to being mistreated, and many began to learn about their status and rights. Their growing awareness was evidenced by occasional outbursts of individual protest, which were of course systematically suppressed. It is generally thought in the region, too, that contact with the villagers, many of whom worked in the fields and the mill, served to arouse, inform, and politicize the ejidatarios.

In particular, the ejidatarios were stirred by the heated campaign for the presidential election of 1940, which pitted the popular Gen. Juan Andreu Almazán of Morelos against the official favorite, Gen. Manuel Avila Camacho, the relatively unknown brother of the heavy-handed governor. Apparently most of the valley's residents favored Almazán,[43] who generally advocated the individual parcellation of lands rather than collective agriculture, a policy that many Atencingo ejidatarios were beginning to desire. The Almazanistas "worked to open the eyes" of the ejidatarios, and with some success.[44] According to Rufino Mejía, then president of the ejidal commissariat and a faithful servant of the mill administration, "All the people had turned against the enterprise. . . . They shot at me a lot also. . . . Two friends were the only ones who stuck by me in that period, because all were against us."[45] Avila Camacho won the election, however, and during the next few years the ejidatarios remained fairly well controlled as the mill administration, with its superior resources and allies, maintained its supremacy.

Meanwhile, the mill workers, another restive group in Jenkins's enterprise, continued to be contained by a long series of "paper syndicates" with such heroic and revolutionary names as Karl Marx, Emiliano Zapata, Miguel Hidalgo, and the like. For all practical purposes these syndicates served the interests of the mill administration, since a pro-mill faction held their key leadership posts, and attempts at reform were quickly subverted.

In theory syndicate members could belong individually either to the CROM or to the FROC, an affiliate of the Mexican Workers' Confederation (CTM). But in fact members of these two groups had been assembled into a single subservient operation.[46] The FROC predominated at the time the cooperative and ejido were founded, but soon afterward its power was challenged by the CROM, which enjoyed Jenkins's support. Following some bloodshed the CROM won, and thereafter it collaborated closely with Jenkins and Pérez.[47] In the words of one ejidatario who witnessed that period, "There was a bad syndicate, a paper one, whose secretary-general did what the owner of the mill told him. It did not matter to him that he was unionized. Manuel Pérez said, 'Run that guy out for me,' and they did it—without compensation, without anything. They said, 'Get going. Beat it. Because the pistol is pointed at you.' "[48] Of course, many of those subjected to such pressures were villagers who supported Doña Lola. A number of them took refuge in the cane regions of the nearby state of Morelos, especially after the unsuccessful presidential campaign of General Almazán and the unsuccessful bid for Jenkins's lands in the 1930's.[49]

By 1945 and 1946, however, circumstances had changed greatly, enabling first the discontented mill workers and subsequently the ejidatarios to organize and mobilize for a vigorous open struggle. In particular, critical changes outside the Atencingo complex dramatically undermined Jenkins's formidable system of control. First, in 1944 a new state governor, Carlos I. Betancourt, entered office; he did not turn out to be the close ally and friend of Jenkins that his predecessors had been. Thus Jenkins not only lost considerable influence at the state level but also lost his most promising channel for influencing the Republic's moderate president, Gen. Manuel Avila Camacho. Second, in 1945 the powerful former governor, Gen. Maximino Avila Camacho, died from food poisoning. Thus Jenkins lost his key political ally and business partner. Third, in 1946 Manuel Pérez became ill, retired, moved to Puebla, and finally died. Thus Jenkins lost the only man who really understood how to run the

Atencingo complex. Without these two associates—Maximino Avila Camacho and Pérez — Jenkins's power was greatly diminished.[50] Fourth, the CTM and then the CNC (National Peasants' Confederation), the unionizing sectors of the government party, based in Mexico City, were becoming interested in establishing affiliated organizations in the Atencingo area among the mill workers and the ejidatarios respectively.

During 1945 and 1946 leaders of the anti-mill forces, having mustered a sizable following that included both villagers who supported Doña Lola and ejidatarios who had rights to work in the mill, established contact in Morelos with key leaders of the new National Sugarworkers' Syndicate, an affiliate of the CTM. Next the opposition force among the mill workers demanded effective unionization, the affiliation of the local syndicate with the CTM, and a labor contract with the mill administration. A fierce and bloody struggle ensued for control and organization of the mill workers. To aid in the struggle, labor leaders and union organizers were brought in from the cane regions of Morelos.[51] Moreover, they were joined by many former Atencingo workers who had been forced to flee to Morelos but now began to return to their homeland. General Acosta apparently lent his support to the movement as well.[52] Even Doña Lola, at the age of 64, prepared to return, but she was assassinated in May 1945.[53] In addition, many ejidatarios who did not themselves work in the mill (especially those who lived in Lagunillas and Atencingo, where most of the mill workers lived) saw a common cause in their own plight and that of the workers.[54]

Thus the rebellious workers pressed for victory. Soon they constituted a majority of the mill's labor force, with their ranks reinforced by the returning refugees and by their local allies, the ejidatarios, and with outside leadership and assistance from the CTM affiliate. After considerable agitation and violence, combined with a formidable strike threat against the mill, they succeeded. In February 1946 local Section 77 of the National Sugarworkers' Syndicate of the CTM was founded at a major assembly and celebration attended by the CTM secretary-general, Fidel Velásquez.[55] Thus the mill workers had won their power struggle against the weakened Jenkins, though conflicts with the mill administration would continue over contract issues and other lasting disputes.

Meanwhile, inspired by the mill workers' struggle and knowing they could depend on the mill workers' support, the restless ejidatarios laid plans for a struggle of their own. Sometime during late 1945 or early 1946 insurgent ejidatarios, at that time concentrated in Atencingo and Lagunillas, formed a commission of representatives from their ranks. This commission sent a petition to the president seeking redress of the ejidatarios' grievances. It also sought advice from the leaders of the workers' movement, and on their recommendation consulted in Morelos with leaders of the National Sugarworkers' Syndicate and other agrarian leaders.[56]

In their ignorance the ejidatarios had planned to ask for advice on forming their own syndicate. They were soon told, however, that as ejidatarios they should join the CNC and through it demand that the federal authorities in Mexico City find a solution to their problems. The ejidatarios had not really considered this prospect before, apparently because they had been largely unaware that Mexico City and the authorities even existed. In line with the strategy of the mill workers, the ejidatarios were also advised to invite certain men then active in the Zacatepec region of Morelos—especially Porfirio Jaramillo, the brother of Rubén—to organize and lead them. The ejidatarios agreed, for they realized that they alone did not have the skills and resources to carry out their plans.[57]

One of the principal leaders of the ejidatarios was Luz Mejía, then serving as the manager of the cooperative. He had been appointed not long before by Jenkins and the post-Pérez mill administration. Bruno Castrejano, now head of the mill, lacked Pérez's ability and experience, and the ejidatarios and workers feared him less than the dreaded Pérez. Mejía and his fellow officers agreed that the cooperative and the ejido should be taken away from Jenkins's control and that the ejidatarios should be permitted to exercise their rights. Like other ejidatarios Mejía sensed his own lack of administrative and organizational skills, and favored importing Jaramillo and several other leaders.[58] Thus Jenkins's system of control sustained another major fracture—a rebellion at the middle level in his local chain of command.

Porfirio Jaramillo, as well as some of the other imported leaders, was actually a refugee from the Atencingo complex. During the early 1930's Jaramillo had lived in the Atencingo region and worked in the mill as a mason. In addition he had agitated actively for the distribution of Jenkins's lands among the villagers and for a mill workers' syndicate that would be truly controlled by the workers. Because of his endeavors he had been ejected from the mill-controlled syndicate by the mid-1930's and chased from the region.[59]

Under the leadership of Jaramillo and his associates, the ejidatarios began to mobilize during early 1946 for their decisive confrontation with the mill administration. At first the rebels had majority support only in Lagunillas and Atencingo, where the sympathetic mill workers and the ejidatarios who worked in the mill were concentrated. Next they gained control among the ejidatarios in neighboring Colón. By the middle of 1946 they had also gained control in Rijo, Jaltepec, and San Nicolás Tolentino.[60] Further substantial support came from numerous landless peasants and wage laborers who wanted to become ejidatarios; this time the villagers were siding with Jenkins's former peons.

In the meantime the ejidatarios' long-standing desires came to the fore as the ultimate demands from which their movement drew its strength and meaning. If carried out, the movement's program would radically change the structure of the ejido and the cooperative and their relationship to the mill. The existing operation consisted both legally and practically speaking of a single giant ejido, a collectivized system of agriculture devoted almost exclusively to cane cultivation, and a cooperative controlled at the managerial level by the mill. What the ejidatarios wanted was quite different. First, they wanted the division of the existing ejido into nine ejidos to correspond with the nine villages in the Atencingo complex. Then the peasants of each resulting ejido could elect their own officers and manage their own affairs. Second, they wanted the ejidal lands to be parceled out into individual plots, apparently in the legal sizes specified in the 1938 decree: four hectares of irrigated land or eight hectares of seasonally cultivable land per ejidatario. Thus each ejidatario would own a particular plot, even though the work might still be done collectively. For many, this goal was paramount. Third, they wanted the old co-operative replaced by a new one, to be controlled and managed directly by the ejidatarios. Thus the ejidatarios, and not the mill administration, would elect and install their own officers, assign the work, disburse the wages and salaries, calculate the dividends, negotiate the contract with the mill, and plan for future operations. Fourth, and last, they wanted permission to grow at least some crops other than cane, whether individually or collectively. By diversifying their crops they could reduce their dependence on the mill, subsist to a greater extent on the fruits of their own labor, and in some cases earn higher profits than were possible from cane production. Together these became the ultimate demands and goals of the ejidatario movement. Most ejidatarios believed that only these measures would truly answer their needs.

In order to carry out such a program, the Agrarian Department would first have to rectify its original census of peasants eligible for ejidal rights; issue certificates of agrarian rights to each ejidatario; survey and map the ejidal lands; and declare the original ejidal grant to have been definitive rather than merely provisional. Such steps not only were essential as preliminary technical measures for any division or parcellation of the ejidal lands but were required by law as routine procedures. In fact, the Atencingo ejido should have been surveyed and mapped years before, as we have already noted. The census badly needed rectification, since the original one was grossly inaccurate and since the law provided that new ejidatarios should be admitted to replace those who had left the region or died. Thus these measures became the preliminary objectives of the ejidatario movement.

Federal Investigations

The administration of President Avila Camacho had taken steps to protect and institutionalize the sugar industry as a vital sector of the national economy. Its most important measure along these lines was a major decree promulgated in 1943 governing relations between the sugar industrialists and their sources of supply, the cane fields and the cane producers. According to the decree the productive areas around a sugar mill were officially designated supply zones for the mill. The Secretariat of Agriculture was to fix the boundaries of these zones in accordance with the capacity of the mill in question. The fields within the zone were to be used strictly for growing cane. All other crops were prohibited, except for those necessary to sustain the fertility of the fields, such as rice. The mill was obligated to buy at standardized prices all the cane produced within the zone, though the sale did not necessarily have to take place the year the cane ripened. Clearly such terms favored the industrialists, and in Atencingo's case they only added to the already considerable restrictions of the 1938 ejidal grant. Nonetheless, it was still legally possible that at least some of the ejidatarios' demands could be met. For example, the supply zone had never actually been defined; if it were, maybe some space would remain for other crops besides cane. In addition, another 1943 presidential decree specified that peasants had the right to grow corn for subsistence purposes on at least 10 percent of their ejidal lands.

Ultimately the future of the ejido and the cooperative depended on the stance of federal officials, for no changes could be made without their authorization. Thus one of the first moves made by the new ejidatario leaders, aside from local organization efforts, was to conduct commissions to the offices of the CNC and the Agrarian Department in Mexico City. There the ejidatarios laid their case directly before the federal authorities, and were sympathetically received. CNC leaders and the Agrarian Department decided to undertake on-the-spot investigations of the ejidatarios' grievances.[61] Meanwhile, less sympathetic replies were apparently received from officials in the Secretariat of Agriculture, who were responsible for overseeing Mexico's cane production.

At first, in April 1946, the Agrarian Department chief, Silvano Barba González, simply ordered his delegate in Puebla to prepare a study of the Atencingo problem, and especially to rectify the census as well as survey and map the ejido.[62] The delegate replied, however, that in the governor's opinion such activities would disrupt the area's

tranquility,[63] and further that "the established interests in the Aten-
cingo region seek the suspension of the work authorized by you."[64]
For his part, the state governor conveyed directly to President Avila
Camacho his fear that such a study would alter and even destroy the
Atencingo region's industrial unity.[65]

Despite this discouragement, in May the secretary-general of the
CNC, Gen. Gabriel Leyva Velásquez, urged the Agrarian Department chief to discuss the Atencingo case with the president so that the
president might authorize the study measures. To persuade the chief,
Leyva pointed out that in recent cases elsewhere agricultural-industrial units had not suffered losses in production either as a result of
the division of a large ejido (as in the case of Nueva Italia, Michoacán), or as a result of the limited distribution of collective cane lands
to form individual plots for growing crops other than cane (as in the
case of Los Mochis, Sinaloa). According to him the majority of the
ejidatarios in Atencingo did not favor cane cultivation only, and
needed land for growing other crops. The CNC secretary-general thus
believed that the proposed study measures, once carried out by the
state delegate, would end the Atencingo ejidatarios' problems. Furthermore, if the matter was properly handled, the ejidatarios' problems could be ended without bloodshed:

> We expect that, with the approval of the president, your department
> will confirm the authorization already given to your delegate in Puebla
> —giving him the necessary equipment to accomplish the work entrusted
> to him, and above all the necessary support—so that the established in-
> terests in the Atencingo region do not react with hostility and violence
> against the persons commissioned by the department . . . and against the
> peasants, who are fighting in order that their rights be respected.[66]

There was no doubt about whose side the CNC was on.

Secretary-General Leyva also argued that the cooperative's contract
should be thoroughly revised, so that the Atencingo ejidatarios would
enjoy the same prerogatives as ejidatarios in Los Mochis, Sinaloa, and
other parts of the Republic. Wages were very low in Atencingo, and
so were dividends, which came to about a hundred pesos a year. The
secretary-general was confident that the secretary of agriculture would
inform the president about the inequities of the contract.[67]

In the meantime the secretary of agriculture, Marte R. Gómez, was directing a different kind of appeal to the Agrarian Department chief. The secretary believed that harmony should be established within the ejido before any new contract was arranged. To this end he called on the Agrarian Department to rectify the census promptly, with the help of one of his own representatives, and afterward to issue certificates of agrarian rights. By this procedure the adjusted census would determine who deserved to be an ejidatario, thus blocking pressure for ejidal rights from the many landless peasants still remaining in the region as well as discouraging agitation for parceling out the ejido into individual plots. Parcellation, according to the secretary, "would impede the collective form of work, which is the one that is most suitable in said zone." Therefore the certificates of agrarian rights should indeed affirm each ejidatario's claim to a typical parcel—but they should not specify the size or location of the parcel. By such means the secretary of agriculture proposed to "consolidate the rights of the authentic ejidatarios, without destroying the harmony within the ejidal unit, which prospers around the mill."[68]

Late in May 1946 the Agrarian Department chief, after consulting with the CNC-affiliated ejidatarios and apparently having received the president's approval, decided to send an official investigator from the Mexico City offices to Atencingo rather than entrust the investigation to his worried delegate in Puebla. The Agrarian Department investigator was to be accompanied by a special CNC investigator, also to be sent from Mexico City. The two would attend special assemblies of the ejidatarios, collect petitions, and hear complaints; then they would report their findings to their superiors. They were not to promote specific solutions or to mobilize the peasants in any way.[69]

Meanwhile, other agents were also being dispatched to Atencingo. The secretary of agriculture commissioned an investigator, who went alone.[70] A representative of the Bureau of Cooperative Development of the Secretariat of National Economy visited Atencingo at the ejidatarios' request. He went only to the management offices, however, and not to the villages.[71]

The investigators from the Agrarian Department and the CNC visited the Atencingo complex during early June. The first day they

attended a general assembly of ejidatarios on the sports field at Atencingo proper. About six hundred residents from five villages—Atencingo, Lagunillas, Colón, Jaltepec, and Rijo—came to state their principal demands. The following day the investigators met with smaller
groups of ejidatarios in each of the same five villages. How many
attended the meetings at Atencingo and Rijo is uncertain, but at
Lagunillas about fifty persons attended; at Jaltepec, about seventy;
and at Colón, about one hundred fifty, the meeting there having
been expanded by neighbors from another ejido with a separate list
of demands.[72]

The interviewing did not proceed easily, however, for government
officials could not intervene in Atencingo without arousing the hostility of the established Atencingo interests. Having successfully visited five of the villages in the Atencingo complex, the Agrarian Department and CNC investigators suspended plans to visit the four
remaining ones—Raboso, La Galarza, Teruel, and San Nicolás Tolentino—after being informed by reliable sources that an attempt
would be made on their lives if they tried to go there. Moreover, the
peasants from these villages had not attended the general assembly
in Atencingo for fear of being suspended from their work or even
physically attacked as a result. Fortunately the investigators were
able to meet in Chietla with representatives from these villages, who
affirmed that they fully agreed with the demands made during the
general assembly.[73]

Those demands had been the following: first, that the ejidal lands
be surveyed and mapped; second, that the original census be rectified
to determine who held and who might hold ejidal rights; third, that
certificates of agrarian rights be issued to each ejidatario, in order to
document his status; fourth, that a specific parcel of land be assigned
to each ejidatario, in accordance with the ejidatarios' reading of the
1938 presidential grant, so that they would no longer be debased to
the condition of wage-earning peons; and fifth, in view of the expiration of the cooperative's contract with the mill, that the existing cooperative be disbanded and that a new one be formed under the direct
control of the ejidatarios themselves. The new cooperative should be
empowered to negotiate contracts with the mill after every harvest,

subject to the mediation of the CNC and in accordance with the recent presidential decrees granting all ejidatarios the right to cultivate at least 10 percent of their lands with the basic family staple, corn.[74] The division of the ejido into nine separate ejidos had not been specifically listed, though the ejidatarios did ask that agrarian executive committees be formed in each ejido village, presumably to lobby for independence.[75] In any case, this demand must surely have been conveyed to the authorities, for they generally understood it to be an important one.[76]

Returning from their three-day trip, the investigators submitted their reports. The Agrarian Department investigator's observations were contained in a lengthy confidential memorandum and follow-up letter to the top department officials.[77] Although the investigator made no specific recommendations of his own, he transmitted the ejidatarios' demands and thoroughly described their wretched living and working conditions. The mill administration, he wrote, "exploited the fieldworkers iniquitously" and had "converted the ejido into a feudal fiefdom, terrorizing and persecuting any peasants who claim their rights."[78] It totally controlled the ejido's labor force, dismissing recalcitrant ejidatarios from work at will or even evicting them from their homes, and replacing them with wage laborers from outside the ejido. The so-called cooperative consisted in reality of trusted mill employees, and it distributed no dividends to the ejidatarios. There was no person in authority to defend the ejidatarios' interests. "One can only suppose," the inspector concluded, "that throughout the region controlled by the mill there is unrest, malaise, misery, and rebelliousness among the people of the countryside."[79] He feared that unless the government took strong measures to improve the lot of the peasants, they would eventually resort to violence against the mill administration.

On the basis of such findings the Agrarian Department chief, with the backing of the secretary-general of the CNC, drew up a report and a set of recommendations very much in line with the ejidatarios' major demands. These documents were then presented to President Avila Camacho, who approved the recommended course of action in a written agreement on July 31, 1946. According to the president the Atencingo problem could be solved primarily by the Agrarian Department. The department would first rectify the census, with the help of the CNC and the Secretariat of Agriculture; second, reorganize the ejidal cooperative, with the help of representatives of the Secretariat of National Economy, the Secretariat of Agriculture, and the CNC; third, help negotiate the new, preferably two-year contract between the cooperative and the Civil and Industrial Company of Atencingo, with the mediation of the Secretariat of Agriculture; and fourth, survey and map the Atencingo ejido.[80] Subsequently, in August, officials in these various agencies were given urgent orders to carry out the president's instructions.

Meanwhile, William Jenkins was quite perturbed about the government's intervention in his domain, though in general little information is available about his counteractions. In September he expressed deep concern in a telegram sent directly to President Avila Camacho. Jenkins argued primarily that the president should put a stop to the activities of the Agrarian Department and the CNC in the Atencingo region until a forthcoming report was submitted by the secretary of agriculture, Marte Gómez. The Agrarian Department and the CNC had begun to reorganize the Atencingo cooperative without waiting for the report, which was evidently based on the investigations ordered the previous May. As far as Jenkins was concerned, they were supporting a group of agitators: "Without taking into consideration the cooperative's true leaders, or myself as financier and director of works, they are carrying out a labor of true agitation, with imminent danger of ruining the industry of Atencingo, sowing discord among all the elements of the cooperative, and for my part lack of confidence in the future." Jenkins further informed the president, as he had previously informed the state governor and the various federal agencies, that he was "entirely agreeable to delivering the management and financing of the cooperative to the person or institution you order." But, he added, "I cannot continue in this direction if the Agrarian Department and the CNC, in the reorganization that they intend to do, do it with elements completely hostile to all order and discipline. I see the inevitable decline in production, to the great harm of the national economy, if these elements continue with their work." Continuing on this note of impending disaster, he then declared: "I do not make this request for my own personal benefit, but rather for the welfare of Puebla and the national economy, for I am sure that in the hands of incompetent persons the production of Atencingo will decrease by one-half within a year."[81]

Whatever the president's personal reaction, the telegram was passed to Agrarian Department officials for an investigation of its allegations. The officials later concluded that their representatives had done no more than carry out the president's July 31 decision. There was no evidence of any "labors of agitation."[82]

The Crisis of 1946–1947

In the meantime the Atencingo ejidatarios, allied with the workers and the landless villagers, continued their campaign. The ejidatarios wanted to assume official control of the ejido and the cooperative, and the workers demanded that the mill administration finally sign a collective labor contract. Agitation and violence were openly resorted to by all parties in the struggle, while the government maneuvered to reestablish order on its terms.

Of the various tasks to be undertaken in Atencingo by the government authorities, rectifying the census was clearly the first order of business. The adjusted census would determine who held ejidal rights and thus who was legally eligible to elect officers and manage the cooperative. On September 12, one day after Jenkins's telegraphed appeal to the president, the Agrarian Department's field agents by special order convened the first general assembly of the ejidatarios, apparently with the blessings of the president, the state governor, and the CNC. The results of the census were announced for all the villages except Raboso and Rijo. With the rights of most of the ejidatarios thus established, the assembly proceeded to elect the councils for both the ejido and the cooperative.[83] For the first time in their history the ejidatarios were able to assemble and to hold a popular election—a great moment for them, for it signified the defeat of Jenkins. At last they had won control over their ejido and cooperative.

Or had they? As things turned out, for some procedural reasons the assembly was not considered an entirely legal and authoritative body. Additional assemblies would have to be called in the ensuing months before the new councils were officially invested with authority,[84] and in the meantime the mill administration did not give up. Perhaps part of the procedural problem was the absence of the ejidatarios from Raboso and Rijo at the main assembly, combined with the Agrarian Department's inability to finish rectifying the census for those annexes. Both difficulties could be traced to the hostility and dictatorial control of the mill's local administrators, especially in Raboso. There the administrator had evidently threatened that the ejidatarios would lose at least their jobs and potentially their lives if they attended the assembly and then tried to return home. As a result the CNC and the Agrarian Department requested the secretary of national defense both to disarm the sixteen mill employees attached to Raboso and to reassign the army soldiers stationed there who were siding with those employees.[85]

Sometime afterward the formal census was completed. The final results showed a total population of 7,139 persons (including women and children) in the ejidal complex. As a result of the investigations, only 2,012 were deemed qualified to receive rights as ejidatarios, which meant that 31 of the possible total of 2,043 rights were to be left unclaimed for the meantime.[86] Indeed, the Agrarian Department's field representatives discovered that only about 560 of the original 2,034 founders (excluding nine school parcels) were still in the region and deserved their rights.[87] The heavy rate of attrition was due to nine years of deaths, voluntary emigration, displacement, and flight from terrorism. All but 31 of the vacant rights were filled by numerous peasants who claimed them on grounds of inheritance and succession, or who had worked in the region long enough to claim eligibility on their own. Among those now admitted to the ejido— and thus to the cooperative—were Porfirio Jaramillo and other imported leaders, plus a multitude of landless peasants from the surrounding area who had participated in the struggle. In the process Pérez's peasant collaborators in the mill, who had previously been granted membership in the cooperative, were forced off the rolls. Of course, the ejidatarios working in the mill retained their rights.

Evidently an agrarian census was as much a political as a technical

undertaking; at least that was the case in Atencingo. In any fieldwork
for a census, government officials ordinarily added and omitted names
according to the evidence they gathered about individual peasants. In
theory the officials were guided in their decisions by the Agrarian
Code, but in practice they proved susceptible to other kinds of in-
fluences. For one thing, officials in the field were supposed to work
through the ejidal commissariat, taking into account the majority
view expressed by the ejidatarios in assemblies. Thus if a dominant
group of ejidatarios favored or opposed a particular individual, the
officials would usually include or exclude him according to the group's
wish, regardless of the status he legally deserved. For another, bribery
was always a possible way of influencing a decision. Apparently these
political factors played some role in the 1946 revision of the 1938 Atencingo census. Of course, it hardly seems surprising that the ostensibly
technical census procedures became such a political matter. Owing
to local population pressures and the inviting prospect of membership
in the cooperative, the competition for rights in the Atencingo ejido
was keen.

Meanwhile, the presidency changed hands, for 1946 was an election year. In December President Avila Camacho turned over his
office to his chosen successor, Miguel Alemán Valdés. One of the first
moves of the freshly inaugurated president was to enact a major constitutional reform that expanded considerably the maximum legal
size of private properties. As a consequence Jenkins received an enlargement of his rightful zone of protection from 150 to 300 hectares.[88]
He had already had 150 hectares, assigned as a result of the 1938 grant
to Atencingo; the additional 150 would come from large tracts that
he had illicitly retained since 1938, and that the peasants would soon
openly demand.

Aside from this happy outcome for Jenkins, the immediate effect
of the succession on Atencingo is unclear. At the least, it meant that
the parties in the struggle had to reaffirm their stands before the new
president, since he might decide to alter the course initiated by his
predecessor. It also meant that new officials would soon take command of the federal agencies, though at the state level Governor
Betancourt would remain in office until 1950.

Whatever the presidential succession's effect, the ejidatarios' determined campaign continued. Not only was bureaucratic pressure maintained in Mexico City, but a work stoppage took place at the very time when the harvest should have begun. The objective was to gain formal recognition of the new cooperative and its councils by Jenkins and the mill administration, and secondarily a new daily wage of 3.50 pesos. The Section 77 mill workers joined the ejidatarios to force the mill administration to sign the collective labor contract.[89] According to one account of the strike, whenever a leader of one of the ejido villages had to travel to Mexico City as part of a committee of representatives, contributions of twenty centavos or more would be collected from each ejidatario in order to obtain the forty or so pesos needed for the journey. Another leader would remain behind to guard against reprisals by Jenkins's pistoleros.[90]

While this difficult and sometimes bloody local strike continued, Jenkins's forces sought a bureaucratic victory at the federal and state levels of government. Jenkins himself refused to hand over to the new cooperative councils certain legal documents—a gesture that would have amounted to formal recognition. Further opposition to the installation of the new ejidatario regime came from certain peasants headed by Maximiliano Sánchez and certain supporters of the mill administration headed by Juan Criollo. Sánchez was apparently an old-time ejidatario leader who had not been included in the new census and who cooperated with the mill forces. Now he represented numerous wage-labor fieldworkers who had not gained rights as ejidatarios, numerous displaced ejidatarios who like him had been included in the original 1938 census but not in the 1946 census, and other former ejidatarios who had lost their rights for various legal reasons.[91]

Criollo was evidently a former associate of the cooperative and a loyal servant of the mill administration. Apparently he headed a group of the old cooperative's salaried workers who were now being displaced by the new regime. Moreover, he was allied with two congressional deputies.[92] According to the president of the new ejidal commissariat, Criollo represented "a group of 'unconditionals' who have always been at the service of the mill, ... a group of pistoleros. ...

These elements are responsible for the disasters the cooperative has suffered since its founding."[93] More than likely, Criollo and Sánchez and their followers were all part of a larger group led by Jenkins.

If their main objectives were to prevent the reorganization of the cooperative and the normalization of ejidal affairs, Jenkins's forces were too late. Criollo and his group apparently lodged strong complaints with the Agrarian Department and with the Secretariat of National Economy's Bureau of Cooperative Development. They objected in particular to the actions of Gustavo Funés, the inspector commissioned to install the reorganized cooperative, and to the displacement of persons who had served the cooperative under the old regime.[94] In further complaints to President Alemán and the Agrarian Department, Sánchez and his adherents similarly focused on faults in the new census. They claimed that returned ejidatarios whose rights dated from the founding of the ejido and deserving wage laborers had been displaced by unqualified peasants from outside villages. Many of these new ejidatarios already had parcels in their home villages, and many had gained their ejidal rights by offering friendship and bribes to the undesirable leaders from Morelos, especially Porfirio Jaramillo. These outside leaders did not deserve membership in the cooperative, the argument continued, let alone official posts. Indeed, in collusion with the ejidal commissariat, they were proceeding to allocate some of the lands to crops other than cane, thus endangering the national economy. As a general solution Sánchez and his associates demanded another revision of the census. As a further measure they demanded the expulsion of "that Mafia of leaders presently living from quotas our compañeros are contributing week by week," so that the ejidal commissariat and the vigilance council would "fulfill their responsibilities" and the cooperative councils would "be made responsible for their acts."[95]

But despite all these tactics—Jenkins's dire warnings of economic disaster, his initial refusal to recognize the new councils, the protests of those adversely affected by the reorganization of the cooperative and the ejido, even acts of violence—Jenkins's forces were defeated. The ejidatarios prevailed, with the support and help of imported leaders and outside agitators, villagers and other sympathizers, the

Agrarian Department and the CNC, the pro-CTM mill workers, Gustavo Funés, and the president and the state governor—and through sheer determination. The councils they elected for the ejido and the cooperative were duly installed in January 1947. The reorganized cooperative was officially recognized on January 1, and Jenkins soon delivered the documents he had previously tried to withhold from the new councils.[96] The councils of the cooperative named the popular leader Porfirio Jaramillo manager of the cooperative, in accordance with the General Law of Cooperative Societies. He took office on February 23.[97] Thus for the first time the peasants controlled the ejido and the cooperative. They had won the power struggle, though the policy struggle would continue.

Jenkins had lost—at least this round. His mill manager was no longer authorized to appoint the cooperative manager. Nor could Jenkins any longer keep a staff of mill employees in the ejido villages or appoint the ejidal officers and cooperative councils at will. But he still owned the mill, which remained the most powerful economic enterprise in the region. The ejidatarios were still obliged to produce cane. And the giant ejido was not yet parceled out or divided. Had he really lost the power struggle, then? Or was it only beginning?

Conclusions

In many respects the Atencingo ejidatarios' movement exhibited the features of a classic peasant struggle for liberation from systematic exploitation and subjugation. At first the ejidatarios as a whole were thoroughly exploited and subjugated—economically, administratively, politically, physically, socially. They had virtually no control over the land and its produce or over their own livelihood. Nor was it difficult to keep them in that condition. Historically they had become accustomed to oppression and rule by fear. They were ignorant, and lacked political and organizational skills. They undoubtedly saw few opportunities and few alternatives to cooperation—except futile outrage, flight, or even death. For that matter, they were grateful to have jobs and to be able to eke out a subsistence.

Though the Atencingo ejidatarios, like many peasant groups, were easily exploited and subjugated, they nonetheless could not have been kept under control without a powerful institutional structure. In Atencingo this structure was provided by the administrators of a monopolistic economic enterprise, who worked their will largely by means of cooptation and coercion. The economic and political stability of the enterprise itself depended essentially on the establishment of a regional power domain by its owners and beneficiaries for protection against local unrest and the even more dangerous threat of outside interference. In particular, two critical elements in the system were political influence outside the immediate power domain and the organizational effectiveness of the local chain of command. Especially striking in the case of Atencingo was Jenkins's dependence on his friendship and alliance with the state governor and state agrarian officials, not to mention the influence he apparently wielded among some officials of the Secretariats of National Economy and Agriculture. By embedding his enterprise in a network of political alliances, Jenkins protected it from unwelcome reformist measures that might have descended from the presidency, from other federal authorities, or from the still weak unionizing organs of the official political party. Within the local power domain the key man was the able manager of the mill, Manuel Pérez, whose regime became very effective at suppressing outbreaks of unrest.

Aside from the multitude of other changes that helped to politicize, organize, and mobilize the ejidatarios, the decisive political break came with the disintegration of Jenkins's network of state-level alliances and his local chain of command. In the space of two years, 1946 and 1947, a new governor took office and proved to be more amenable to the president and less amenable to Jenkins than his predecessors; Jenkins's key political crony, a powerful former governor, died; the manager of the mill died and was succeeded by a less able man; the new manager of the cooperative defected; and the ejidal commissariat virtually ceased to exist.

Moreover, the ejidatarios were spurred on by allies among other local oppressed groups: the rebellious mill workers, the landless wage laborers, and other village residents. Undoubtedly the mobilization of these groups also owed much to the disintegration of Jenkins's chain of command and network of alliances. Ultimately the mill workers and the ejidatarios combined forces in a classic worker-peasant alliance against the mill administration.

The ejidatarios' mobilization and eventual victory depended not only on Jenkins's loss of power within and without his domain but also on the intervention of outsiders. Important leaders and organizers were brought in from the state of Morelos, in part on the recommendation of leaders of a local CTM organization. Surely even more important were the contacts established with the CNC and the Agrarian Department in Mexico City, for both provided channels to the president. In addition, the new governor went along with the ejidatarios' efforts—or at least he did not obstruct them. Clearly, then, the assault on Jenkins's power domain depended decisively on efforts by CTM, CNC, and Agrarian Department officials to assert their influence in the Atencingo region. Clearly, too, these efforts would not have been successful without the president's firm backing. As it happened, he was directly involved in making the interventionist policy decisions.

Thus we see how strategically dependent on outside political developments were the major protagonists in the regional power struggle, Jenkins and the ejidatarios: Jenkins in order to maintain his power domain and economic interests, and the ejidatarios in order to mobilize themselves and to obtain outside help for an open power struggle. Once the struggle was under way a combination of direct action at the local level and lobbying at the government level became the tactical approach of both sides. Such a combination was important not only for fighting the adversary directly but also for attracting the government's attention. As the 1939 land invaders had demonstrated, threats to productivity and order could definitely stimulate a government response.

So far the principal issue in the Atencingo ejidatarios' struggle had been power—that is, control of the ejido's institutions. Yet basically the struggle was predicated on a number of demands by the ejidatarios for more radical policy changes concerning the ejido's structure and purpose. Now that they were in power, the ejidatarios could begin to fight for these more basic changes—the division of the ejido, the parcellation of its lands, and the diversification of its crops.

CHAPTER FOUR

The Movement in Power, 1947-1952

The second period in the history of the Atencingo ejido and cooperative, extending from 1947 to 1952, was the era of the ejidatario movement in power. During this time the ejidatarios, led by Porfirio Jaramillo, directly controlled the operations of the ejido and the cooperative without domination by the mill. As a result of their reformist
policies, however, the relationship between the cooperative and the
mill, shaky at best from the start, deteriorated to the point of crisis.
Ultimately federal and state authorities intervened. A special government commission was created to take charge of the cooperative, thus
ending the crisis by subjecting the ejidatarios once again to outside
rule.

The Establishment of the Jaramillo Regime

In general the ejido's new organizational structure resembled the
old one, with some important modifications. The ejidatarios were still
governed by the ejidal commissariat and vigilance council, now duly
elected every three years. The original six-man system, however, was
replaced by a nine-man system, so that each member village had an
official representative on each body.[1] The cooperative's two councils,
now duly elected every two years, were similarly expanded to include
nine representatives, one from each village. In accordance with the
General Law of Cooperative Societies, the council of administration
named the manager of the cooperative, subject to the veto of the

vigilance council. The manager appointed the field staff, as in the past, but in each village this staff now included one or two supervisors as well as the mayordomos and capitanes of the old system. The supervisors became the top leaders at the village level, replacing the administrators formerly installed by the mill.

By February 1947 the members of the four elected councils and the new manager of the cooperative, Porfirio Jaramillo, had all taken office and were enjoying virtually unanimous popular support. The ejidatario movement had finally come to power. In the succeeding months its leaders set about the final consolidation of their new regime. The critical tasks were to employ an accountant for the cooperative and to appoint the managerial field staff. In both cases the decisions made aroused bitter protest from the small pro-mill opposition.

As the new accountant Jaramillo hired Gustavo Funés, who had previously been the inspector commissioned by the Secretariat of National Economy to reorganize the cooperative and to teach the officers how to manage its affairs.[2] The announcement of his new career immediately aroused opposition from several quarters. Juan Criollo, leader of the displaced cooperative associates, denounced Funés to the secretary of national economy. Jenkins stalled in handing over certain accounting materials. Even the Secretariat of National Economy tried to interfere by sending two new inspectors to visit the cooperative, though this move was thwarted when the cooperative associates obtained an amparo against it.[3] Despite these obstacles Funés remained securely in office, protected by the Jaramillistas.

Meanwhile, Jaramillo moved to install loyal supporters as the field staff in the ejido villages. Again there was immediate opposition. The peasant leader Maximiliano Sánchez and his followers energetically implored the authorities not to allow experienced mayordomos and capitanes—namely, themselves—to be supplanted by "unconditional" followers of the privilege-seeking majority leaders. These newcomers lacked technical agricultural knowledge and practical ability, it was argued.[4] Their induction would bring "grave detriment to the economy of the ejidatarios and the tranquility of the region." Moreover, charging that the new Jaramillistas had no claim to ejidal rights, Sánchez again demanded a new census.[5] Nevertheless, Jaramillo and his fellow leaders successfully installed the staff and then favored their multitude of supporters in assigning work, though apparently some local violence and bloodshed resulted from the continuing feud with the mill forces.[6]

Thus the leaders of the ejidatario movement accomplished an important task faced whenever top offices are wrested from an old regime—that of consolidating a new regime. Having its loyal supporters in the top offices put the movement in power, to be sure; but regimes consist of more than the top offices. They include the middle and lower levels of the administrative structure, in this case the positions of the field staff and the accountant. Once they, too, were controlled, Jaramillo had a viable regime. Failure to have supplanted appointed personnel of the old regime at these levels might have put strong constraints on the new regime's durability and effectiveness.

The Census and the Survey

Meanwhile, the reform program of the ejidatario movement awaited action. Ultimately it called for the division and parcellation of the ejido and the diversification of crops. Any of these changes alone, not to mention all of them, would constitute a major, even radical, revision in the ejido's structure and functioning as ordained by the 1938 presidential decree. To be legal, such changes would require high-level official approval and even presidential authorization, since only presidents could modify the decrees of past presidents. In fact, presidential decrees were never supposed to be modified at all. Below the president, according to the Agrarian Code, the responsibility for the division and parcellation matters lay with the Agrarian Department, and that for crop diversification with both the Agrarian Department and the Secretariat of Agriculture.

As essential preliminary steps for division and parcellation, the ejidatarios' reform program demanded, as we have seen, that certain basic technical tasks be completed: the ejidal census, with the subsequent issue of certificates of agrarian rights, and the cadastral survey and mapping of the ejidal lands. For these tasks the Agrarian Department simply had to commission a brigade of engineers, order them and the state delegation to do the fieldwork, and then approve or disapprove the results, subject to the president's confirmation. Once approval had been granted, the president and the Agrarian Department could finally authorize the definitive possession of the ejido. In general, as prescribed by the Agrarian Code, these procedures were routine technical, bureaucratic, and legal steps to be taken for any ejido. In the case of Atencingo and annexes, however, they were highly political steps, too—and thus far from routine.

Of all these procedures, two were fundamental: the census and the survey. If they were not in order, then the authorities could not proceed to issue certificates of agrarian rights or grant definitive possession of the ejido, not to mention instituting the major reforms. The peasants knew this. So did the government bureaucrats. So did the mill administration.

In 1946 President Avila Camacho had specifically ordered that the 1937 census be rectified and the survey of the ejidal lands be completed. As we have seen, the census rolls were adjusted in late 1946, with results that satisfied the leaders of the new regime and permitted the reorganization of the cooperative. Nevertheless, the 1946 census was soon attacked as defective. Complaints about exclusion—commonly voiced by opposition leader Sánchez—came from former ejidatarios who had left the ejido and now demanded readmittance, from former peons who had held rain-check rights since 1937, from ejidatarios who had just been displaced by the 1946 census, and from landless wage laborers who now claimed ejidal rights. These groups charged that preferential treatment had been improperly given to undeserving peasants from outside the area, including Jaramillo and other leaders.[7] But though their complaints were officially acknowledged,[8] additional work on the census was postponed.

Meanwhile, the 1946 survey effort immediately encountered problems in the field. In September the ejidatarios complained that the engineers had demanded a payoff of one thousand pesos apiece in advance to carry out the survey work and protect the ejidatarios' interests. The engineers had allegedly backed up their demand by claiming that they had already turned down a substantial offer from Jenkins, who wished them to withdraw, and that the ejidatarios were being asked to pay much less.[9] As a result these engineers were quickly removed, and work was temporarily suspended. Unlike the census, at least the survey was not needed in order for the ejidatarios to take charge of the cooperative.

Thus, immediately after the Jaramillo regime took office in early 1947, the census was under fire and the survey was stalled. President Avila Camacho's 1946 orders consequently could not be fully carried out. For that matter, now that President Alemán had come to office, the orders were no longer in force, since they had never been put on a formal basis. Fieldwork came to a virtual halt. The ejidatarios' officers responded by filing new petitions for prompt action on their demands.* As a result, in April 1947 the Peasant Affairs Coordinating Commission, attached to the presidency and headed by Gen. Cándido Aguilar, ordered an investigation and then directed the Agrarian Department to proceed with the survey, settle boundary and water disputes, and consider dividing the ejido.[10] Later the commission added to this list a census revision to provide a basis for distributing certificates of agrarian rights.[11] Consequently, at the urging of the ejidatarios and under orders from a presidential commission (though not specifically from President Alemán himself), the Agrarian Department once again seemed prepared to resolve most of Atencingo's problems during 1947, the Jaramillo regime's first year in office.

But the situation soon became very complicated and problematic. In April the Agrarian Department promptly commissioned new engineers to finish the survey. By June, however, the chief engineer had been transferred elsewhere, and work was suspended.[12] Then matters

---

* As usual the major reform demands depended on the survey issue. The ejidal commissariat, in a letter to the DAAC chief on January 20, 1947 (FNDA, pp. 99–100), requested that the survey be completed in order to stop mill administrators from using ejidal lands for their own crops and to help correct the ratio between the number of ejidatarios and the size of the ejido. The commissariat's president, Guadalupe Sandoval, in a letter to President Alemán dated February 10, 1947 (FNDA, p. 99), requested the survey in the interest of avoiding any recurrence of a recent land invasion led by the former ejidatario Alberto Espinosa, who refused to recognize any authority other than the president and his own pistols. Furthermore, Sandoval favored the division of the ejido, which obviously could not be accomplished without a survey. In a letter on the same subject to a DAAC official sometime in 1947 (FNDA, p. 40), Sandoval mentioned the threat of land invasions again and cited the need to locate urban zones in the various sections of the ejido. Other evidence suggests that boundary disputes between Colón and Chietla were also a serious argument for the survey.

took a different turn. From the middle of 1947 on, surveying and mapping the total ejidal complex became a distant objective. The immediate objectives were reduced to specifying the urban zones and surveying and transferring lands occupied since 1937 as part of the ejido but still really owned by Jenkins.

As the valley's residents and state agrarian authorities had apparently known for years, Jenkins's company still owned extensive agricultural tracts. In the 1937 preliminary survey for the Atencingo grant, these tracts, many of them now irrigated, had been either ignored or classified as arid brushlands and building zones.[13] Then, during the Pérez regime, the tracts had been surreptitiously cultivated and passed off as part of the ejido. Jenkins would later attribute the irregularity to those who had proceeded with the grant "without measuring the area, and without fixing the boundaries, basing it only on a badly calculated estimation"—as though the fault rested with the Agrarian Department.[14] Meanwhile, since 1938 various petitions for ejidal grants and enlargements, both by outside villagers and by landless residents in the various ejido villages, had been turned down by state authorities as though no land were available.

Now the tenure problem became an open issue. In July a major study by the agrarian delegate revealed that the Ejido of Atencingo and Annexes in reality embraced an estimated 11,169 hectares rather than the 8,268 specified by the 1938 presidential grant. Each of the ejido's nine sections was in fact larger than the documents stipulated. Moreover, not only the Atencingo complex but also most other ejidos in the region remained unsurveyed and unmapped. The agrarian delegate counseled, though, that "in practice it would not be easy to rectify the boundaries of those ejidos." Such a move, he feared, would be "the pretext or motive for agitation in the villages," besides requiring time and personnel.[15]

In October the ejidatarios of Atencingo and annexes formally petitioned the state governor for the expropriation of Jenkins's remaining lands so that their ejido could be enlarged for the benefit of numerous landless residents.[16] Accordingly, during 1947–48, on orders from the Agrarian Department and the Mixed Agrarian Commission, a brigade of engineers under the supervision of the agrarian delegate did do survey work.[17] Then, during 1949, the delegate and his crew kept the survey figures in their offices while they resisted demands from the ejidatarios, the landless peasants, and the federal authorities for information. Indeed, the situation was highly problematic: forty other villages or peasant groups had also filed petitions for the same lands and vigorously challenged the claims from Atencingo and annexes.[18] On being requested for maps, the agrarian delegate temporized to his superiors. Since there were private and political as well as ejidal interests that wanted the maps for their own purposes, he wrote, the surveyors had decided to keep the maps secret for the time being. Only after the applications for the lands had been processed, and only after the decision on how to distribute the lands had been approved by the president, would the maps be given out.[19] A similar explanation was also provided to the ejidal commissariat in Atencingo, which had been applying pressure in concert with Jaramillo, as manager of the cooperative, with the CNC, and with certain officials who wanted to delimit the cane supply zone.[20]

Leaders in Atencingo blamed the temporizing on their enemies and feared that the survey's outcome might not be in their favor, even though the ejidatarios had occupied the lands continuously since 1938 and had regularly paid the annual state property taxes.[21] In a long letter sent in August 1949 to President Alemán and the Agrarian Department chief, the ejidatario leaders expressed their concern about "the chaotic situation created artificially by the enemies of the economic and social liberation of the ejidatarios." The agrarian delegate and his team of engineers were singled out for criticism. They had been given food, lodging, and travel expenses, the letter noted, to encourage them to carry out their mission. Moreover, to speed up the work, the ejidatarios had also paid the draftsmen to prepare the survey maps. "But in spite of having received advance payment for their work, and in spite of already being finished, the Agrarian Department delegation refuses to send us a copy of said maps, though they were made a year ago." At the root of the trouble, the letter charged, was Jenkins's company, which as the former owner of the ejidal lands had been secretly contriving to have the delegation suspend its work and withhold the survey maps. The company was also inciting outside villagers to demand Jenkins's excess lands, thus detracting from the Atencingo ejido's claim. The writers of the letter claimed to have information that the company was trying to regain control of its former lands, by "resorting to underhanded bureaucratic claims, even though it has its zone of protection in Atencingo." Finally, as for the general mood in the Atencingo ejido, the letter reported that all the ejidatarios, on becoming aware of the threat to their interests, had agreed in general assembly to defend their lands to the utmost, "without permitting a single piece to be wrested from us."[22] With such insistent language they raised the probability of turmoil and bloodshed if the government did not extend de jure possession to their de facto occupancy.

In the meantime work proceeded on a related task. If the ejido were enlarged, there would be room for additional ejidatarios. Accordingly a census was taken in 1948 for the pending enlargement. Its results showed a total of 766 inhabitants, including 197 heads of families, who lacked ejidal rights. Of the total, 433 were deemed qualified to receive a place in the ejido.[23] Among them, apparently, were peasants who had protested their exclusion from the 1946 census. In 1949, moreover, officials finally examined the rolls of the existing ejidatarios of Atencingo and annexes, who were awaiting their certificates of agrarian rights. Apparently there were no major incidents.[24] None of the entrenched "outsiders" from Morelos was displaced. Qualified peasants were admitted to fill vacancies, and as a result the number waiting to be admitted by means of the enlargement was revised downward to 286.[25] Thus by late 1949, with work well advanced on the census and the survey, the enlargement of the ejido and the issuing of certificates of agrarian rights seemed at last in sight. Indeed, the agrarian delegate reported to the department chief, "I estimate that by the end of the year all the agrarian problems of the important system of Atencingo and annexes will be resolved."[26]

Such optimism was not entirely unrealistic, for in 1950 a few problems did resolve themselves. First, in January, the Agrarian Department finally sanctioned the distribution of 2,043 certificates of agrarian rights.[27] Then, in May, after another firm demand from the leaders in Atencingo,[28] the Mixed Agrarian Commission submitted its report to Governor Betancourt. He quickly signed it into law and awarded provisional possession of the additional lands on July 4. Thus the Ejido of Atencingo and Annexes was provisionally enlarged by 3,229 hectares, of which 1,973 were irrigated, 420 were seasonally cultivable, and 836 were brushlands.[29] In line with recent constitutional reforms, new ejidatarios were to be added at the rate of one for every ten irrigated hectares or twenty seasonally cultivable hectares, now the minimum legal parcel sizes. Accordingly, the enlargement benefited 218 of the 286 qualified peasants, with the remaining 68 receiving rain-check rights.[30] In addition, 300 hectares of choice lands, some in Atencingo and some in San Nicolás Tolentino, were designated for Jenkins's private property.[31] No maps appeared, however, either for official inspection and approval or for public use.

Thus the Atencingo ejidatarios gained legal possession of lands that they had already occupied and worked for twelve years and that they had refused to relinquish. Indeed, those two facts were not only the bases for their claim but also the reasons for the official decision in their favor. The lands had been invaded in 1939 by the outside villagers who claimed them, and during 1949 and 1950 the threat of invasion had arisen again. This potentially violent situation helped convince the governor to legalize the existing situation. As the agrarian delegate later explained to his superiors, any move to take the lands away from the ejidatarios in order to process the applications of other villagers of the region would lead to "great agitation and clashes among the villages, because of the opposition of the ejidatarios involved."[32]

To summarize, then, from 1946 through 1950 government officials compiled a mixed record with respect to the elementary technical tasks essential for the Atencingo ejido's organization and legal status. The basic census rolls were put in order. The 2,043 certificates of agrarian rights were distributed. A number of peasants were provisionally given new ejidal rights. The ejidatarios were told the location of some urban zones for building homes and stores. And they were granted provisional possession of lands they had always occupied and worked anyway. Yet by 1950 there were still no authorized maps of the ejido, and no authoritative drafts; certainly the primitive efforts from 1938 were unreliable. The 1947–48 survey for the enlargement was in fact defective, the engineers never having surveyed large portions from the original 1938 grant. The enlargement had not yet been approved by the president; hence the new ejidatarios could not be issued their certificates of agrarian rights. The urban zones had not yet been given official approval; hence the rights to the lots in these areas could not be distributed. And needless to say, the original 1938 grant was still not authorized as definitive. Despite an eager beginning in 1946, the Jaramillo regime on balance was not faring very well with the Agrarian Department officials.

The data have especially illuminated the role of the agrarian delegate and the field engineers in the Atencingo survey proceedings. The Agrarian Code stipulated, however, that within the Agrarian Department offices in Mexico City, the primary responsibility for surveying and mapping ejidos rested with the Bureau of Lands and Waters. Further research would probably show, as seems to have been the case in later periods, that efforts to get the work done were no better than halfhearted at all three levels—those of the field engineers sent to Atencingo itself, the Agrarian Delegation in Puebla, and the Bureau of Lands and Waters in Mexico City. In a case like that of Atencingo, it appears that resolute determination and constant prodding by authorities at the highest levels of government are required to compel lower- and middle-level officials to do their jobs, and to do them effectively—unless, of course, the top-level authorities are not really committed to getting the job done either.

The Reform Program

Meanwhile, little was happening in official arenas with regard to the ejidatario movement's demands for the division of the ejido, the parcellation of the ejidal lands into individual plots, and the diversification of the ejido's crops. Of course, the technical disorganization obstructed such refoms. But there was also another obstruction, for after 1947 it began to appear that the top leaders of the new peasant regime were not as interested in division and extensive parcellation as they had initially claimed.

Once in office in 1947, the new ejidal commissariat president, Guadalupe Sandoval, had officially requested federal authorities to authorize the division of the ejido, arguing that he could not possibly oversee all nine sections.[33] Then, during April, the ejidatarios received major support for this objective. Within the Agrarian Department the general director of ejidal organization, Contran Noble, was developing a plan for the rational diversification of crops in the ejido. As part of the plan he suggested the possibility of dividing the Atencingo ejido.[34] Also in April, and far more important, Gen. Cándido Aguilar, head of the president's Peasant Affairs Coordinating Commission, proposed that the Agrarian Department seriously consider division as part of a general plan for the Atencingo ejido. According to him, dividing the ejido into nine ejidos would not alter the functioning of the Atencingo complex, since each of the ejido's nine sections constituted a separate agricultural unit that had no effect on the others. Noting that the proposal for division had been made by interested ejidatarios, General Aguilar went on to suggest that it be presented to all the ejidatarios in each section for their approval. The matter could then be put before the Agrarian Department and the president, in the hope of eventually obtaining a presidential decree appropriately modifying the terms of the 1938 decree.[35] Thus in 1947 at least some high-level officials cautiously advocated the division of the ejido.

After 1947, however, the ejidal commissariat seems to have stopped pressing the issue, and consequently the authorities did little themselves to pursue it. Perhaps all parties were simply more concerned then about the survey and other technical prerequisites to reform. Yet there is evidence to indicate that some leaders of the Jaramillo regime altered their priorities or even opposed the division of the ejido. Sandoval, of course, was a major proponent of division. His term as ejidal commissariat president should have lasted from 1947 to 1950, but for some reason he was supplanted after 1947 by Gregorio Maldonado, originally the alternate for the office. Throughout the rest of the term, as far as the evidence shows, Maldonado apparently made no diligent effort (if he made any effort at all) to obtain division.

Instead, two separatist movements developed during Maldonado's incumbency in opposition to further domination by the central offices in Atencingo. In the more serious case, during 1948 a popular leader of San Nicolás Tolentino who was a member of the cooperative's administration council organized ejidatarios in his section of the ejido for a separatist invasion of their own lands. Only a bloody shoot-out enabled Jaramillo and his supporters to regain control.[36] In the second case, also during 1948 (or possibly earlier), six ejidatarios living in the Raboso annex seized the lands around their small ranch and petitioned the authorities for an independent ejidal grant. They refused to rejoin the rest of the ejido until early 1950, when the president rejected their petition.[37] Future research may reveal that the separatist movements were instigated by the mill administration in an effort to weaken Jaramillo's regime. Whatever their origins, they forced Jaramillo to fight to keep the ejido together rather than seek division. In 1950 a new ejidal commissariat was elected. Its president, Carlos Galarza, also made little or no effort to secure the division of the ejido—and behind doors may actually have opposed the idea. In fact, he was more interested in the ejido's enlargement.

To the mass of ejidatarios, having individual parcels was even more important than having nine separate ejidos. During 1946 Jaramillo and his fellow leaders had identified themselves strongly with this longstanding aspiration. Yet the ejidal commissariat under Jaramillo never filed a formal petition for parcellation with the proper authorities. Certainly the government never promoted the reform, and the mill administration was singularly opposed to it. Both feared that parcellation would endanger cane production and ruin the sugar industry.

Thus the Jaramillo regime failed to reach either of its two major goals for land reform in the ejido: division and parcellation. Among local residents two general explanations for this failure have persisted. One finds fault with the government and the mill. According to this view Jaramillo and the other leaders, at least at first, did try to get the government to respond. Division was to be the first step, and then the ejidatarios would press for parcellation. But the government stalled, and never performed a proper survey. According to one former ejidal officer, "The government authorities listened only to money, but we had only spit to offer. . . . They kept us calmed down, telling us, 'Compañeros, we'll see about it,' and 'This is the way to proceed.' And so we passed the time away."[38] Later, when the cooperative incurred a huge debt to the mill, the authorities refused to consider parcellation until relations between the two institutions were normalized.[39]

According to the second explanation, during later years of the Jaramillo regime some of the top ejidal and cooperative officers obstructed Jaramillo's efforts to achieve division and parcellation. Although Jaramillo had opportunities to accomplish these reforms, his closest associates gave him conflicting advice. One would tell him to do one thing, and another would tell him to do something else: "So he found himself between the sword and the wall, and when the moment came, they were undecided."[40] In this way Jaramillo's fellow leaders immobilized him. In particular, Carlos Galarza, the president of the ejidal commissariat from 1950 to 1953, is reputed to have opposed the popular reforms—and to have accepted bribes from mill administrators.[41]

Furthermore, even Jaramillo's own position was unclear. Parcellation was virtually his slogan. Yet, as the most powerful figure in the ejido, he never raised the issues of division or parcellation in a general assembly so that the mass of ejidatarios eager for reform could authorize formal petitions to be sent by their ejidal commissariat.[42] A pessimistic view maintains that Jaramillo only used the issue to bring himself into power and then reneged on his promises, despite popular pressure for action.[43] Another view—probably correct—maintains that Jaramillo decided against the division of the ejido because it might have weakened the position of the ejidatarios vis-à-vis the mill. Instead he preferred a single ejido parceled out into individual plots, with collective work on the cane crop and individual work on other crops. However, the authorities rejected this idea,[44] besides not completing the technical preliminaries.

With respect to the third major reform objective, crop diversification, the ejidatarios were somewhat more fortunate. The 1938 grant decree had prescribed the exclusive production of cane and rice. Yet the ejidatarios needed permission to cultivate at least some corn and beans, if only for subsistence purposes, and argued their case convincingly on the basis of the 1943 presidential decree extending to all peasants of the nation the right to cultivate at least 10 percent of their lands with the basic staple, corn.[45] Moreover, they hoped to cultivate certain other lucrative crops for the market, despite objections from the mill administration.

As we have seen, the Agrarian Department's general director of ejidal organization, Contran Noble, laid plans to delimit the fields that had to be planted with cane for the mill and those that could be used for other crops, whether permanently or in rotation with cane. To complete the plans, however, he needed maps of the ejido.[46] Needless to say, despite requests from him and others, no maps were forthcoming. Moreover, by 1949, prodded by the ejidal commissariat,[47] officials in the Secretariat of Agriculture had drafted a plan for delimiting the cane zone. They had also assembled appropriate topographical, agricultural, and economic data on the ejido, including not only figures on the area cultivated with cane but figures on the area available for other crops and on the costs of cultivating them.[48] At least some officials in the Agrarian Department and the Secretariat of Agriculture, then, were prepared to consider crop diversification for the Atencingo complex. But their plan for diversification remained useless owing to the inability of other Agrarian Department officials to provide the necessary maps.

No doubt the ejidatarios grew tired of all this fruitless official maneuvering. At any rate, in 1947 they proceeded on their own by seizing and apportioning small plots for individual use. As a result, and in line with the 1943 decree, those who held certificates of agrarian rights were officially conceded the right to cultivate corn and beans on a limited basis for subsistence purposes, so long as they did not turn irrigated fields that were to be sown with cane or rice that season over to this use.[49] Thus formal progress was made toward one of the ejidatario movement's three major goals. Even in this case, however, the victory was only a partial one, for diversification extended only to corn and beans, and not to the lucrative commercial crops. Moreover, legally even the ejido's subsistence agriculture was supposed to be organized collectively and controlled by the cooperative society. In sum, the ejidatario movement in power, with two defeats on its major reform program and one partial victory, had fallen far short of expectations.

The Cooperative Versus the Mill

While the Jaramillo regime was having doubtful success with its reform program in the official arena, back in the Atencingo region it was pursuing policies that resulted in some material improvements to the cooperative, some de facto parcellation, and some further crop diversification. Unfortunately, the regime's policies also resulted in low cane production and huge debts to the mill. As Jaramillo struggled to reduce the cooperative's dependence on cane agriculture and Jenkins's mill, a crisis developed between the two institutions.

Data on economic conditions during the Jaramillo regime are scarce, though the ejidatarios claim that their overall incomes and living standards improved a little. The typical daily wage for fieldworkers was raised from 3.00 pesos to 3.50 pesos as a result of the work stoppage in late 1946.* By the early 1950's it had been raised further to 4.50 pesos, and by 1952 to 5.00 pesos.[50] Following the first harvest credited to the new regime, that of 1946-47, Jaramillo distributed the first annual dividends in years—about half a million pesos altogether, or some 200 pesos per ejidatario. Comparable dividends were evidently announced the second year, but after an assembly vote they were reinvested in the cooperative for construction and mechanization.[51] In succeeding years, however, the Jaramillo regime paid out no more dividends,[52] whether because of the decline in cane production, the cost of material improvements, the low market price of sugar, or the increase in salaries and wages. Fortunately, by then many ejidatarios had additional incomes from various other crops, some of which had a higher market value than cane.

The Jaramillo regime also spent some 916,000 pesos on material improvements for the benefit of the cooperative and the ejido. According to a February 1952 inventory, the improvements consisted of twenty Fordson tractors, at a total cost of 280,000 pesos; five other vehicles, at 151,000 pesos; one office building, at 130,000 pesos; four

---

* The peso was valued at about $.21 until 1949, and then became worth about $.11.

schools finished in Teruel, Colón, Rijo, and Jaltepec, at 115,000 pesos; one school begun in Atencingo, at 22,000 pesos; two cooperative stores, at 70,000 pesos; one casino, including nine pool tables and other items, at 45,000 pesos; one machine shop building and machine shop tools, at 60,000 pesos; two houses for employees at Atencingo and Raboso, at 28,000 pesos; and one building in La Galarza, at 15,000 pesos. In addition the cooperative now provided a medical service for its associates.[53] As a result of the various expenditures, the real patrimony of the cooperative increased in value from zero in 1946 to more than 435,000 pesos by early 1952, when Jaramillo was ousted.[54]

The large new two-story office building, which replaced the small old office maintained in Matamoros by the Pérez regime, was located in Atencingo along with the machine shop. On one wall inside the new office building an artist painted a timely mural. It depicted Jenkins concealed behind Pérez and whispering conspiratorially, while Pérez handed a pistol and a purse to their commissariat president, who eyed the peasants in the canebrake. The tractors and other equipment were purchased for the purpose of mechanizing the cooperative, which became a primary goal of the Jaramillo regime.[55] By contract, the cooperative's officials were ordinarily required to rent all agricultural machinery from the mill, as well as use the mill's railroad system for hauling harvested cane—all at high costs to the cooperative. Thus the new machinery enhanced the cooperative's independence from the mill. In particular, it aided in the production of crops other than cane, for which the mill administration refused to lend equipment.*

In the meantime Jaramillo and his fellow leaders embarked on a popular policy of de facto parcellation and crop diversification, beyond the token limits set by government authorities. In 1946–47 the ejidatorios started small individual plots of corn and beans on the seasonally cultivable lands as well as on some fallow irrigated lands, apparently with the indulgence of the authorities. In 1948 this practice was expanded, partly in reaction to serious problems with the mill. Thus each ejidatario eventually controlled from one-half to a full

---

* Nevertheless, it is my impression from talking to various ejidatarios that the mechanization did not get under way until the final years of the Jaramillo regime, and that even then there were actually fewer than twenty tractors delivered and operating.

hectare of good land.[56] Tomatoes, melon, and rice, as well as corn and beans, were cultivated on an individual basis, beyond the jurisdiction of the cooperative as such. In fact, after 1949 the area devoted to cane was reduced in favor of these other crops, some of which returned higher profits.

Financing and sales were not handled through the cooperative. Instead the ejidatarios dealt with private parties in the area and with the expanding National Ejidal Credit Bank, which authorized the formation of a local ejidal credit society in mid-1948. Most of the ejidatarios joined. Jaramillo was popularly elected chief delegate, and in general the credit society was run by the same persons that ran the cooperative.[57] The purpose of the society was to finance rice cultivation, which in the past the mill had always financed on credit through the cooperative. For the other crops, and for some additional rice, the ejidatarios organized themselves into small associations and then arranged through private parties for joint credits and sales.[58]

At first the main justification offered by Jaramillo and other leaders for these activities was that the ejidatarios needed small corn plots for family subsistence purposes. Later, however, the leaders said that crop diversification and parcellation had become necessary because cane production was unprofitable, owing to nationally low cane prices. Other crops simply earned more money. In addition, of course, the de facto agricultural reforms reduced the ejidatarios' dependence on the mill and fulfilled some of their long-standing aspirations—as well as endangering the mill's productivity.

If the Jaramillo regime made some unofficial headway in achieving reforms, its official performance in the areas of cane production and financial management was in the long run a failure. The record for the harvests credited to the Jaramillo regime, as well as for the mill in general, is shown in Table 3. Actually, the 1946–47 harvest, though credited to Jaramillo as manager of the cooperative, was in large part planned and executed by Jenkins and his administrators in the mill.[59] The Jaramillo regime was responsible for the 1947–48 and the 1948–49 harvests, however, and the figures show that its performance was on a par with that of the Pérez regime; indeed, the total output for 1948–49 was the best in years. But on the heels of this success, production

TABLE 3

Sugar Cane Produced and Processed by the Atencingo
Cooperative and Mill, 1946–1951

| Harvest | Mill | | Cooperative: |
	Total milled from all sources (tons)	Av. yield of all sources (tons/ha.)	Total delivered to mill (tons)
1946–47	330,570	100.8	294,500
1947–48	327,932	101.7	304,415
1948–49	371,866	99.3	342,674
1949–50	202,537	63.3	186,818
1950–51	197,720	66.1	159,972

SOURCES: For the cooperative, memorandum of the local ejidal credit society of Aten-cingo and annexes, July 12, 1967, MAEM. For the mill, Unión Nacional de Productores de Azúcar, *Estadísticas azucareras* (Mexico City, 1965), p. 44.

plummeted to disastrously low levels for the regime's two remaining seasons in office.

The cause of this sudden failure was not just agricultural and financial mismanagement but more fundamentally a serious feud between the cooperative and the mill. By law the mill was the only agency authorized to finance and purchase the cooperative's cane crop. The cooperative functioned by incurring debts each harvest year for the capital equipment and services furnished by the mill—debts that annually amounted to some eleven million pesos. Accounts were settled each year with the proceeds from the sale of the harvest. Profits gained by the cooperative could be allocated to dividends or capital improvements; any remaining debts had to be charged against the proceeds of future harvests.

Within this context the Atencingo cooperative fell into debt specifically because of unharvested cane. According to the 1943 presidential decree concerning the sugar industry, the mill was supposed to reimburse the cooperative for the value of any cane left standing in the fields for reasons attributable to the mill. When cane was left unharvested in Atencingo, however, the cooperative leaders were unable to obtain compensation from the mill. Indeed, the mill administration refused to reimburse the cooperative but accepted that unharvested and aged cane the following year, meanwhile charging the cooperative interest on the debt. During the Jaramillo regime cane was left standing in the fields after every harvest. In the 1946–47 season the main reason was crop disease. The estimated loss, borne by the cooperative, was 1.2 million pesos. In 1947–48 the main reason was breakdowns in the mill's machinery. The estimated loss was 1.6 million pesos, and the cooperative's total debt to the mill mounted to 1.8 million pesos. In 1948–49 further breakdowns in the mill's machinery caused further losses due to unharvested cane, and the cooperative's total debt mounted to 2.8 million pesos.[60]

The experience with the 1947–48 harvest was especially galling to the ejidatarios. Beforehand Jaramillo and his team foresaw that the mill could not process all their cane, so they lined up a buyer, another mill in the state of Morelos. Then they requested permission from the mill manager in Atencingo to sell about 100,000 tons of cane elsewhere. The manager, Manuel Espinosa Yglesias (now one of Mexico's foremost bankers), roundly opposed the idea, claiming that the Atencingo mill would use all the cane. Besides, he insisted, the cane—even if left standing—served as collateral for the mill's annual loan to the cooperative. When harvest time came around a considerable quantity of cane was again left uncut in the fields, and the mill administration again charged the deficit (plus accrued interest) to the cooperative— even though the deficit could have been liquidated by selling the cane to a third party. The cooperative's leaders demanded that the mill administration adjust its accounts in accordance with the 1943 presidential decree by reimbursing the cooperative and reducing the total 1947–48 debt to only 200,000 pesos. But their demands went unheeded.[61]

The 1948–49 harvest went much the same, as one retrospective account relates:

> From 1948 to 1949 they required us to sow a lot of cane in our ejido, and at the beginning of the harvest of those two years, it so happened that the mill could not make its milling machinery work normally, and because of this it did not succeed in milling all the cane it had ordered us to sow in our ejido. This was a premeditated and cunning act. A little more than 50,000 tons remained standing in the fields. The own-

ers of the mill refused to pay us the value of the tons of cane it did not
mill, thus creating for us a debt of more than a million pesos to the mill.
A contract existed between us; and they had an obligation to buy the
cane from us, since it had been sown at the request of the mill and since
the contract obligated them to buy the harvest. Well, they did not comply, and the authorities sided with them. As in the times of the Porfiriato, it was not even possible for us to get them to pay the expenses.
Now it was not the peon who was put into debt. It was the ejido. What
a profitable business the Revolution turned out to be![62]

It appeared that the mill administration was deliberately scheming
to bankrupt the cooperative by means of mechanical breakdowns.

Unharvested cane was not the only reason for the cooperative's
mounting debt. Beginning in 1948–49 the cooperative's leaders complained, though to no avail, about excessively high rental and mainte-
nance charges for tractors and other equipment and about the high
rates for transporting cane from the fields on the mill's private railroad. Later they protested that the mill's scales gave inaccurate read-
ings, naturally to the mill's benefit.[63] Moreover, according to them,
the cooperative's debts were compounded by the regrettably low sugar
price set by the federal government for the national market.[64]

Facing financial ruin at the hands of the mill, Jaramillo and the cooperative's administration council took their case to the highest state
and federal authorities, including President Alemán. As they wrote
to Governor Betancourt in 1949:

> Our first interest is producing cane and rice, but we cannot continue
> working to produce sugar cane, because its cultivation brings us enor-
> mous losses. . . . We have been carrying on talks in Mexico City with the
> mill, despite the cost of transportation. . . . They have given us nothing
> but refusals, which has only aggravated the situation of our peasant as-
> sociates in this region, who above all remain resolved not to sow more
> cane if the mill does not agree to the deal we have proposed. . . . They
> say they are going to do something about this, but they do not. And this
> makes us think of the idea: We live in a society in which the poor be-
> come poorer and the rich richer every day.[65]

But such pleas fell on deaf ears. Neither the government nor the
mill administration did anything to alleviate the financial woes of the
beleaguered cooperative, and the mill's machinery was not improved.

The ejidatarios accordingly decided to take drastic steps, as their letter had threatened. "This show of bad faith on the part of the mill forced us to reduce the area planted with cane until they modernized their plant."[66] In the wake of this decision the 1949–50 harvest was a production disaster, yielding only 226,627 tons. Even so, cane was once again left standing in the fields—approximately 40,000 tons of it, for the mill accepted only some 187,000 tons.[67] The cooperative's debt to the mill mounted to 3.5 million pesos.[68] Then, in the 1950–51 harvest, production diminished to some 160,000 tons, or approximately one-half the normal amount. At that level the mill was no longer an economically viable enterprise.

Thus the disastrous drop in cane production was engineered by the ejidatarios as a reprisal against the mill administration, and incidentally as part of the de facto crop diversification that had taken place. But ironically enough, it also appears that the financial and production crisis was just as deliberately brought on by the mill administration for a quite different purpose—that of precipitating government intervention against Jaramillo. The breakdowns in the mill's machinery served this purpose; moreover, according to popular belief, the mill administration subverted the members of Jaramillo's field staff and gave them bad technical advice:

[Jaramillo] had people working with him, and these were the ones who had led him into bankruptcy. Yes, those around him. His cabinet. We were a united mass, but apart from us were the managerial leaders. And apart from them was Jaramillo, who found himself in the middle.[69]

Many led him astray, his friends and other persons behind the scene who made him fail.... They forced him to fail in the administration. That is, the mill and persons close to him, who he believed to be trustworthy.[70]

The mill gave bad orders to the mayordomos about not irrigating, in order to try to get the cooperative to fail. Porfirio Jaramillo did not always see what was going on; he could not be in all the annexes at the same time. The mayordomos, though ejidatarios, were accustomed to following orders. Because of this, and much sabotage, the society could not progress. The mill wanted the government to think that the peasants did not have the ability to look after themselves.[71]

In fact, it is generally recognized that Jaramillo and his fellow leaders did lack administrative ability and even technical knowledge about cane agriculture. Apparently Jaramillo himself was only partially literate.[72] These shortcomings put the Jaramillo regime at a disadvantage to the mill administration. In sum, then, the production disaster was brought on not only by the ejidatarios' countermoves against the mill administration but by the mill administration's strategy of undermining the Jaramillo regime. As a group of ejidatarios later recalled, "It was in the interest of the Atencingo industrialists to make us fail."[73]

The Regime Beleaguered

By 1950 the cooperative and the mill had reached a crisis. The dismayed mill owners and administrators insisted to the government that the ejidatarios were an incapable lot who did not know how to manage their own affairs or the ejido's production. Consequently the mill was in economic trouble, and the government must intervene.[74] The authorities listened. The mill remained a critical component of the state and national economies. In addition Jenkins was now even more influential than before, having substantial investments in Mexico City and other parts of the Republic. These outside ventures more than made up for any loss of influence he might have suffered owing to the expropriation of his Atencingo domains. In fact, in recent years he had apparently pretended to sell the Atencingo mill to his two Spanish business partners, Moises Cossío and Lorenzo Cue—probably to protect it from any further expropriation pressures.

To make matters worse, by 1950 the Jaramillo regime was also having trouble with the state and federal governments. Until then the state governor, Carlos I. Betancourt, had not openly turned against the regime, though he had evidently offered little support aside from the provisional enlargement. But after the 1950 elections Betancourt was succeeded by Gen. Rafael Avila Camacho, the brother of Maximino and Manuel. This new governor was not disposed to tolerate what he regarded as the disorderly conduct of the cooperative's officials or to allow the economic collapse of the mill. As a result, in 1951 the Jaramillo regime's difficulties with the state government—and by extension with the federal government—assumed crisis proportions.

Beset on all sides, the Jaramillo regime had no allies for the show-down. Even its former supporters, the local villagers and the mill workers, now defected, the villagers seizing the opportunity presented by the crisis to renew their bid for land and the mill workers seeing the regime's economic failures as a threat to their own jobs. For many years the villagers petitioning for land had been loosely represented by a number of separate local executive committees, one for each petitioning village or group. During 1950 and 1951, however, this loose aggregation of the land-hungry became impressively organized. Evidently the motive for the new organization effort was to intensify lobbying against the Jaramillo regime so that the federal government would not make the provisional enlargement grant to the Atencingo ejido a definitive grant.

The first opposition association to appear among the villagers was the Regional Caneworkers' Circle 83 of the new National Cane Producers' Union, an affiliate of the CNC. The local head of the caneworkers' circle was the prominent former ejidatario Alberto Espinosa. Espinosa had been among those who lived and worked in neighboring Morelos during the early 1940's but returned to the Atencingo region in 1946 to join the struggle against the mill administration in the hope of regaining their ejidal rights. Now he was the influential leader of the local executive committee for former ejidatarios and peons of the Atencingo complex who were petitioning for land. He was also reportedly in league with the mill administration.[75] The second opposition association was the Puebla Peasants' Federation "General Miguel Alemán," formed in 1951 and named after the president's father. The federation drew together under one front a number of villages and groups that years before had formed local executive committees to press for the enlargement of their own ejidos.

Outraged by the provisional enlargement granted to the Atencingo ejido during 1950–51, these villagers demanded that the federal government nullify that grant and give them all or part of the lands as a definitive grant in the form of individual ejidal parcels.[76] More radical ideas were added to this basic approach as the landless peasants sought to capitalize on the cooperative's disorganization and poor production record. First, Espinosa's two organizations, the caneworkers' circle and the Atencingo local executive committee, called for the liquidation of the cooperative and for the division and parcellation of the giant ejido.[77] These ideas were basically seconded by the federation, which also proposed the formation of a special committee of mill representatives and peasants to regulate regional agriculture.[78]

Both the caneworkers' circle and the federation claimed that their petitions had the support of the majority of the ejidatarios of the Atencingo complex, who were allegedly disillusioned with the Jaramillo regime.[79] The leaders of the caneworkers' circle even asserted that their organization represented these ejidatarios. Unfortunately there is no substantial evidence to indicate whether or not it did, though it is safe to say that a program calling for division and parcellation was virtually guaranteed to attract some following in the ejido.

What happened to the parcellation proposal is unknown, but the caneworkers' petition for division was turned over to a subordinate in the Agrarian Department for study. He reported to his chief that despite difficulties the agrarian laws might be interpreted to allow the division of the Atencingo ejido. Of course, there were major legal obstacles to the modification of any presidential decree, including the 1938 ejidal grant, but the official located precedents in the cases of the El Yaqui ejido in Sonora state and the Laguna ejidal region of Coahuila state. Thus it appeared that the authorities might now respond to a petition for division from adversaries of the Jaramillo regime.[80]

While making these far-reaching proposals, the various groups of villagers also demanded that the Agrarian Department undertake another survey to locate lands to accommodate them.[81] Indeed, as the governor's provisional enlargement order was passed upward to federal officials, it became clear that the 1946 survey was not acceptable. Large areas from the original ejidal grant had never been surveyed at all, and there were some questionable figures for the areas surveyed for the enlargement.[82] Espinosa even charged that some of Jenkins's holdings might still be transferable.[83]

Immediately after the provisional grant the agrarian delegate had counseled against further surveying, saying that the information already gathered was sufficient and that further survey work would stir up conflicts in the region.[84] Yet, after a new spate of requests to the president from the villagers, the responsible officials of the Agrarian Department asked the agrarian delegate to begin yet another survey. His reply was firm: "Given the situation and the agitation that prevails in the region as a result of intergroup conflicts, for now it is not advisable to order survey work . . . in the villages of Atencingo and its vicinity."[85] So no work was begun. Moreover, as we have seen above, the agrarian delegate defended the decision to grant the enlargement to Atencingo and annexes in view of the ejidatarios' determination to continue occupying the disputed lands.[86]

Back in Atencingo the ejidal commissariat also defended its right to the provisional enlargement. In particular, commissariat president Carlos Galarza objected strenuously to Espinosa's maneuvers, charging that Espinosa's only objective was "to seek the division of the peasants of the region and to foment antagonism among the people of other ejidos.[87] Thus, owing to the land dispute, the Jaramillo regime not only was becoming isolated from its former peasant allies but was becoming a target of attack.

The old camaraderie between the ejidatarios and the mill workers had also subsided since 1947. At that time the CTM faction, which was sympathetic to the ejidatario movement, had had the upper hand among the workers, but by the 1950's its strength had diminished owing to a resurgence of the CROM faction.[88] Moreover, though evidence on this point is sparse, even the CTM mill workers were apparently alienated from the cooperative because the low levels of cane production posed an economic threat to the mill—and thus to their livelihoods. Whatever the full reasons, the high-level CTM leader Blas Chumacero, who had taken an active part in obtaining the original ejidal grant, went to the new governor, Rafael Avila Camacho, and helped convince him that the government should intervene in the cooperative's affairs and end the disorder in the ejido.[89]

Thus by the middle of 1951, and especially after the disastrous 1950–51 harvest, the Jaramillo regime was virtually surrounded. Looking for a way out, yet implicitly defending their cutback in cane cultivation, Jaramillo and the administration council (headed by Jesús Aguilar, in his second two-year term) published a lengthy open letter to President Alemán in a major newspaper. Complaining about the general condition of cane agriculture and the sugar industry, the cooperative society officers publicized their support for recent CNC proposals for an increase in the government-regulated price of sugar. In view of the present miserable conditions, they noted, and since no one should be forced to work without just compensation, "The peasant has a right to search for other means of living, including turning wetback."

Moreover, the letter asked that cane production be mechanized in order to lower costs. While the necessity of this move had been acknowledged for several years, nothing had been done. Now mechanization was more difficult than ever, the letter noted, because the Korean War had made machinery more expensive. In fact, cooperative society officers had asked for machinery two years before, without results to date. The letter further noted the need for the government to locate new lands for peasant farming, but it expressed doubt that the government would do so.[90]

Despite such efforts the Jaramillo regime remained under siege, with no relief forthcoming. Ejidatarios would later charge that the mill administration had conspired with the federal government, "then in notoriously dishonest hands," to bring about the regime's fall.[91] Moreover, the mill's new owners "redoubled their pressure against us and our representatives, making accusations against us before the federal authorities, naturally charging the cooperative with all the blame for the failures of the inexpert managers of the Atencingo mill."[92] In official circles the regime was opposed by the National Cane Producers' Union of the CNC and evidently got little sympathy from the CTM. The Agrarian Department, the Secretariat of National Economy, and the state government were all unfavorably disposed toward it as well. But the key government figures who apparently convinced President Alemán to intervene were Governor Avila Camacho and José Antonio Cobos, general director of the Bureau of Cooperative Development of the Secretariat of National Economy.[93]

Even within the ejido the Jaramillo regime evidently lacked sufficient support to impress the authorities. Jaramillo's popularity was apparently waning because of his failure to achieve division and parcellation, and more ejidatarios were beginning to support anti-Jaramillo leaders and organizations in the region. Attacks on Jaramillo's character even began to spread to the effect that he was embezzling the cooperative's money and had purchased a ranch in Morelos.[94] Thus, as one ejidatario later noted, "Certain elements spurred by envy began to look for problems, putting themselves on the side of the Atencingo milling enterprise, . . . which had always looked for the way to regain control of our ejido."[95] And as another said, "The mill, persuading with its money—and with power from above—got its faction to increase."[96]

Federal Investigation and Ouster

In late 1951, both the governor and the president now being convinced of the need to intervene in the ejido's affairs, two federal investigators were commissioned to make a joint inquiry into Atencingo's problems. One was José Antonio Cobos, general director of the Bureau of Cooperative Development of the Secretariat of National Economy. The other was Contran Noble, now general director of the Bureau of Ejidal Development of the Secretariat of Agriculture—and also the official who had earlier tried to plan for crop diversification in the Atencingo complex. The Agrarian Department was not represented on the investigative team. The investigators were ordered to determine why cane production had diminished and why the cooperative society functioned inadequately, and to propose measures to correct these difficulties. That is to say, the primary institutional focus was the cooperative, not the ejido. Moreover, very little attention was given to the cooperative associates' grievances against the mill.[97]

From their experience with the Atencingo case, and from their familiarity with the interests and objectives of the cooperative, the mill, and the state government, the federal investigators synthesized the basic goals of each.[98] The goals of the cooperative were exhaustively described, as follows:

1. The continuation of the cooperative system.
2. The continuation of the existing group of staff leaders.
3. The continuation of the existing system of operation: collective work on the cane; individual work on the other crops (rice, tomatoes, beans,

melons, and corn); the collective sale of the cane; the individual sale of the other products; the continuation of the same manager; the continuation of the present accountant; agreements with third parties for producing individual crops.

4. The continued freedom of the management and operation from any official supervision and intervention.

5. The continuation of the existing pattern of obtaining credit for the cane and other crops (through the mill, the agency of the National Ejidal Credit Bank, and private parties).

6. An increase in non-cane cultivation.

7. The reduction of cane cultivation, because of low returns in comparison with other products, or because it is to the advantage of the staff to produce other crops individually, or for both reasons together.

8. The soliciting of official intervention (as has already taken place) exclusively for the liquidation of the unharvested cane ... ; the reduction of the mill's hauling charges; and an increase in the price of cane.

Naturally, the goals of the mill administration were quite different:

1. To continue financing the cooperative for the cultivation of cane.

2. To finance the cultivation of rice (currently financed by the National Ejidal Credit Bank and by private parties).

3. To halt the cultivation of crops other than cane and rice.

4. To increase cane production (up to 400,000 tons per harvest).

5. To reduce costs.

6. To continue lending its agricultural equipment to the cooperative (supposedly deriving from this practice not only the amortization but also additional profits).

7. To continue hauling the cane at the expense of the cooperative.

8. To exercise some control in the cooperative, so as to ensure as much as possible the supply of cane.

In other words, the mill administration desired a near return to the original economic relationship between the cooperative and the mill, and opposed Jaramillo's attempts at diversification and mechanization.

The investigators separated the goals of the state government into economic, social, and political categories. The economic goals were as follows:

1. To increase the cultivation of sugar cane, by extensive and intensive means, in accordance with the capacity of the mill.

2. To intervene in order to perfect the functioning of the cooperative, or the organ that replaces it.

3. To restrict the cultivation of other products that affect cane production.

4. To diminish the operating costs.

The social goals:

1. To increase the personal incomes of the peasants.
2. To construct facilities and establish social services.

The political goals:

1. To break the control of labor organizations in the peasant sector of the Atencingo region.
2. To break the cacique-type control of the present managerial staff.
3. To increase the intervention of the local government in the cooperative, or the organ that effectively replaces it.

According to the investigators' description, then, the state government in effect sided with the mill on the need for intervention and for the restoration of cane production, and struck a middle course on the issue of diversification. Moreover, it sought to reap political as well as economic advantages by intervening, one of its major goals being to regain regional political power.

The investigators leveled three major accusations against the cooperative society and its current management, charging that both the 1938 presidential decree authorizing the ejidal grant and the cooperative's constitution were being violated. First, the ejidal lands were supposed to be worked collectively; yet the ejidatarios grew only cane collectively, cultivating rice, beans, corn, melon, and tomatoes in individual plots. Second, the cooperative was supposed to see to the production and sale of all crops, again on a collective basis; yet the cooperative performed these functions only in the case of sugar cane. Part of the rice crop was financed by the National Ejidal Credit Bank and produced individually; the rest of the rice crop and the beans, corn, melon, and tomatoes were financed by third parties, and then produced and sold on an individual basis. Third, only ejidatarios listed in the census were authorized to be cooperative associates. Yet according to the investigators, the membership rolls included 374 persons who were not actual ejidatarios and excluded 874 of the 2,043 who were.[99] Strangely enough, the report did not mention that the presidential decree's clause reserving the ejidal lands for the exclusive cultivation of cane and rice was also being violated.

In addition to making the three major accusations, the investigators criticized the way the ejidal institutions were run. Within the ejido were three formal institutions, each associated by law with a different government agency: the ejidal commissariat, corresponding to the Agrarian Department; the cooperative society, corresponding to the Secretariat of National Economy; and the local ejidal credit society, corresponding to the National Ejidal Credit Bank. The investigators observed that frequently the cooperative society was opposed by an alliance of the ejidal commissariat and the leaders of the local ejidal credit society. This opposition, they said, created conflicts that were damaging to the collective interests represented by the cooperative.[100] At the same time the investigators also pointed to what they regarded as improper collaboration among officials in the three institutions. Locally, Porfirio Jaramillo was the head of both the cooperative and the local ejidal credit society. Moreover, the leaders of all three institutions seemed to be unofficially involved in planning and financing the production of crops other than cane by various small groups. "Because of the influence they exercise, and because of the assurances and opportunities they give to whoever finances these crops, it is to be supposed that they make sizable personal profits."[101]

The cooperative came under fire for its financial practices. The investigators found that it was misusing funds provided by the mill solely for cane agriculture. In particular, the cooperative had spent some of this money on operating and maintaining machinery used for crops other than cane. Over the years this improper practice had added considerably to the mounting debt. Furthermore, the investigators found serious fault with the cooperative's accounts. An audit revealed that the accounts were rudimentary, defective, incomplete, and not up-to-date—and therefore unsatisfactory for an enterprise that managed millions of pesos a year. So disorderly were the accounts that the audit, made in 1951, could only proceed as far as the records for mid-1950, when the debt to the mill had amounted to 3.5 million pesos. Discrepancies were repeatedly uncovered between the cooperative's accounts and the mill's accounts. No records had been kept of expenditures related to crops other than cane, nor was there any break-down of costs for cane production in the various sections of the ejido. Indeed, the investigators concluded, the accountant and the managerial staff seemed unqualified to keep the accounts properly, if they had not intentionally kept them in disorder.*

At the conclusion of their report the investigators proposed three major plans for the long-run solution of Atencingo's problems and one interim plan. Of the three major plans,[102] one provided for the survival of the cooperative, given several conditions. First, the cooperative must comply strictly with its constitution. Second, new councils must be elected and an honest, capable managerial staff installed. Third, all ejidatarios included in the census must be admitted as associates of the cooperative. Fourth, all who were not ejidatarios must be excluded. Fifth, the cooperative must control all agricultural production, and thus all credits must be channeled through it. Finally, the accounting system must be totally reorganized. (This plan was eventually put into effect in 1961.)

The second major plan proposed the liquidation of the cooperative. The credit society would then take charge of the financing and cultivation of all crops, as well as attending to the social needs of the former cooperative associates. (This measure was taken in 1965.) Under the third major plan the ejido would be divided and a local ejidal credit society would be established in each of the resulting ejidos. Left open was the possibility of dividing the ejido into fewer than nine ejidos. (This appeared to be the direction of events in 1969.)

The investigators did not compare the ramifications of these three plans or recommend any one plan as superior. It is clear, nevertheless, that the first preserved the official authority of the Secretariat of National Economy over the ejido, whereas the second and third put the

---

* José Antonio Cobos and Contran Noble, investigative report to superiors, January 3, 1952, FNDA, pp. 26, 29, 33. Actually, two prior visits to the cooperative had been made by accounting inspectors at the behest of the Secretariat of National Economy's Bureau of Cooperative Development. The cooperative's accounts were found to be in order on both occasions, according to an unsigned memorandum, probably by Jaramillo, sent to President Adolfo Ruíz Cortines sometime in 1953 (FNDA, p. 57).

ejido under the authority of the National Ejidal Credit Bank. It seems significant that the investigators did not call for the restriction of the ejido's crops to cane and rice, as prescribed in the 1938 ejidal grant. Rather, the emphasis was on "cane and its rotative crops," with implicit sanction for diversification.[103]

As an interim plan the report recommended that the federal government take action in accordance with the statement in the 1938 ejidal grant obligating the ejidatarios to comply with any directives the federal government might give concerning the ejido's administration and organization. The investigators proposed the creation of a government commission that would supervise the operations of the cooperative society in concert with the Secretariat of National Economy and subject to the General Law of Cooperative Societies. The commission would be composed of representatives of the state government, the Secretariat of National Economy, the Secretariat of Agriculture, and the Agrarian Department. It would be empowered to name the cooperative's manager and staff, who should be persons of sufficient ability to put the cooperative on the same technical level as the Atencingo mill. Finally, the commission would make a systematic study of the Atencingo ejido's problems—agricultural, economic, and social—to determine the type of organization most appropriate for the ejido in the future. In particular, the study should investigate the feasibility of dividing the ejido, whether into nine ejidos or into a fewer number; of parceling out the ejidal lands; and of installing one or more local ejidal credit societies.[104]

Such were the terms of the report submitted by the two investigators. The original was signed on January 3, 1952, and was 21 pages long. But it may not have been the final version, for Noble later had some interesting revisions made on his copy, presumably reflecting some considerations that arose after the fieldwork had been completed. Most important, the reference to studying parcellation was suppressed —implying that it was an unacceptable alternative.[105]

Not too many days later, on January 29, President Alemán and three other officials—the secretary of national economy, Antonio Martínez Báez, the secretary of agriculture, Nazario Ortíz Garza, and the

Agrarian Department chief, Mario Sousa—signed a joint decree submitted by the secretary of national economy that created a special commission to oversee the administration of the Atencingo ejidal complex. The members of the commission were to be the state governor; one representative each from the Secretariat of National Economy, the Secretariat of Agriculture, and the Agrarian Department; the president of the administration council of the Atencingo cooperative society; the president of the ejidal commissariat; and a representative of the Atencingo mill.[106] The inclusion of these last three members expanded the commission's membership beyond that recommended by the field investigators.

The reasons given for the measure closely paralleled the investigative report's conclusions, with one significant exception: the decree strongly emphasized the ejidal grant's stipulation that the lands be used exclusively for the cultivation of cane and rice, a point passed over by the field investigators. Aside from repeating the report's criticisms of the ejido, the decree emphasized that the existence of three separate institutions within the ejido had created conflicts prejudicial to the collective interests, and that the local ejidal credit society and its head had encouraged the cultivation of crops other than cane. It argued also that the disagreements between the mill and the cooperative could only be settled by an outside agency. Of course, federal intervention had been provided for in the 1938 ejidal grant. On such a basis, then, the new commission was given wide-ranging powers over the cooperative, the most important being the power to name the cooperative's general manager. The decree left no doubt about who was in charge of the ejido and the cooperative now—namely, the government, and not the ejidatarios.

The decree was published in the federal government's *Diario Oficial* and became law on February 15. On February 24 the cooperative's administration council presented a demand for an amparo before a high-level judge in the Federal District. The Jaramillista leaders protested that the decree's terms grossly violated the General Law of Cooperative Societies, and likewise the right of the administration council to name the cooperative's general manager. The government was quick to respond: "A few days later, in the late hours of the night, the plaintiffs were compelled, by means of arms, to sign papers of compliance."[107] Meanwhile, the agrarian delegate, probably accompanied by other officials, "went through the nine sections of the ejido, working to convince the people and overcoming the difficulties that showed up." But, he reported, "All the ejidatarios accepted the execution of the decree."[108] Finally, on March 5, an extraordinary assembly was convened, presided over by the state governor, to authorize the transfer of power to the commission and the new manager. As a group of ejidatarios later reported, the governor told them that under the new regime "we, our women, and our children would eat better, that we would have milk to drink, that we would sleep on mattresses, and that we would wear shoes. What alluring promises!"[109] Yet many ejidatarios and a number of their leaders were prepared to protest the intervention, which they regarded as unjust. Again the threat of protest was met by the threat of violence. According to one ejidatario, the authorities "intimidated the manager, and they told him, 'If you do not accept, and if there is a disruption there, we'll get you.' "[110] Forced to sign his resignation and threatened with bodily harm, Jaramillo stepped down without attempting to incite the assembled ejidatarios. Not only that, he rallied a vote of confidence for the man named to be the new manager, Col. Félix Guerrero.[111] Thus ended the unfortunate reign of the ejidatario movement in power.

Conclusions

In general, one might say that the government was the key to the Jaramillo regime's rise and fall. The regime rose, despite the hostility of the mill administration, because it had government support as well as popular support; it fell, despite enduring popular support, when the government joined the mill administration in opposition. More precisely, the Jaramillo regime was essentially struggling for a liberation based on local institutional power and agrarian reform. The two goals were separate and equally essential to full liberation. Yet institutional power was in a practical sense the prerequisite for agrarian reform, if only because government authorities scheduled their response to popular demands in that order for their own political reasons. Moreover, local power did not necessarily lead to reform. Both required resolute government support, and government support was contingent on whether or not government interests were being served. There lay the difficulty. In 1946 and 1947 government interests were served politically and economically by helping the ejidatario movement take control over local institutions, despite mill opposition. Those interests were not served either politically or economically, however, when the Jaramillo regime persisted in trying to achieve agrarian reform at the expense of the mill. The government accordingly intervened on its own and the mill's behalf. Having initially won power without achieving reform, the Jaramillo regime lost power because it continued to struggle hard for reform rather than subordinate itself to the established political and economic interests.

At the heart of the conflict over agrarian reform was the inevitable clash between official and populist conceptions of economic development. After the 1910 Revolution as much as before, the sugar industry constituted a valuable sector of the state and national economies, and hence a critical interest of certain powerful economic and political elites. As such it was also a primary concern of government officials at all levels, who took steps to protect the industry from any loss in production or profits. In Atencingo this official policy of protection resulted in the requirements that only cane be grown on the surrounding lands and that all lands be owned and worked collectively—the most economical system, but also the most restrictive. In effect, the federal government officially licensed monopoly capitalism and exploitation for the benefit of the sugar industry. Moreover, a complex agrarian bureaucracy with the president at its head was committed to institutionalizing and defending this official conception.

These conditions did not suit most ejidatarios. They preferred a populist economy and life-style based on some combination of subsistence agriculture and local market capitalism, with each ejidatario personally controlling a specific plot of land. Cane was not always the most profitable or most useful crop they could grow. Jenkins himself often chose to grow melon and tomatoes privately; the ejidatarios quite naturally felt they should be allowed to do the same. Corn and beans met family subsistence needs and also brought an easy profit at the market. Parcellation would satisfy long-standing desires among the peasantry for personal control over their means of making a living. In other words, an economy allowed to develop in an open market based on local values would have been entirely different than the one institutionalized by the government and the mill.* Thus on the agrarian reform issues the ejidatarios were ultimately opposed not only by the mill administration but by the government.

On the issue of local institutional power over the cooperative and the ejido, no comparable disagreements existed between the ejidatarios and the government. To be sure, in line with their conflicting economic interests, the ejidatarios and the mill administration were singularly opposed to each other, each ultimately preferring to exclude the other from local policy control. But from the viewpoint of the government, and especially the federal government, economic interests were not the only consideration in determining policy on local institutional power. The government also had distinct political interests it expected the ejidatarios' local institutions to serve. In particular, it was vitally interested in expanding bureaucratic and official-party control over the ejidatarios and in continuing to command their loyalty and respect—if only for the sake of maintaining political stability. For these purposes the ejido and cooperative, the local institutions of the Atencingo region, could basically be considered outposts of the federal bureaucracy. The greater the government's political and institutional controls, of course, the greater its ability to constrain the ejidatarios to serve the mill administration and official economic development policies in a pattern of mutual reinforcement between the economic and political interests. As a result of these combined interests, the government, unlike the mill administration, was generally prepared to support the ejidatarios on the issue of local institutional power, so long as established interests were not endangered.

During the 1946–47 struggle that led to the founding of the Jaramillo regime, then, the government supported the ejidatarios even though they threatened regional economic and political stability, for

---

* Of course, such a populist economic development might also have spawned new forms of land fever, power struggles, and exploitation—but these possibilities were not the immediate concern of the ejidatarios.

they still evinced loyalty and respect for the government. In the long run this strategy promoted the government's interests, both political and economic. It returned political stability to the region without immediately endangering productivity. It strengthened the ejidatarios' ties to the government. It channeled the reform struggle out of the fields and into the bureaucracy, where official controls were best exercised and elite interests were best protected. And it produced all these benefits without changing the region's basic economic structure.

Having actually helped the ejidatario movement seize local institutional power, the government proved less than eager to pursue economic reform in the succeeding years, aside from unofficially permitting token crop diversification on small plots seized by the ejidatarios. Despite some promises and plans for substantial reform, official procedural obstacles appeared in the form of the uncompleted ejidal census and survey. The state Agrarian Delegation showed itself to be peculiarly and perhaps even deliberately inefficient in these matters, partly because Jenkins's maneuvers to retain the ownership of certain lands had confused the tenure issue to his benefit and set peasant against peasant throughout the region. When high government officials did seem prepared to consider one reform, the division of the ejido, Jaramillo apparently retreated, probably because he feared that division might ultimately work to the mill's advantage.

Meanwhile, apparently satisfied to be in power, the Jaramillo regime at first cooperated with official precepts, produced a couple of good harvests for the mill, and took only limited steps toward crop diversification. This very minor reform was apparently acceptable not only to the National Ejidal Credit Bank but also to middle-level officials of the Agrarian Department and the Secretariat of Agriculture. The mill administration took a different view, however. Evidently feeling threatened by Jaramillo's local power and by any reformist endeavors, it took advantage of certain provisions in the contract with the cooperative to protect its monopoly interests, thereby plunging the Jaramillo regime into debilitating debt. The cooperative's financial failure discredited it to government officials, making them even less willing to entertain more substantial reform proposals.

In view of the ruinous hostility of the mill administration, the

Jaramillo regime opted for a compromise counterattack—a mixed system whereby some lands were still reserved for cane agriculture and others were freed for other crops, thus opening the way for a form of populist capitalism. That move was too much not only for the mill administration but for the government: productivity was endangered, and such loss of control by the mill also meant loss of control by the government. In addition to its financial machinations, the mill administration evidently subverted the Jaramillo regime and provided faulty technical advice in order to create a disaster that would compel the government to intervene. Without the strategic aid of government support, the Jaramillo regime's tactics, when exposed, were politically counterproductive. Confronted with de facto reforms and with what it regarded as the abuse of local power, the government intervened and ousted the peasant regime.

Of course, the Jaramillo regime's lack of administrative competence contributed to its fall. But it seems likely that this factor was only secondary. In an atmosphere of cooperation, skillful technical assistance from the mill and the government might have compensated for any managerial incapacities on the part of the Jaramillistas. Given the conflicts that prevailed, however, those incapacities only made it easier, for the mill administration especially, to bring about the cooperative's failure and later to blame that failure on the ejidatario regime.

Thus, in a pattern often repeated in Mexican politics, the government helped reformists come to power, but only in order to coopt and control them. When the reformists persisted in their struggle for fundamental changes, the government rejected them. Strategically, the government and the mill had the advantage. Over the long run the rebellious ejidatarios could not hope to match them.

CHAPTER FIVE

Peasants Against the State, 1952-1957

The third major period in the political history of the ejido and the cooperative spanned nearly a decade, from 1952 until 1961. Its definitive characteristic was imposed state control of the cooperative by means of a special government commission and the manager the commission was empowered to appoint. Of the two appointed, Col. Félix Guerrero held office from 1952 until 1957, and Congressional deputy Manuel Sánchez Espinosa from 1957 to 1961. During this period the government commission replaced the mill administration as the primary target of a new opposition struggle for power and reform.

The Establishment of the State-Controlled Regime

The government commission and Guerrero did not assume command under auspicious circumstances. Both the ejido and the cooperative were in a troublesome state of disarray. The cane fields and the agricultural equipment had deteriorated greatly from neglect and misuse, and as of June 1952 the cooperative's debt to the mill totaled 3.2 million pesos.[1] To complicate matters, the majority of the ejidatarios, and especially the incumbent leadership, received the government commission and Guerrero with reluctance, if not open hostility.[2] Nevertheless, the new administration resolutely shouldered its responsibilities.

Certainly the commission had been given broad power and authority. According to the presidential decree of 1952, its functions were as follows:

1. To oversee the administration of the property and interests of the ejidal complex. . . .
2. To study and make proposals for . . . the division of the ejido into appropriate units. . . .
3. To study and make proposals for the legal and economic organization that should be imposed on the ejidal system of Atencingo and annexes, whether by reorganizing the existing cooperative society or by adopting the type of society or arrangement that best suits the characteristics of the ejido and the nature of its problems.
4. If suitable and proper, to promote the dissolution and liquidation of the local ejidal credit society.
5. To authorize the non-cane cultivations that may be undertaken on lands of the ejidal complex. . . .
6. To ensure that . . . all the agricultural products harvested in the ejidal complex . . . are delivered and sold through the ejidal cooperative society or the body that replaces it.
7. To ensure that all the debts that are contracted for all types of crops . . . are registered with the cooperative, with the consent of the commission.
8. To intervene in and oversee the functioning of the cooperative society of Atencingo and annexes. . . .
9. To designate the general manager of the cooperative, assigning his responsibilities as well as the auxiliary personnel that are required in the running of the cooperative.
10. To intervene in disputes arising between the enterprise that owns and administers the Atencingo mill and the ejidatarios. . . .
11. To study and install the regulations and system of social services that best suit the interests of the ejidatarios of the ejidal unit.[3]

Clearly the peasants were no longer in charge of their own affairs.

The seven members of the government commission, as we have seen, were the state governor; representatives from the mill, the Agrarian Department, the Secretariat of Agriculture, and the Bureau of Cooperative Development of the Secretariat of National Economy; and the presidents of the ejidal commissariat and the cooperative's administration council. The presidency of the commission was conferred on the state governor, and the office of secretary on the representative from the Secretariat of National Economy. The commission was to meet regularly once a month. Beyond those directives, however, the commission was empowered to write its own procedural rules and regulations, subject to federal approval.[4]

According to the procedural document eventually authorized by President Alemán, the commission was formally titled the Reorganizing Commission of the Ejidal Cooperative Society of Atencingo and Annexes. For a meeting to be official, the governor (or his alternate) and the representative of the Secretariat of National Economy (or his alternate) had to be present, along with two other members, to make up a minimum quorum of four. Measures were to be officially adopted according to the majority vote of those present. Any tie votes would be broken by the single vote of the commission's president, the governor. These rules could be altered only by the president of the Republic at the commission's request.[5]

Thus the ejidal complex was now subject to a system of combined state and federal planning and control aimed primarily at ensuring the mill's economic well-being. In both theory and practice, the state governor had replaced the cooperative manager as the single most powerful figure in the ejido's affairs. Second in command was the representative of the Secretariat of National Economy, who was sent directly from the federal offices in Mexico City. For many years the Agrarian Department's representative on the commission was simply its state-level agrarian delegate—a choice that may have lessened the relative influence of the department somewhat. Furthermore, the commission was structured in such a way that the two peasant representatives could never outvote the other participants. Indeed, meetings were usually held in Puebla, removed from both peasant agitation and federal concern. For most practical purposes, then, the real decision-making power over the Atencingo region was now vested in the state government, and specifically the governor, with day-to-day decisions being left to the cooperative manager.

The new manager appointed by the commission, Col. Félix Guerrero, was actually the choice of Gen. Rafael Avila Camacho, who as the state governor was acting as the president of the commission.

Guerrero had attended Mexico's Heroic Military College when General Avila Camacho was head of the college. He had also fought in the Spanish Civil War and had won renown as Mexico's foremost artillerist. At the time of his appointment as manager, he was serving as the chief of Governor Avila Camacho's personal aides.[6] In effect, Guerrero was chosen for his loyalty to the governor, in addition to his administrative ability. He was not chosen for his knowledge of cane agriculture, which was minimal.

Like the managers who had preceded him, Guerrero concentrated his attention on consolidating a dependable regime embracing the elective as well as the appointive posts. The terms of the elected incumbents for the ejido and the cooperative did not expire until early 1953. Yet hostile activities by the administration council were apparently curtailed, if only by means of threats, after its unsuccessful bid for an amparo against the 1952 decree, and the council president, Jesús Aguilar, eventually saw fit to collaborate with Guerrero.[7] Also, the president of the ejidal commissariat, Carlos Galarza, evidently began to collaborate, reportedly as a result of bribes or at least loans.[8] Then, in 1953, Guerrero-backed candidates won the elections and took office.[9] In particular, the president of the new ejidal commissariat, Agustín Valle Cuenca, proved to be a staunch partisan of the state-controlled regime. Following the elections the influential Aguilar continued to support Guerrero, whereas the opportunistic Galarza began to work with the opposition faction.[10]

In appointing his field staff in the ejido villages, Guerrero retained many competent incumbents from the Jaramillo regime but replaced others. Although there was some initial hostility, the retained staff worked well with the manager in the succeeding years.[11] As staff members they at least enjoyed the benefits of a regular salary. Moreover, as many ejidatarios who worked with Guerrero have reported, they also came to respect Guerrero as a manager and as a person.

Thus Guerrero structured a regime over both the cooperative and the ejido by coopting selected leaders, many of them recruited directly from the old Jaramillo regime. Satisfied especially with the performance of the field staff, Guerrero in later years steadily reappointed the same team to office—thus creating a fairly closed elite of former

Jaramillistas now loyal to the Guerrero regime. If most ejidatarios submitted to state intervention with reluctance or even animosity, their discontent was tempered by the combination of fear and respect with which they regarded Colonel Guerrero as a representative of both the military and the government.[12] The potential for rebellion was apparently moderated further by the sense of disappointment with which many ejidatarios regarded the ousted Jaramillo regime. Besides, the authorities were backed by police squads and army troops—always potent obstacles to open protest. At least for a few years, then, the majority of the ejidatarios ranged between acquiescence and reluctant cooperation in their behavior toward the state-controlled regime: thus work went on as usual, and collaborators remained in office.

Acquiescence to Guerrero and the state commission was not unanimous, however. In selecting his officers and consolidating his regime, Guerrero in effect divided the leaders from the old Jaramillo regime into two camps: those who collaborated and those, like Jaramillo, who did not. At first this cooptive, divide-and-conquer strategem weakened the prospects for opposition to the state-controlled regime. But wise as this approach was, it created a natural target for any opposition struggle in the entrenched former Jaramillista collaborationists, as well as a leadership nucleus for opposition in the displaced Jaramillistas. Although they had been ousted from office, the Jaramillistas did not give up; instead, they banded together with a few followers to form the major opposition. A small and quiescent group during 1952, the Jaramillistas began to engage in vocal opposition and agitation during early 1953, and by mid-1955 they had secured majority support in the ejido. At first their overriding objectives were the revocation of the 1952 decree, the return of the cooperative to the ejidatarios, and the parcellation of the ejido; later the division of the ejido was added to their list. Almost as soon as the state began to control the Atencingo ejido's affairs, then, a vital opposition was born, drawing strength from the ejidatarios' long-standing reform aspirations.

Planned Economic Development

In contrast to the Pérez and Jaramillo administrations, the Reorganizing Commission made a specific effort at developmental planning, as prescribed by the 1952 decree. The commission's plan proposed three stages of development.[13] In the first stage the regime would take steps to restore the cooperative as a viable economic institution by returning the neglected cane fields to productivity and gradually liquidating the cooperative's debt to the mill.

In the second stage it would bring about "integral" development by strengthening and diversifying the ejido and the cooperative as complex agricultural enterprises. Specifically, the objectives were high cane productivity on sufficient lands to meet the mill's full capacity (then about 400,000 to 450,000 tons) and the cultivation of cash crops on the remaining lands. The means were to be good credit, increased water supplies from new wells, mechanization, and advanced techniques of intensive agriculture. The end result would be considerable independence from cane agriculture and the mill. Finally, in the third stage, the developmental emphasis would shift from agriculture to social and community conditions. Now housing, electrification, potable water supplies, educational facilities (including vocational schools), roads, health services, and recreational facilities would receive top priority. Thus, if completed according to plan, the economic development of the Atencingo complex would enable the peasants to live very well indeed.

It was envisioned that to carry out the plan would require about fifteen years, or five for each stage. During his five and one-half years in office, Guerrero followed the plan earnestly and did a commendable job of revitalizing the cooperative. Steady economic progress became the norm, interrupted only by political agitation. Table 4 shows the levels of sugar cane production achieved in the harvests managed by Guerrero. The figures reveal that the productivity of the cooperative and the mill was restored to respectable, profitable levels comparable to those achieved before the production disasters of 1949–51. Only in the 1955–56 harvest did the cooperative falter, failing to meet the quotas assigned by the mill because a number of ejidatarios who opposed Guerrero's regime at the time refused to work.[14]

Along with productivity, financial vigor and good relations with the mill returned to the cooperative. Whereas annual financing for the cane harvest rose modestly, from 11 million to 13 million pesos, the

TABLE 4

Sugar Cane Produced and Processed by the Atencingo Cooperative and Mill, 1951–1957

	Cooperative		Mill	
Harvest	Total delivered to mill (tons)	Average yield (tons/ha.)	Total milled from all sources (tons)	Average yield of all sources (tons/ha.)
1951–52	210,454	—*a*	271,831	94.6
1952–53	283,330	—	341,185	118.0
1953–54	271,705	98.0	370,267	111.7
1954–55	304,145	129.3	392,664	118.2
1955–56	290,589	—	425,866	122.2
1956–57	316,998	—	426,321	114.4

SOURCES: For the cooperative's total production, memorandum of the local ejidal credit society, July 12, 1967, MAEM; for the cooperative's average yield, Guerrero, annual report for 1954–55, July 31, 1955, FNDA, p. 128. For the mill, Unión Nacional de Productores de Azúcar, *Estadísticas azucareras* (Mexico City, 1965), pp. 44–45.

a Figures for 1951–53 and 1955–57 are not available.

3.2-million-peso debt to the mill inherited by the Guerrero regime was entirely liquidated by 1957. Financial problems due to cane left standing after a harvest were settled amicably, and the mill claimed no more mechanical breakdowns.

Although he restored the cooperative to its former role as a major supplier of cane to the mill, Guerrero did not return it to a status of submission to the mill's rule. Instead, with the authorization of the Reorganizing Commission, he actually strengthened the meager autonomy initiated by Jaramillo. To be sure, the cooperative still had to transport the harvest on the mill's private railroad and still depended on the mill for equipment loans—all at high costs. Nevertheless, the Guerrero regime made small but significant purchases of trucks, tractors, and other equipment for the mechanization of agriculture, a goal Jaramillo had pursued without success. The cooperative's fixed assets accordingly more than quadrupled in value, from just under one million pesos in 1952 to 4.3 million pesos in 1956.* The new equipment

* Guerrero, annual report for 1955–56, November 17, 1956 (MAPBAC). A devaluation of the peso in 1954 changed its exchange rate from about $.11 to $.08, where it remains today.

was especially useful for non-cane agriculture, for which the mill was reluctant to lend its own equipment. Furthermore, general credit relations and practices for paying wages were rationalized to the cooperative's advantage[15] and institutionalized with a new contract signed in 1956.

In the meantime the ejidatarios' incomes rose. The wage for a typical day's labor increased from five pesos in early 1952, to six in 1953, to seven in 1955—though some ejidatarios might be given only a few days of work during the week. The supervisors earned salaries of 100 pesos a week. Moreover, profit dividends were now sizable. During Guerrero's term in office the following sums were distributed among the peasants:

Harvest	Total dividends	Harvest	Total dividends
1951–52	1.1 million pesos	1954–55	2.0 million pesos
1952–53	1.2	1955–56	.4
1953–54	2.0	1956–57	3.0

Such a record was excellent, especially when contrasted with the records of the Pérez and Jaramillo administrations. As prescribed by the General Law of Cooperative Societies, the commission prorated these dividends according to the number of days each ejidatario worked on the cane harvest. This system meant, of course, that those who had regular employment, such as the field staff, garnered higher dividends than those who worked only occasionally, such as some members of the opposition faction.[16]

Under the auspices of the Reorganizing Commission, the ejidatarios earned additional income and produced extra food from the limited cultivation of crops other than cane. Despite popular outcries, during 1952–53 the commission had sharply curtailed the cultivation of other crops while Guerrero revived the cane fields.[17] Afterward, though, it permitted a return to the practices initiated during Jaramillo's administration, though on a much more regulated and restricted basis. As a rule the ejidatarios were now allowed one-half hectare of irrigated land to grow rice (in rotation with cane) and one-half hectare of seasonal land to grow corn and beans for family use. In addition, smaller plots of melons, tomatoes, peanuts, and wheat were sometimes authorized in rotation with cane.[18] Individual as well as collective work was permitted, and all credits and sales were apparently channeled through the cooperative. Yet, despite the mill administration's original protests, some credit for rice still came from the National Ejidal Credit Bank—though apparently the old local ejidal credit society was liquidated. As a special privilege for the ejidatarios, moreover, Guerrero sometimes allowed them to sell their rice on the open market at a profit, even though legally the rice was supposed to be sold to the National Ejidal Credit Bank at a lower price in exchange for the financing.[19]

In sum, the Reorganizing Commission and Guerrero succeeded in advancing the cooperative through the first and into the second stage of their development plan. Annual cane production was restored to profitable levels, and the old debt to the mill was liquidated. To enhance the cooperative's autonomy and profits, and to meet the ejidatarios' needs, steps were taken toward mechanizing and diversifying the ejido's agriculture, and individual farming was reintroduced on a limited basis. The ejidatarios' incomes generally increased, except perhaps in the case of members of the opposition faction. Thus, apparently acting on their own intentions as well as responding to popular pressures, the commission and Guerrero moved the cooperative by stages in the directions initiated by Jaramillo, though without jeopardizing the mill's cane supply.

Guerrero's opponents, the Jaramillistas, tried to claim credit for compelling him and the commission to carry out the limited parcellation and crop diversification. In fact, however, Guerrero saw the wisdom of promoting extensive diversification and even total parcellation over the long run, as long as the cooperative met its obligations to the mill. Though he favored collective agriculture for economic reasons, Guerrero believed that even for cane agriculture, parcellation was preferable economically and politically for ejidos like Atencingo and annexes, where a natural basis for cooperation was lacking. Indeed, he felt that parcellation could end many of the ejido's difficulties, as demonstrated by the examples set at the major sugar complexes of Zacatepec and El Mante in other states.[20] Furthermore, he definitely planned to expand crop diversification in the years ahead, after the ejido's cane agriculture had became more intensive and production had reached optimal levels for the mill.

For both parcellation and crop diversification, however, there was one simple prerequisite: more water, both to prevent water disputes and to increase production. By the time of Guerrero's administration less water was available than the 1938 grant had allocated to the ejido, in part because peasant settlers and neighboring property owners had invaded uncultivated boundary plots legally belonging to the ejido, and now farmed them with the ejido's river waters. As a result the ejido no longer controlled enough water to irrigate all its own irrigable lands, and already there were disputes over water distribution among the ejido villages.[21] Guerrero had planned to regain control of the border plots and river waters, and to drill new wells, pursuant to diversification and even parcellation. These steps would have brought the ejido considerably closer to the very goals advocated by the Jaramillistas in their attempt to attract ejidatarios to the opposition. But Guerrero was compelled to resign before he could carry out his plans, in part because of the Jaramillistas' unrelenting protests against his management.

The Politicized Technical Tasks

During the Guerrero administration the Reorganizing Commission, Guerrero, the ejidatarios, and the landless villagers all asked the government to complete the standard technical tasks for the ejido. Most had gone uncompleted for fourteen years, to the general disadvantage of the ejidatarios—and to the advantage of the mill administration, neighboring property owners, and outside political actors whose involvement is very unclear. By now the list of tasks had become quite familiar. As a type of property, the ejido required proper surveying, mapping, and boundary adjustment. As a type of community, it required another census revision and subsequently another redistribution of certificates of agrarian rights. Once all these preliminaries were accomplished, then the government could at last authorize the definitive execution of the original grant and the enlargement—and the ejido would finally exist as a legal entity. Only then would the way be clear for structural reforms.

As before, the critical tasks were the survey and the census, now complicated by the pending enlargement. After some procedural confusion between the state agrarian delegate and Agrarian Department officials, accompanied by the general confusion surrounding the presidential succession in late 1952, a complex decision favored by the state Agrarian Delegation was made to postpone further survey work until after the definitive granting of the enlargement—even though the 1947–48 survey was admittedly inadequate.[22]

In early 1953, however, the state Agrarian Delegation and ejidal officers undertook new census work. The new census aroused strong agitation, for it became the occasion for a contest between the various political factions within the ejido to increase the size of their ranks. Aside from striking ejidatarios who had died or left the area from the rolls, the secure collaborationists evidently made some attempt— whether properly or improperly—to deprive certain ejidatarios of their rights. Demanding that the fieldwork be immediately suspended, the opposition Jaramillistas protested that it was illegal and discriminatory: it favored the established interests; it had been undertaken without the official consent of the ejidatarios; and it was improperly stripping fellow ejidatarios of their rights, with the backing of federal troops.[23] Evidently their strategy of common defense worked, for the Jaramillistas survived with their ranks intact; certainly none of their main leaders lost his rights. Yet in view of the apparent collusion between the collaborationist officers and the state Agrarian Delegation, the Jaramillistas demanded that all future fieldwork be carried out only by federal engineers commissioned directly from the Agrarian Department.[24]

Additional protests against the census came from the well-organized outside peasants who had complained rancorously ever since the Jaramillistas eliminated them from the ejido with the 1946 census: the displaced founder-ejidatarios who had once collaborated with the Pérez regime, the former peons who had received rain-check rights in 1946, and the sons of these two groups.[25] Numbering about three hundred and still led by Alberto Espinosa, the outsiders claimed to have helped the government oust Jaramillo in the hope of having their former ejidal rights restored to them as a reward.[26] Indeed, they asserted that the governor had installed the Reorganizing Commission to end the abuses they had allegedly been subjected to, and that the governor and the commission explicitly intended to use the current census to restore their rights.[27] Now their claims had been shunted aside, allegedly because of collusion among the Agrarian Delegation's engineer, ejidal officers, Jaramillo's accomplices, and "the eternal leaders."[28] The hundred or so vacancies were being filled once again with landless wage laborers who had arrived and worked in the ejidal complex in recent years,[29] and who probably enjoyed the friendship of the entrenched ejido leaders. Confronted with such complaints, the field engineer temporized that the plan was to admit the former ejidatarios and peons later, as part of the pending enlargement.[30]

Meanwhile, attuned to the unrest in the Atencingo region, Agrarian Department officials advanced cautiously toward the definitive enlargement decree. Their major problem was to determine how many new ejidatarios could be admitted. The 1950 provisional grant had accommodated 218 out of 286 qualified peasants and their families—obviously not enough to satisfy or even curtail the land hunger rampant throughout the overpopulated region. Moreover, as Espinosa and his followers claimed, during 1950–51 government officials or the mill administration had apparently encouraged the landless villagers and former ejidatarios to help oust the Jaramillo regime, with promises that afterward they might be accommodated within the enlarged ejido. In early 1952 Espinosa had even presented calculations, based on a once-official ratio of acreage to men, showing that there was really room for 571 new ejidatarios—presumably including his following of former ejidatarios and peons.[31] Yet the existing ejidatarios, whether Jaramillistas or collaborationists, had no desire to share their land with any extra peasants.

In the wake of Jaramillo's ouster in 1952, the administration of President Alemán may have seriously considered Espinosa's proposal, but a presidential succession in late 1952 forestalled any action that might have been in the offing. Instead the new president, Adolfo Ruíz Cortines, and the new Agrarian Department chief, Castulo Villaseñor, adopted a compromise approach. On August 12, 1953, they decided in favor of a definitive enlargement that would grant ejidal rights to all

286 of the qualified peasants—with no mention of any legal ratio of acreage to men. Such a measure would ease a little more of the population pressure without requiring a new census, and hence without stirring up new agitation.

In accordance with improved computations from the old survey data, the definitive enlargement totaled 3,262 hectares, consisting of 2,174 irrigated hectares, 179 seasonally cultivable hectares, 880 hectares of brushland, and 29 hectares for urban zones. As in the past the lands were to be used expressly for collective cane agriculture.[32] The Ejido of Atencingo and Annexes now had 2,329 ejidatarios and on paper, at least, a giant total of 11,528 hectares, of which 10,249 hectares were irrigated. Table 5 shows the official figures on the ejido's size. Actually, the total acreage was slightly less, since the enlargement regranted as additional lands a few ejidal plots that had been in dispute since 1938.[33] In any case, the ratio of acreage to men was quite good indeed, with more than four irrigated hectares per ejidatario. Each of the ejido's nine sections consisted of some 1,200 to 1,300 hectares on the average, with 250 to 300 ejidatarios and their families, whereas elsewhere in the region the average ejido consisted of 80 to 100 ejidatarios, with less land per ejidatario.[34] In other words, the individual sections of the Atencingo complex were much larger than most ejidos in the region.

For some reason the definitive enlargement decree was not publicly printed until April 13, 1954, and not officially executed until December 5, 1954.[35] More than likely, the authorities delayed partly because of the agitation produced throughout 1953 and 1954 by the former ejidatarios, as we have seen, and by the power-hungry Jaramillistas, who lobbied intensively—though separately and even competitively—for the definitive enlargement.[36] More than just an immediate procedural goal, it was also the prerequisite for further fieldwork and hence for parcellation—the ultimate goal of most ejidatarios and the ultimate fear of the mill administration and most government authorities.

With the execution of the enlargement decree, the way was finally cleared for rectifying the census of the 286 new ejidatarios. The fieldwork was completed in early 1955, and certificates of agrarian rights

TABLE 5
TABLE 5
Size of the Atencingo Ejido After the Enlargement of 1953 (Hectares)

| Section | Type of land | | | Total |
	Irrigated	Seasonal	Brushland, urban zones	
Atencingo	1,056	64	71	1,191
Lagunillas	2,399	0	0	2,399
Jaltepec	1,650	0	0	1,650
Colón	468	205	122	795
Rijo	444	0	451	895
San Nicolás Tolentino	1,176	0	0	1,176
Raboso	921	102	126	1,149
La Galarza	1,203	0	0	1,203
Teruel	932	0	138	1,070
Total	10,249	371	908	11,528

SOURCE: "Resolución sobre ampliación de ejido al poblado Atencingo y anexos en Chietla, Puebla," *Diario Oficial de la Federación*, April 13, 1954, pp. 2–4.

NOTE: Many of the hectares listed as irrigated were actually farmed seasonally, owing to lack of water, even though they were irrigable.

were distributed to the new ejidatarios some months afterward, despite protests from Jaramillistas that the census figures had been altered within the bureaucracy to their disadvantage.[37] As for Espinosa's followers, government officials and ejidal leaders once again barred them from ejidal rights, no doubt fearing that they would become a divisive influence and add to the popular pressures for parcellation. Despite all the earlier promises made to them, the former ejidatarios and peons were technically outmaneuvered and rejected again,[38] essentially for political reasons (or so it appeared). Afterward the Agrarian Department chief told them that their readmission was no longer possible.[39] This defeat dashed the hopes of that faction of landless outsiders, at least for a few years.

Meanwhile, ten Agrarian Department engineers began survey work in early 1955, with orders to map both the 1938 and the 1954 grant.[40] But progress was slow, primarily because of boundary disputes and problems within the ejido. For example, a collaborationist ejidatario and a Congressional deputy each illegally monopolized large plots, reportedly with the connivance of the ejidal commissariat and a group of entrenched leaders who did not actively support the survey work.[41] Moreover, the discovery was made that Jenkins still owned 288 hectares more than his legal limit, though the ejidatarios had invaded them anyway.[42] Guerrero paid the engineers 90,000 pesos,[43] but in the face of the legal and political complications, the work came to a halt once the engineers retired with their data into the confines of the Agrarian Department's bureaucracy. Two years later, after a lengthy review of the survey results, an official finally judged that the survey and the maps were technically unacceptable because they contained innumerable errors, such as the failure to specify the size of certain plots. The engineers retorted that "the peasants of the place do not want this notation to be made."[44] Thus another survey was deemed defective, and still another would be needed.

Throughout the Guerrero administration, then, as in earlier periods, government functionaries made little progress on the technical tasks. As before, the chief problem was that the tasks were far more than simply technical in nature: they were inextricably politicized, embedded as they were in larger struggles for power and reform. The individual parties involved in the struggles saw in each task an opportunity to promote or protect their own divergent interests—whether in gathering supporters, securing private control of a plot of land, or improving the prospects for land reform. Accordingly, technical accomplishment was supplanted by agrarian agitation, political feuding, bureaucratic temporizing, official irresponsibility, and—undoubtedly —simple corruption. Tactically, Guerrero's collaborators relied on the state government and the Agrarian Delegation for protection, and so the Jaramillistas appealed to the superior federal authorities. Strategically, however, the real advantage apparently lay with outside government and economic interests that showed no interest in changing the status quo.

The Jaramillista Opposition: Minority to Majority

As we have seen, the Reorganization Commission and Guerrero administered the Atencingo ejido by an authoritarian patronage system. Elements of such a system had been apparent during the Pérez and the Jaramillo regime, but now each ejidatario's livelihood clearly depended on collaboration with the Guerrero regime. Those who worked hard and cooperated readily were assigned the better jobs, accordingly earned higher dividends, and apparently were given better and even larger plots for individual use. All the top leadership posts were reserved for able collaborationists. They in turn used their office and their patronage powers to perpetuate their own ascendancy and that of the state-controlled regime that had benefited them. Meanwhile, those who were economically or politically uncooperative were deliberately kept at the bottom, receiving only low-level and infrequent work, and accordingly lower dividends. Outsiders were even hired to do the fieldwork of ejidatarios who were considered especially lazy or uncooperative.

Porfirio Jaramillo and his remaining supporters were now at the bottom of this system, stripped of their powers and privileges. Having been offered a chance to cooperate with the new regime, they had determined to fight it instead. They had therefore begun a new opposition struggle for power and reform, based preeminently on two highly popular objectives: first, the revocation of the 1952 decree to permit the return of the cooperative to the ejidatarios; and second, the parcellation of the ejido's lands into individual plots. According to the Jaramillistas' interpretation the 1952 decree and the Reorganizing Commission were highly illegal; there was no reason or right for either to exist. In addition they saw collectivization as the root of the ejidatarios' economic problems, for under the collectivized system the ejidatarios were treated like wage laborers. Liberation from exploitation thus depended on parcellation. Indeed, the 1938 grant had specified the measure—or so the Jaramillistas claimed. Inherent in their arguments for parcellation was a third objective—diversification to permit the cultivation of crops other than cane for profit. Yet the Jaramillistas denied any intention of ruining the ejido's cane agriculture. Later, in 1954, they also emphatically demanded a fourth reform —the division of the ejido—but only after the idea had won some semiofficial sympathy and popular support. The division of the ejido was perfectly legal, they said, because the work within each new ejido could still be collective, as prescribed by the 1938 grant; moreover, division had been authorized by the 1952 decree. The Jaramillistas' goals, in other words, were essentially the same as those that had inspired the 1946–47 struggle, also led by Jaramillo.

Whatever they may have claimed, though, once again the Jaramillista leaders apparently did not consider the division of the ejido a desirable goal. Instead they favored parcellation within a single giant ejido, so that intensive cane agriculture on some lands farmed collectively would suffice to supply the mill's needs, and the remaining lands could be distributed as individual plots for growing other crops. To manage this system the Jaramillistas favored the development of a strong, well-equipped cooperative or credit society, run by themselves, that would receive credit from the government rather than the mill. They apparently feared that the division of the ejido would ultimately weaken the cooperative and the ejidatarios in relation to the mill.* Nevertheless, division was still a popular goal with some ejidatarios, and the Jaramillistas were unwilling to risk losing support by openly rejecting it.

On a more personal level the Jaramillistas unceasingly protested against the economic discrimination and political repression they suffered owing to the state-controlled regime's patronage system, and specifically to Guerrero and his field staff in the ejido villages. In the economic area the Jaramillistas pointed to their lack of work, low wages, low dividends, insufficient opportunity to grow their own crops on individual plots, and displacement in the fields by outside day laborers. By the same token they deplored the injustice of the extra amenities enjoyed by Guerrero and his field staff: high salaries, high dividends, and reappointment to office year after year. In the political area the Jaramillistas complained of dictatorial impositions, death threats, expulsions, beatings, forced labor, and assassinations— all inflicted by the Reorganizing Commission, Guerrero, the field

---

* Future research may confirm that the Jaramillistas hoped the sugar mill would eventually be nationalized for the benefit of the mill workers and peasants of the Atencingo complex, as once proposed by Lombardo Toledano. To exert pressure for this move would require not only a strong worker-peasant alliance (of the sort, incidentally, that Jaramillo had been unable to sustain during his administration) but a strong alliance among all the ejidatarios in the Atencingo complex. From this point of view it was essential that the ejido remain a single unit; otherwise the mill administration could easily pursue a divide-and-conquer strategy to defeat nationalization demands.

staff, municipal authorities, and police agents. The only sure remedy for these alleged injustices, they said, was to remove the collaborationists and Guerrero from office or revoke the 1952 decree, or both.

It took months for these stands to develop, of course, but the major reform issues for the emergent opposition struggle were defined immediately after the state-controlled regime was established. As soon as the 1952 decree was promulgated, the top officers of the old Jaramillo regime appealed for an amparo against it. Moreover, in another major reaction, 186 lesser spokesmen for the ejidatarios filed a major petition for the parcellation of the ejido, in the hope that the government would now concede what the Jaramillo regime had failed to secure.[45] Not surprisingly, the federal and state officials denied the requests—in the case of the amparo, at gunpoint. They had no reason to respond favorably. President Alemán and other authorities were certainly not about to undermine the powers of the commission they had just authorized, and legal and economic arguments against parcellation in the Atencingo case apparently won ready acceptance in government circles, if only in deference to the mill administration's wishes.

As the new patronage system took hold under the Reorganizing Commission and Guerrero, popular opposition dwindled both in quantity and in quality. Many of Jaramillo's former co-leaders became collaborationists, and the vast majority of the ejidatarios acquiesced to the state-controlled regime. Indeed, many now lacked faith in the Jaramillistas, who were in the questionable position of trying to rally support with exhortations about the very reforms they had failed to achieve during their own term in office.[46] As the realignment proceeded, the Jaramillista opposition leaders ended up with a weak minority of only several hundred followers.[47] Jaramillo himself was virtually expelled from the ejido by the state government, and drove off in an old Chevrolet ejidatarios had given him from the cooperative's holdings. He went to lobby in Mexico City and rarely visited the Atencingo ejido again. After his departure the local leadership of the opposition forces fell to his top associates, notably Teodoro Sánchez, Francisco Coronel, and J. Guadalupe Ramírez Vargas, three ambitious men who had entered the ejido after 1946.

Forced into submission by the state and federal governments, the Jaramillistas lay low throughout the remainder of 1952. They could hardly do otherwise, since they lacked both popular support and government support, the strategic essentials for a successful struggle. But 1952 was an election year, and by early 1953 the new administration of President Adolfo Ruíz Cortines was entrenching itself in office. Thus the Jaramillistas' strategic position changed. Spurred by the threat of the census revision in early 1953, the Jaramillistas ventured into open opposition and hastened to appeal their case to the new federal authorities.

In the succeeding months the Jaramillistas repeatedly condemned the Guerrero regime and the government perpetrators of the 1952 decree, and petitioned the new president for intervention on their behalf.[48] They contended that the decree "has consummated the greatest betrayal of the agrarian law, the most ungrateful slap at the Constitution, and unqualifiedly the worst abuse in our history."[49] One petition was accompanied by more than one thousand signatures,[50] indicating that either the Jaramillistas or their demands enjoyed heavy popular support—even though the Jaramillistas could not win the ejidal or cooperative elections that year.

Thus the opposition leaders probed for a breach in the ranks of officialdom. It appeared in September, with the election of Gen. Lorenzo Azúa Torres, a progressive congressman, to the post of CNC secretary-general, replacing the incumbent from the final years of the unsympathetic Alemán regime. After studying a new petition from the Jaramillistas to the president, Azúa ordered his secretary of cooperative action, José María Suárez Téllez, to make an investigation for the CNC's National Executive Committee.[51] Suárez went to Atencingo, apparently the first official to take the Jaramillista opposition's complaints seriously.

What Suárez saw and heard in Atencingo displeased him. According to his report,[52] ejidal and cooperative officers were virtually the manager's lackeys, to the disadvantage of the ejidatarios. Work was not distributed equitably: the mass of ejidatarios earned only 12 to 18 pesos a week for piecework, whereas favorites of the well-paid staff earned 30 to 36 pesos a week for regular work. Moreover, Suárez said, the restrictions imposed on the individual cultivation of crops other than cane aroused "profound disgust" among the ejidatarios. By contrast, he was favorably impressed by what the Jaramillo regime had accomplished economically and materially before being overthrown.

Suárez believed that the 1952 decree was illegal and violated the General Law of Cooperative Societies in many respects, just as the Jaramillistas had argued in their rejected request for an amparo. Accordingly, he attacked the Secretariat of National Economy for acting arbitrarily and capriciously, overstepping its legal right to exercise a modicum of supervision. As a result of the Reorganizing Commission's having been imposed on the ejido, he wrote,

> what has been done to the cooperative of Atencingo is not supervision but a blatant intrusion in its direction and management, with the aggravating factor that the commission is under the charge of a political personage, the governor of the state. And in consequence the principle of liberty that is the inspiration and norm for the cooperative institution remains practically annulled by the presence of an authority contrary to the fundamentals and the destiny of a body with a strictly economic character, the cooperative.

Struck by the "curious," contrived character of the 1938 grant, Suárez advocated the division of the ejido among the nine villages, "because that conforms more to the aspirations of the peasants and with the text of Article 27 of the Constitution, which orders the granting of lands to villages and not to aggregations of villages." In his opinion, division would not conflict with the original 1938 ejidal grant, since the agriculture could still be organized collectively. Precedents certainly existed, especially in the multi-ejido collective agriculture found around the sugar mill at Zacatepec in Morelos. Division would certainly be popular, Suárez noted, because the ejidatarios "have been shouting for it for a long time." Nevertheless, in contrast to the hard-core Jaramillistas, Suárez opposed parcellation, on the grounds that it would violate the 1938 decree and severely harm the sugar industry. With regard to the relationship between the cooperative and the mill, he revived an idea originally put forth by Lombardo Toledano and perhaps harbored by the Jaramillistas: "The source of the malaise prevalent in the agricultural-industrial unit that concerns us resides in the fact that the mill continues to be the property of the old hacendado." He did not advise expropriation, however, because the deteriorated machinery broke down too often. Instead he recommended the construction of a new mill that would be owned by the workers, peasants, and employees.

Based on these findings and on "considerations of legality and public order," Suárez then proposed a specific series of substantive and procedural measures for resolving the problems of the ejidal complex. The critical measures were the revocation of the 1952 decree and the full restitution of the cooperative's legal faculties; presidential authorization of the definitive enlargement and of the definitive possession of the entire ejido; the division of the ejido into nine ejidos, one for each ejido village; and the construction of a new sugar mill for the region. He submitted his lengthy report in mid-December of 1953. Four days later it was approved by the CNC's National Executive Committee. The report now represented the official position of the government's peasant defense organization, and thus Suárez and Secretary-General Azúa became major spokesmen and supporters of the Jaramillista opposition. In succeeding months Azúa urged President Ruíz Cortines and other authorities to study the report and act on its recommendations.[53]

One notable difference existed between the Jaramillistas and their CNC supporters: the latter advocated the division of the ejido but not parcellation, whereas the former continued to demand parcellation but not division—at least not yet. Heartened nonetheless by the resolute support of their new ally, the Jaramillista leaders began to toughen their opposition. During early 1954 they appealed again for presidential intervention and complained about the unfavorable responses they had received from other federal authorities.[54] Next, especially after the April publication of the enlargement decree, they agitated to rouse the ejidatarios against the state-controlled regime. Some partisans of the opposition evidently refused to work on the cane harvest, then under way and vulnerable to disruption: as one explained, "We consider that at present it is not to our advantage to work with all our might."[55] Of course, the reaction to such tactics was firm. According to the Jaramillistas the new regime began to use pistoleros for protection as well as to threaten the opposition and "dispossess the peasants of everything, even their own homes."[56] In a word, the situation was growing tense.

Suddenly, during the agitation, one of the most prominent Jaramillista leaders—Teodoro Sánchez of San Nicolás Tolentino—disappeared. Somehow he had not long before been appointed supervisor of his annex, where the opposition had a very strong following. Perhaps his appointment was a concession by Guerrero; perhaps it was an attempt at cooptation. Whatever the case, once in office Sánchez had continued to lead the struggle against Guerrero and the commission. Now he was missing, having been seized by police agents and secretly jailed in Puebla, as rumor had it. Needless to say, Sánchez's disappearance fueled the unrest. Blaming Guerrero for the "repressive methods used against the peasants" and for attempts "to take away our right to free speech," the Jaramillistas hastened to organize a collective protest.[57] In an open assembly they resolved to stop work throughout the ejido until Sánchez was free.[58] Moreover, in a measure that enhanced the impressiveness of their local agitation and government lobbying, the leaders organized themselves into the Committee for the Revindication of the Rights of the Ejidatarios of the Ejidal Cooperative of Atencingo and Annexes, with the veteran Francisco Coronel as president and with representatives in all the ejido villages.[59] From that base they continued to appeal for help from the president, knowing they could expect no concessions from the state government.

The work stoppage never materialized. According to the Jaramillistas, its failure was to be blamed on repression by federal army troops. The ejidal commissariat and Guerrero's supervisors argued, however, that the failure was due to the Jaramillistas' lack of support among the ejidatarios, and not to any action by troops: "The federal forces in this area have confined themselves exclusively to maintaining order, so that blood is not spilled."[60]

Meanwhile, the report came that Sánchez was not in prison. Suspecting foul play, the peasants began to search in the canebrake for his body. In the middle of June it finally turned up, miles away from the Atencingo complex: Sánchez had been brutally assassinated. Thus the Jaramillista opposition was deprived of one of its best leaders, and thus pistolerismo returned to Atencingo as an answer to agitation. Of course, no real evidence was available to charge anyone with the murder, but from the beginning of the incident the Jaramillistas had blamed Guerrero, claiming that he was Sánchez's only enemy and that he had threatened Sánchez with death on several occasions in the presence of others.[61] Basically an honest man, Guerrero was probably innocent. Still, the assassination and the accompanying agitation undermined popular acceptance of the Guerrero regime. More ejidatarios now began to side with the Jaramillistas' minority opposition.[62]

The Revindication Committee's popular appeals for parcellation also rallied new support. The Agrarian Department chief had taken the position that parcellation was impossible because the collectivization clauses of the 1938 and 1954 grants could not be modified.[63] Nevertheless, at the height of the agitation, the Jaramillistas started an optimistic rumor that they had convinced the federal government to concede the long-awaited reform. This news surprised and worried the collaborationist ejidal commissariat and field staff.[64] Though a few officials in the Guerrero regime actually favored parcellation, the majority objected that such a move would be inadvisable because the region lacked sufficient water and because there would be problems in allocating the use of the cooperative's machinery. Accordingly, the collaborationist officers asked the Agrarian Department chief for clarification.[65] Though Governor Avila Camacho and Colonel Guerrero did not share the officers' concern, the governor arranged for them to have an audience with the chief, and Guerrero hired a bus to take them to Mexico City. When the officers arrived, they found that the leaders of the Revindication Committee, including Jaramillo, had already been waiting several days for a similar conference. The chief invited both parties into his offices together, and there he told them that no parcellation was planned, since the 1938 decree ordered collectivization.[66] With that issue settled and with the harvest in, the crisis subsided. Guerrero, the collaborationist officers, the state and federal authorities, and the army had rather easily protected their interests. Yet the Jaramillistas had finally demonstrated a tactical capacity for disruption, and they were gaining in popular support.

During the succeeding months the Revindication Committee leaders returned to a war of words. They vigorously continued sending their customary petitions to federal and state authorities. They pressed legal arguments against the 1952 decree and even tried to impeach the cooperative councils.[67] They published open letters in the press attempting to discredit the Guerrero regime as an illegal return to methods of rule used during the Porfiriato.[68] Yet such legal and political jousting was ineffectual: the frustrated Jaramillistas lacked sufficient popular and official leverage to sway the authorities, who continued to support the commission firmly. Moreover, even the enduring support of the CNC brought no relief. Deputy Arturo Luna Lugo, standing in as secretary-general for Azúa, who was ill, continued to ask the president to study Suárez's report and dictate a new decree accordingly.[69] Yet the CNC was now making no major effort to aid the rebellious Jaramillistas. Basically the organization was designed for controlling and coopting peasants, and lacked the power to wring significant concessions from the authorities. The CNC was a broker for lobbying, and little more.

For some reason, no doubt political in nature, around late 1954 the Jaramillistas' principal sympathizer and spokesman within the CNC, Suárez, resigned from his government post and became a top leader of the National Zapatista Front, an independent, moderately leftist peasant defense organization based in Morelos. As a result the Jaramillistas shifted to the National Zapatista Front too. They did not entirely forsake the CNC, but they openly used Suárez as their formal representative before the government. Thus the Jaramillistas began lobbying through an unofficial peasant organization as well as an official one—a change that clearly lessened the government's control over the rebellious faction.

The leaders of the Revindication Committee soon registered just how distressed they had become over the government's unresponsiveness. On December 31, 1954, just after the definitive execution of the enlargement and at about the time of Suárez's job change, they once again addressed themselves to the president. This time the message was a ranting open letter of five thousand words, printed as a fourteen-page propaganda booklet and signed by 121 Jaramillistas. In un-

commonly disrespectful language the letter bluntly criticized the top
political and economic institutions and elites involved in the Atencingo case—the Agrarian Department and its chief, the Secretariat of
National Economy and the director of its Bureau of Cooperative Development, the state governor, the three joint owners of the mill (Jenkins and his Spanish partners), the manager of the cooperative, and
the prior federal regime of President Alemán. The signers described
how they had been exploited:

> It is unjust that after we have worked these lands sixteen years, suffer-
> ing thousands of deprivations, they continue trying to deceive us as
> though we were eight-year-old children, keeping us in possession of the
> lands that we were granted *only in appearance,* pretending to respect
> our rights as ejidatarios. But in reality, given the situation in which
> they have put us, we continue in the condition of peons. This we have
> made the agrarian authorities see as many times as has been necessary,
> with the object that our situation as apparent ejidatarios be defined:
> iniquitously exploited with the dissimulation, if not the complicity, of
> the agrarian authorities and the Secretariat of National Economy. This,
> only in order to protect wrongfully the interests—or rather the fabulous
> profits—of a trio of famous captains of industry in that region, in com-
> plicity with the chief executive of the state.

The letter stated that only major reforms, now including the division
of the ejido, would remedy the ejidatarios' plight. Parcellation was
especially necessary, it argued, because experience had shown "that
the exploitation of which we are the victims, as much by the mill as
by professional politicians, is due to the fact that we have been required to work collectively." Of course, the 1952 decree was attacked
as a highly illegal "instrument of exploitation."[70]

Although they argued that the Constitution, the Agrarian Code,
and the General Law of Cooperative Societies had all been clearly
violated, the Jaramillistas also wrote that they had exhausted the possibilities for a legal remedy to their plight. Now there was only one
remedy left—"the justice of the Chief Executive." Hence they pleaded
for direct intervention by the president: "The agrarian reform was
done for the good of the peasants. You should not allow enslaving
foreigners, in collusion with immoral politicians, to rob the peasants,
because that would be to betray the Revolution." The plea was backed

up with a veiled threat: the president should intervene, the Jaramillistas added, because "it is impossible for us to continue working with all the zeal and enthusiasm that in these moments our fatherland requires from us."[71]

Thus murders, pistolerismo, and threats at the local level, not to mention government unresponsiveness at the state and national levels, had only led the relentless Jaramillista leaders to carry on their campaign with increasing vigor. Discouraged by the failure of legalistic tactics and reinforced by fresh (though still minority) popular support, they were prepared to renew direct action politics. As for the government authorities, who were surely shocked by the Jaramillistas' disrespectful criticism of the government (which is quite unusual in public discourse in Mexico), they held their ground on the major reform issues. But now that the enlargement had been executed, they did return to the technical tasks with surprising speed.

The survey and the census were well under way in February 1955, when Porfirio Jaramillo once again traveled to Mexico City to consult with officials in the Agrarian Department. Some say privately that Jaramillo, having discovered that Jenkins still owned more property than the law allowed, was about to create a scandal involving the millionaire and his two Spanish partners. Others say that Jaramillo was on the verge of securing government acceptance of his plan for parcellation, and that the officials had even quietly completed maps for the eventuality.[72] Certainly new data were available from the fieldwork then in progress. Whatever the full motives behind Jaramillo's lobbying, his efforts this time were suddenly halted. He and a fellow opposition leader, Fortunato Calixto, were kidnapped from their hotel room and murdered. Thus the Revindication Committee and the discontented peasants of the Atencingo complex were deprived of their major source of inspiration and leadership. Altogether three top leaders of the peasant struggle—Sánchez, Jaramillo, and Calixto—had been assassinated, not to mention lesser figures.[73]

Again accusations were hurled in all directions, and again no one was ever formally charged with the crime. At the time the opposition leaders focused their rage on Guerrero, the state governor, and the mill owners; they also asked the president to "end the terror in Atencingo and annexes, and concede definitively the parcellation."[74] In the aftermath, however, many came to believe that employees of the mill, in collusion with state police, were the parties directly responsible for the deaths of Jaramillo and Calixto.

These assassinations signified a change in the system of control between late 1953 and 1955. At first the Guerrero regime had permitted considerable freedom of expression and action for virtually all the ejidatarios, including those in the opposition. There had been the imposition of outside authority, to be sure, but little repression. Guerrero himself had maintained no pistoleros and had not even interfered with the commissions repeatedly sent by the opposition minority to government offices in Mexico City.* Instead the principal method of control had evidently been economic in nature: by means of the patronage system, the Guerrero regime rewarded those who cooperated with it, and penalized those who opposed it. During 1954 and early 1955, however, as the opposition mobilized for struggle, pistolerismo and political assassination augmented the economic controls, if only to make the ejidatarios keep working hard. Guerrero was probably not the initiator of these tactics, especially since he regarded himself strictly as the instrument of the Reorganizing Commission. Because of the murders, nevertheless, Guerrero and his collaborators lost important allegiance among the ejidatarios. Indeed, so many ejidatarios defected to the ranks of the opposition in reaction to Jaramillo's assassination that the Revindication Committee now commanded majority support.[75]

Federal Investigations

At just about the time Jaramillo was shot, a CNC investigator was writing up his report about the problematic fieldwork for the Atencingo survey and more generally about the ejidatarios' problems. The

* That Guerrero's rule had been firm but not particularly repressive is my general impression, despite the accusations of the Jaramillistas. Even today the ejidatarios vary widely in their interpretations according to whether they supported or opposed Guerrero at the time. Probably the most balanced local point of view I encountered was that of Guillermo Covarrubias, who said that Guerrero had not used pistoleros (interview, June 5, 1969). That Guerrero did not interfere with Jaramillista commissions was stated by Efraín González and Benito Ojeda (interview, August 13, 1969).

investigator's observations in many ways corroborated the charges made by the Jaramillistas in their lengthy open letter to the president only two months before. The report said that the ejido and the cooperative were run by a "small privileged group"; that the administration of the ejidal commissariat was "completely bad"; and that the civil authorities were in collusion with the administration council. The peasants were being subjected not only to extortion but also to "a wave of terror" at the hands of the field staff, the manager of the cooperative, and the civil authorities. Moreover, agricultural work was inequitably distributed: the majority of the ejidatarios were either suspended from work or given work only a couple of times a week, whereas fieldworkers, "who have no right to substitute," flocked in from other areas and were hired as wage laborers, to the great detriment of the ejidatarios' economic well-being. While struck by their misery and poverty, the CNC investigator also admired the ejidatarios' efforts to better their own lot. Though the general population was timid, he said, the opposition's struggle was "tenacious and untiring."[76]

"To alleviate the situation a little," the investigator proposed that the CNC intervene with the authorities so that elections would be promptly held for the cooperative's council members when their terms expired in March. He also proposed that the CNC send a representative to Atencingo at election time to assist the Jaramillista candidates. Then, addressing the ejido's problems more broadly, he suggested that the CNC delegate a permanent representative to the Atencingo ejido to "intervene in all the problems that afflict no less than two thousand families ... from the distribution of the work, to the distribution of the dividends to which they have a right at the end of each harvest."[77]

In spite of this advice, the CNC sent no permanent representative, and the cooperative elections were officially postponed. The Jaramillistas continued their struggle, however, by interfering with the cane harvest, even to the point of sabotage, while demanding a federal resolution of their problems.[78] Finally, in May, the top officials of the CNC, the Agrarian Department, and even the Secretariat of the Interior, undoubtedly owing to the political assassinations that had taken place, determined to make a thorough investigation and jointly commissioned a special team for the purpose. As was normally the case with major investigations, the final decision to send the team to Atencingo probably came from the president and not just from the heads of the three government agencies.

The investigative team spent four days in the Atencingo region and held extensive interviews with parties on both sides of the conflict. Each member of the team then wrote a report for his own superiors; no joint report was made.* The Agrarian Department investigator had held lengthy separate interviews with Guerrero, the collaborationist ejidal commissariat, and leaders of the Jaramillista opposition, and his report gave remarkably complete and candid descriptions of their responses.[79] The major demands and grievances of the opposition faction received thorough treatment, especially the allegations about political repression, economic discrimination, and the failings of Guerrero's regime—its unresponsiveness, its irresponsibility, its corruption, its elitism, and the simple illegality of its existence and conduct.

According to the report Colonel Guerrero cooperated very well with the investigative team. Indeed, he seemed pleased at the opportunity to present his side of the case. He especially thanked the CNC representative for coming to him, noting that on three past occasions CNC investigators had interviewed the opposition leaders without interviewing him. Besides making a vigorous defense of the cooperative's development policies, on a more personal level Guerrero denied the accusations against his field staff. In his opinion they were reliable and capable leaders, and he had expended considerable effort in selecting them. They were well paid because they had shouldered heavy responsibilities and were conscientious about their work. Moreover, he said, municipal police and security agents were not controlled by his field staff and were not on the cooperative's payroll as employees; they were paid only for any agricultural work they might do.

Guerrero denied that he persecuted or discriminated against mem-

---

* Unfortunately, the author saw only the report of the Agrarian Department's representative, but at least it reveals the information that was communicated to the department chief, and through him, to President Ruíz Cortines.

bers of the opposition, assuring the investigator that any who had fled could return whenever they wished. He was not an assassin; he had no pistoleros; and he did not abuse his powers as a military officer. On the contrary, on one occasion he had rejected an opportunity to surprise persons plotting his assassination. Lately he traveled with a bodyguard because he had received information that Porfirio Jaramillo's radical brother, Rubén, was in the area. In particular, Guerrero denied that he harassed those who demanded parcellation. The investigator wrote: "It does not interest him that his associates promoted parcellation. The only thing that matters to him is that they perform the work entrusted to them, aside from whether they petition for parcellation." But among the opposition faction were many who did not work. Some were "agitators," according to Guerrero; since they had begun to demand parcellation, they had "sabotaged the plots entrusted to them, so that it may be proved that collectivization is a failure." These persons he considered enemies of the cooperative. Others were simply lazy and negligent about their jobs. Still others had occupied leadership posts in prior administrations and had actually opposed parcellation then; now they supported it "because they know that they will not be leaders again and have the privileges they once enjoyed." Since such ejidatarios would not do their assigned work, Guerrero had to hire outsiders, much to the chagrin of the "saboteur ejidatarios."[80]

(Indeed, Guerrero generally believed that the opposition's real objective was not reform but power. The Jaramillistas were mere opportunists in his view, using the reform issues to rally support but having no intention of actually carrying out reforms. Instead their aim was just to regain their posts and to control the purse strings of the cooperative and the ejido once again. More broadly speaking, Guerrero theorized that in valuable patronage systems like Atencingo's there was a natural tendency for individuals to divide into two opposing parties, one led by those in power and the other led by a coalition of those who were ambitious but out of power; he further theorized that there was a natural tendency for the opposition struggle to be highly demagogic. Both the two-party model of patronage systems and the view that the Jaramillistas were mainly interested in power have been widely accepted as fundamental explanations for the development of opposition struggles within the Atencingo ejido—as we shall see.)[81]

The opinions of the members of the ejidal commissariat, as reported by the Agrarian Department investigator, generally resembled those of Guerrero. On the volatile issue of parcellation, commissariat members acknowledged that the proposal was universally popular among the ejidatarios and even expressed sympathy for it themselves. Nevertheless, for the present they preferred the collective system. They understood how collectivization worked, they said, whereas those who attacked it were ignorant. Immediate parcellation would make it difficult to allocate the ejido's inadequate water supplies, to dispose of the cooperative's machinery, to liquidate the cooperative's sizable annual debt, or to obtain any large amount of credit. Though the commissariat president and one other member had on occasion visited the annexes to hear complaints, they generally admitted that they rarely made such visits, saying that they were busy and earned no salary. At least some members admitted to the investigator that opposition ejidatarios who campaigned for parcellation were indeed treated roughly and sometimes beaten up, as they had charged.[82]

The Agrarian Department investigator made no recommendations and drew no formal conclusions from his data. Instead, he simply added some personal observations. Most important, he was struck by the absence of ejidal officers in the various annexes:

> On arriving at each annex there was no one with whom to deal, for in reality the only ones who speak and command are the supervisors. Consequently ... these population nuclei should have representation—as the residents wish—so that they may look after not only ejidal matters but also all that pertains to their betterment. This problem is accentuated whenever someone has to arrange a matter. He has to lose a day in going to and from Atencingo, the place where the cooperative administration and the ejidal comissariat are based.

Ultimately the investigator was endorsing the division of the ejido, though that objective was certainly not the Jaramillistas' main concern. His concession to the mill workers was somewhat greater. Finding that they feared parcellation would imperil cane production and thus be detrimental to their own interests, he soothingly promised that their interests would not be threatened by any action the superior authorities might take on the basis of his investigation. In effect, then, he rejected parcellation.[83]

After the investigation, of course, the individual reports of all the members of the investigative team were conveyed to the federal authorities in Mexico City. Apparently the president was also fully informed about the proceedings. The Jaramillistas—or neo-Jaramillistas, after Jaramillo's death—hastened to demand a favorable government response on the strength of the investigation, and their representatives in the National Zapatista Front obtained a special interview with the president in order to plead their case, especially for the division of the ejido.[84]

The Opposition in Office

Confronted with inexorable demands for power and reform by opposition leaders with strong majority support, the federal authorities, after consultation with the president, proceeded to do what they customarily did under such pressures: deny reform, but grant the appearance of power. Specifically, the Agrarian Department chief immediately rejected the division of the ejido as an illegal measure, despite the neo-Jaramillistas' strong case to the contrary.[85] Officials in the Secretariat of National Economy took similar action. Although they continued to refuse to revoke the 1952 decree, they did agree to have it reviewed by their legal experts in the Judicial Section. Then, when the decree was apparently judged illegal, they withheld the information from the ejidatarios.[86] Pestered by legal problems, but guided by political considerations, the federal government staunchly persisted in its support for the Reorganizing Commission and refused to intervene in what was essentially, after all, the state governor's domain.

Nevertheless, in July 1955, immediately after the federal investigation, the postponed election assembly for the cooperative's councils was finally held. In a rare public appearance the Agrarian Department chief himself, Castulo Villaseñor, presided as the president's personal representative. When the election was over, the candidates of the Revindication Committee had won control of not only the administration council but also the vigilance council.[87] Though full evidence is lacking, it seems clear that the authorities decided to permit and even encourage such a resounding victory by the opposition leaders in an attempt either to coopt them or just "to alleviate the situation a little," as the CNC investigator had said.[88]

Impressive as it was, the neo-Jaramillistas' electoral victory gained them little more than prestige. Because of the 1952 decree the cooperative's councils now had few powers or privileges. For one thing, their legal authority had been preempted by the Reorganizing Commission and Guerrero. For another, the collaborationists holding posts in the field staff and the ejidal commissariat still controlled the key components of the patronage system—the salaried posts, the work assignments, the wage disbursements, the dividend distributions, the allotment of plots for crops other than cane, and the census rolls. But if the victory meant little in the short run, it was a significant turning point in the long run. The neo-Jaramillistas had finally obtained majority support, and it had paid off: they were in office, and Guerrero's regime had begun to disintegrate. Since their new electoral power gave them a distinct tactical advantage in the local power struggle, they now devoted their energies to capturing control of the critical posts in the ejidal commissariat and the field staff—posts Guerrero and his collaborators were determined not to relinquish.

The collaborationists had dominated the ejidal commissariat and vigilance council since 1953. Their three-year term expired in March 1956, and new elections were held in a 36-hour assembly filled with heated debate. Of the two major slates, the one headed by leaders of the Revindication Committee won with 560 votes. The slate of collaborationist candidates received just 519—only enough for second place, though still an improvement over the Guerrero candidates' showing in the 1955 elections.[89]

By law the Guerrero faction was now supposed to relinquish its claim to the commissariat and take over just the vigilance council. Instead, a protracted legal battle ensued. On procedural grounds the incumbent commissariat and the losing Guerrero slate refused to acknowledge the neo-Jaramillistas' victory and demanded a new election.[90] The collaborationists charged that their opponents had rigged the election in connivance with a middle-level official of the Agrarian Department, and state police arrested members of the neo-Jaramillista slate.[91] Having secured freedom with an amparo, the neo-Jaramillistas countercharged that state-level Agrarian Department officials were protecting the collaborationist officers in violation of department orders.[92] As a result of the legal and procedural skill of the collaborationists, however, efforts to resolve the dispute bogged down in the middle levels of the Agrarian Department, and the succession was stalled. In early 1957 the neo-Jaramillistas finally obtained an official decision in their favor and took office, but in the meantime the incumbent commissariat had managed to retain control for more than a year beyond its elected term.[93]

Thus the conversion of the power struggle into a legal struggle enabled the pro-Guerrero leaders, evidently in collusion with state officials, to keep their local power for a time. The commissariat was the local authority for controlling individual ejidal rights and ejidal relations with the Agrarian Department. Except for the weaker vigilance council, moreover, the commissariat was the only formal institution of government in the ejido—unlike the cooperative's administration council, whose functions currently had been taken over by the manager and the field staff. By keeping control over the commissariat, the collaborationists prolonged important institutional support for the disintegrating Guerrero regime. They prevented the opposition force from gaining authoritative stature and a strong position from which to present its reform demands. And they guarded the critical right to regulate the assignment of plots for individual use—another source of discrimination and opposition within the ejido. Indeed, the collaborationists derived exceptional benefits from their procedural ploys. For the opposition, however, legal tactics once again proved to be ineffective—even though the neo-Jaramillistas finally won their battle.

Meanwhile, also to take advantage of their new electoral power, the neo-Jaramillista officers in the cooperative councils tried to gain control of Guerrero's patronage system by replacing the appointive field staff with an elective equivalent, to be called the "technical control commission." According to their proposals the General Law of Cooperative Societies permitted such a change.[94] The secretary of national economy disapproved the proposal, however, and ignored the neo-Jaramillistas' complaints about economic discrimination. He simply rejoined that setting all managerial policy was the legal prerogative of the Reorganizing Commission.[95]

In sum, after allowing the neo-Jaramillistas to use their majority support to win office in 1955, the authorities obstructed them from making any further gains in their enduring struggle for power and reform. At every turn the neo-Jaramillistas' legalistic feuding and bureaucratic lobbying proved ineffective. Yet in dealing with the authorities the neo-Jaramillistas persistently returned to the same tactics—ultimately the tactics most easily subjected to government control. Curiously, the neo-Jaramillistas never used their new majority support to mount a militant confrontation or to create a major work disruption, aside from some interference with the 1955–56 harvest. Indeed, the year and a half after their 1955 election victory was much calmer than the previous year and a half. Once in office the opposition leaders clearly moderated their former militancy—just as the authorities had evidently hoped they would do.

It has been intimated that the pleasures of holding office alone softened the militancy of the opposition leaders. According to this view the neo-Jaramillistas were far more interested in personal gain than in the general welfare they had made so much of during their campaign. But it must be remembered, too, that with three of their top leaders assassinated, the rest had good reason to be cautious. On the ejido pistolerismo had once again become a fact of life, and the Reorganizing Commission and Guerrero were using municipal authorities, police agents, and the field staff to impose a brutal system of political repression and forced labor—or so the neo-Jaramillista leaders claimed.[96] If indeed such claims were even partially true, it is no wonder that the opposition forces hesitated to resort to direct action tactics.

In a deeper sense tactical inertia was also dictated by the neo-Jaramillistas' strategic position. Aside from the weak CNC and the National Zapatista Front, the neo-Jaramillistas simply had no political allies. Support from the main CNC officials had recently slackened off after certain collaborationist leaders had joined the CNC-affiliated National Cane Producers' Union. More important, all the federal authorities supported the Reorganizing Commission and generally deferred to the state governor. No major elections or unsettling appointments occurred at the state or federal level, and thus there were no important political shifts from above to affect the Atencingo situation—at least not until after the new governor took office in late 1956. From the middle of 1955 until early 1957, then, the neo-Jaramillistas had no new opportunities to secure major concessions from either the state or the federal government. In addition to these political factors, the economic situation in the Atencingo region favored the continuation of the status quo. Since 1952 cane production, the cooperative's financial status, and the general income level had all improved markedly, and the mill was being properly supplied. With the existing system showing every indication of economic success, there was little reason for the federal government to comply with the neo-Jaramillistas' demands for change.

Guerrero's Resignation

Despite popular opposition Guerrero could remain in office indefinitely as long as he had the support of the state governor, who wielded considerable power as president of the Reorganizing Commission. What finally ended Guerrero's service was not the organized peasant opposition but the election of a new governor, Fausto Ortega, to succeed Gen. Rafael Avila Camacho.

The collaboration between the new governor and Guerrero lasted only about six months, until the end of the cane harvest in the middle of July, while power struggles at the state, regional, and local levels converged on Guerrero. At the state level Guerrero became only one of the many appointees and holdovers from the prior gubernatorial regime that Governor Ortega sought to supplant in order to consolidate and personalize his own control. At the regional level Guerrero evidently became the target of Manuel Sánchez Espinosa, who was a veteran politician and Congressional deputy from Matamoros, and a close associate of Jenkins. According to views current in Atencingo, at least, Sánchez spotted the weakness in Guerrero's position and sought to further his own career by joining the lobbying against Guerrero's continuation as manager. At the ejidal level Guerrero was attacked by the neo-Jaramillistas, who beset the governor's office with commissions and petitions, demanding at least his dismissal and the end of the discriminatory patronage practices. Even the politicized women, organized into "feminine leagues" in the ejido villages, joined in the petitioning.[97]

As a result of all these pressures, not to mention his own interests, the governor finally delegated a special representative to make a political investigation of the problems in Atencingo. The report was unflattering to Guerrero and blamed the local discontent on his management practices, especially that of allowing the same clique of collaborationists to hold the salaried cooperative posts year after year. A few days later Guerrero submitted his resignation.[98] Evidently he could not work with the same liberty and the same trust with the new governor as with the previous governor, and therefore decided to resign.[99] Then, as the new manager of the wealthy and important cooperative, Governor Ortega appointed Jenkins's friend Deputy Sánchez, ironically enough a welcome sight to the neo-Jaramillistas.

Conclusions

The state and federal governments imposed the Reorganizing Commission on the valuable Atencingo ejido in an effort to restore local institutional control and economic development according to the official conception. Clearly the commission and the cooperative manager it appointed both had strong government support. But lasting rule required some popular support as well, if only to get the work done. For this reason the commission and Guerrero pursued a strategy of cooptation and control, a classic strategy of government in contemporary Mexico. Essentially they converted the Atencingo ejido into an authoritarian patronage system in which remunerative participation depended on cooperation with government policy. A regime to preside over the system was recruited by the cooptation of selected leaders from the old Jaramillo regime. This process also served to divide the old leadership into two hostile factions, thus forestalling the or-

ganization of an effective opposition. The leaders who chose to collaborate then helped rally support for the state-controlled regime, or
at least acceptance of it. Most ejidatarios complied, either from fear
of the government or from a simple desire to secure a job and regular
wages within the patronage system.

Since the government needed the collaborationist leaders, and since
the collaborationists naturally wanted to stay in power, a pattern of
elitism and favoritism soon developed within the patronage system.
For political as well as economic reasons, uncooperative Jaramillistas
were shoved to the bottom of the system and kept there, initially by
economic discrimination and later by political repression. When the
Jaramillistas clamored for reforms, moreover, they were branded as
being power-hungry opportunists and demagogues. According to the
collaborationist rulers these rebels sought only power and not reform
—as evidenced by the Jaramillo regime's own failure to carry out reforms in the past. From the collaborationist point of view the Jaramillistas (and neo-Jaramillistas) were merely using popular support as
a pawn in their power struggle against the Guerrero regime. By en-
listing large numbers of ejidatarios in their campaign, it was said, they
hoped to disrupt the system enough to induce government intervention in their favor.

Of course the Jaramillistas gave different reasons for their actions.
From their perspective they were struggling against a system of exploitation and subjugation, rooted ultimately in the enforced commitment to collective cane agriculture. If they were not to submit to
this system or collaborate with it, an opposition struggle was their
only practical alternative. As in the past, the opposition's proclaimed
strategic objectives were local institutional power and agrarian reform. Its proclaimed tactical objectives were the completion of the
technical tasks and participation in the local patronage system. The
overall opposition strategy was to mobilize a winning combination
of popular support and government support. The overall tactics were
legalistic appeals, bureaucratic lobbying, local propaganda and agitation, and varying degrees of direct action against the state-controlled
regime.

From 1952 through 1954 the Jaramillista leaders lacked significant popular support and government support, and accordingly made little progress toward any of these objectives—other than to keep themselves on the census rolls. When a new president took office in 1953, their only allies were some members of the weak CNC. Owing to the murder of Teodoro Sánchez, the Jaramillistas won some new popular support, but they still commanded only a minority. As a result their bureaucratic lobbying and legalistic appeals proved inconsequential, and the work stoppage organized after Sánchez's murder failed.

When Jaramillo was assassinated in early 1955, however, the public reaction gave the opposition majority support. At last the opposition posed a real threat to the stability of the state-controlled regime. The federal authorities now responded according to a classic government strategy of cooptation: they conceded local power but denied reform. Thus the neo-Jaramillistas gained the strategic advantage on their tactical objective of participating in the local patronage system, and consequently won control of the cooperative's elective offices. Beyond that issue, however, they were not given effective government support, as evidenced especially by the procedural obstacles posed to their succession to the ejidal commissariat. Indeed, for the neo-Jaramillistas legalistic and bureaucratic tactics proved remarkably ineffective for making further gains, and from a strategic point of view their opportunities for further progress were temporarily closed. Then, in late 1956, a gubernatorial succession provided a fresh opportunity for further gain. Probing for support by means of a new wave of lobbying and agitation, the neo-Jaramillistas found that their interest in ousting Guerrero coincided with the new governor's interest in establishing personal control over the key management post. Accordingly, having gained a strategic advantage on that tactical objective, they won the replacement of Guerrero with someone more favorable to their interests.

From a broader perspective, then, victory for either the establishment or the opposition on any basic issue depended on gaining a strategic advantage. The strategic advantage went to the side that garnered the strongest combination of popular support and government support on the given issue. Moreover, government support was likely to follow on popular support, and vice versa. Thus when the neo-Jaramillistas won majority support in the ejido, the federal government conceded local power to them, if only to ensure the ejido's continued stability and productivity. Opportunities for opposition leaders to secure some government support usually resulted from a succession in office at a top level of government or from the acquisition of enough popular support to threaten stability and productivity. As for the opposition's tactics, they were only as effective as the support behind them. The less they demonstrated active support, the less likely were they to win any meaningful concessions from the government. Thus the opposition had the least success with the more passive tactics—legalistic appeals for change and bureaucratic lobbying for the completion of the technical tasks—and they had the most success when, given both popular and government support, they combined intensive agitation and the threat, if not reality, of direct action with their lobbying. This strategic principle was demonstrated not only during the Guerrero regime but also during earlier periods in the Atencingo ejido's history.

CHAPTER SIX

Peasants Against the State, 1957-1961

If Colonel Guerrero was the key figure in the first half of the decade of state control in Atencingo, Manuel Sánchez Espinosa was the key figure in the second half. Unlike Guerrero, Sánchez was well known in the Atencingo region before he became the manager of the cooperative. Born in a nearby village to relatives of Doña Lola, he completed the sixth grade and then in the late 1930's or early 1940's went to work in the cane fields of the Atencingo complex. Soon he secured leadership posts from the mill administration, eventually becoming the administrator of the Rijo annex. After the 1946–47 reorganization he worked for a while as a tractor driver for the mill, but then he quit that job to collaborate with his brother and none other than William Jenkins in a profitable tomato-growing venture. During the 1950's Sánchez succeeded in becoming the municipal president of Matamoros. Like a public-works politician he admirably paved the streets, renovated the central square, and built a secondary school in the growing town. Next he was elected deputy congressman for the district, the post he held when he was favored with the appointment as cooperative manager.[1] In contrast to Guerrero, then, Sánchez took office with a background as a cane agriculturist, as a state and local politician, and as a close collaborator of Jenkins. Accordingly his administrative policies were quite different than Guerrero's.

Sánchez's leadership style also differed markedly from his predecessor's. Whereas Guerrero secured at least some strong supporters among the ejidatarios and gave them the exclusive control of the top leadership posts, Sánchez tried to play all sides and ended up with few supporters, if any. Whereas Guerrero, a military officer with a gruff manner, inspired considerable respect and even fear among the ejidatarios, Sánchez, a placating politician and a calculating business-man, generally inspired less respect and no fear.[2] Whereas Guerrero was basically honest, Sánchez used his office for personal gain: an audit later revealed that over two million pesos were embezzled by his administration, though some of the cash went to outside political figures and even to leaders of the peasant opposition. At first these features of Sánchez's style helped him secure control over the ejidal complex, but later, when a crisis arose, they contributed to his rapid loss of control.

The Politics of Pacification

The major immediate consequences of Sánchez's coming to office in the middle of 1957 were twofold. First, it reintegrated the chain of command extending up to the president. Second, it shifted the bal-ance of power within the Atencingo complex in favor of the restive neo-Jaramillistas. As a result of these developments, opposition to the state-controlled regime subsided for a time.

To get rid of Guerrero the neo-Jaramillistas had taken advantage of discord between him and the new governor, Fausto Ortega. With the managerial succession, however, Governor Ortega—the most pow-erful figure in the Reorganizing Commission—established his control over the valuable cooperative. Moreover, like the federal authorities, neither the new governor nor the new manager favored structural re-forms. Once again the ejidatarios confronted a well-integrated state-controlled regime: there were no longer disagreements within the chain of command—from the manager and the governor, to the fed-eral representatives on the commission, to higher federal authorities—that the ejidatarios could exploit to their own advantage. From this point of view Sánchez's coming to office weakened the neo-Jarami-llistas' position. Certainly their prospects of having any petitions for structural reform granted were no better than before.

Within the ejidal complex, however, Sánchez and the commission promptly set policies that gave the popular neo-Jaramillistas broad participation, and hence a new stake, in all levels of the patronage system. After all, the neo-Jaramillistas deserved some reward for having supported Sánchez's replacement of Guerrero. Thus Sánchez did not interfere with their control of the ejidal commissariat and the administration council, and even made a notable effort to cooperate with these two elected bodies. He introduced some circulation in the appointive field staff and other well-paying positions, to the benefit of the neo-Jaramillistas and their followers.[3] Further, he and the governor informally—and perhaps illegally—stopped prorating the dividends and acceded to the popular demand for a return to equal shares.[4] Finally, Sánchez relied on persuasion rather than force as his major control technique. Virtually all sources agree that pistolerismo disappeared from the ejido. In its place were liberal loans[5] and perhaps even bribes that Sánchez apparently used to soothe passions and settle disputes, especially those involving the opposition leaders; in fact, the opposition leaders may have used the same cash later to finance their campaign against the Reorganizing Commission. On all these different counts, then, Sánchez and the governor immediately redressed grievances the neo-Jaramillistas had been voicing ever since 1952–53, thereby shifting the balance of power within the ejido dramatically in the neo-Jaramillistas' favor. As for the collaborationists, they were now weaker than ever. Sánchez kept a top collaborationist leader as his assistant manager, but otherwise the collaborationists were relegated to the vigilance councils, a portion of the field staff posts, and a few other well-paying posts.

These combined changes in government inside and outside the ejido brought new stability to the state-controlled regime. Inside the ejido Sánchez's cooptive concessions placated the neo-Jaramillistas and their majority following, while also settling issues that might have been used as a basis for opposition. Now enjoying greater participation and influence in the patronage system, the neo-Jaramillistas temporarily curtailed their agitation. Outside the ejido the reintegration of the official chain of command into a united front closed any breach that might have enabled them to wrest structural reforms from the government, such as the revocation of the 1952 decree.

Having lost much of their motivation inside the ejido and much of their strategic advantage outside it, the neo-Jaramillistas contented themselves with consolidating their economic and political power against the collaborationists. Indeed, the only serious dispute during 1957–58 concerned precisely the one aspect of the patronage system where the neo-Jaramillistas had not made immediate gains—the distribution of plots for crops other than cane, a matter subject to the authority of the ejidal commissariat. During Guerrero's administration certain collaborators and privileged peasants in collusion with the ejidal commissariat had been given disproportionately large plots, whereas ejidatarios who were out of favor had been given only small plots, or none at all.[6] When the neo-Jaramillista leaders finally took official command of the commissariat presidency in early 1957, they proceeded to equalize the land distribution. Since they generally had majority support, the adjustments were successfully carried out in most sections of the ejido. But in Lagunillas and La Galarza, where their popularity was less certain, the collaborationists put up a resistance with the support of the ejidal vigilance council, the CNC-affiliated National Cane Producers' Union, and local agrarian officials.[7] The Agrarian Department chief, Castulo Villaseñor, sided with the ejidal commissariat, however, and confirmed that the plots for individual cultivation should be apportioned equally.[8] Thus by the end of 1958 the neo-Jaramillistas had made virtually all the gains possible in the patronage system without another change in manager.

Cane Production and the Ejidal Economy

During the Sánchez regime the economic life of the Atencingo complex again revolved around the interests of the complex's former owner, the powerful and mysterious William Jenkins. In fact, Jenkins's exact role has been difficult to determine, since he never let people learn much about his activities. But however elusive he was, by the late 1950's he had become a most formidable behind-the-scenes figure in the state and the nation. Then described as the "mysterious buccaneer-businessman who has built the biggest personal fortune in Mexico," Jenkins was reported to be worth anywhere from 200 million to 300 million dollars. During the middle of the 1940's he had bought an entire five-million-dollar bond issue from the government's holding corporation, Nacional Financiera. In more recent years Jenkins had lent needy contractors 25.6 million dollars so that they could complete the four-lane highway from Mexico City to Querétaro, and he had also offered the government 80 million dollars to finance another superhighway from Mexico City to Puebla. Besides cash his holdings allegedly included "the Bank of Commerce, textile mills, cement plants, an automobile assembly plant, finance companies, and a soap company," plus several hundred of Mexico's best movie theaters. He had also built a hospital in Puebla, and had apparently made contributions to numerous other projects and causes (probably including the official party and political campaigns), thereby endearing himself to Puebla's governors and other important political personages. And, of course, he still controlled the sugar mill at Atencingo, though his two Spanish business partners were listed as the owners.[9]

Jenkins's activities will continue to be obscure. It is certain, nonetheless, that during 1957–61 his interests in the Atencingo complex were given excellent treatment, perhaps the best they had had since 1945. From 1946 to 1952 Jenkins had been forced to struggle desperately against the Jaramillo regime in order to protect the mill's productivity. During 1952–57 economic relations between the cooperative and the mill had improved greatly, but the state-controlled regime had worked to develop the cooperative's autonomy—a process the mill administration had historically resisted and even feared. Now, however, the state-controlled regime was ruled by Sánchez and Governor Ortega, who were both more eager to please Jenkins than to continue developing the cooperative's autonomy. Whereas Guerrero and Governor Avila Camacho had aimed at what they called an "integral" development of the Atencingo ejido as a diversified agricultural complex, Sánchez and Governor Ortega now altered that emphasis. Attentive to the interests of Jenkins, and hence to the needs of the mill, they preferred to concentrate on cane production and construction projects, and showed little concern for long-range development alternatives.

From Jenkins's point of view, indeed, Sánchez performed his main function very well: he managed to produce a great deal of cane. During his regime production rose to the highest levels ever recorded by

TABLE 6

Sugar Cane Produced and Processed by the Atencingo
Cooperative and Mill, 1957–1961

Harvest	Cooperative: Total delivered to mill (tons)	Mill	
		Total milled from all sources (tons)	Average yield of all sources (tons/ha.)
1957–58	347,731	468,682	133.8
1958–59	388,094	527,260	136.5
1959–60	443,890	611,935	186.1
1960–61	427,414	572,118	153.7

SOURCES: For the cooperative, local ejidal credit society memorandum, July 12, 1967, MAEM; for the mill, Unión Nacional de Productores de Azúcar, *Estadísticas azucareras* (Mexico City, 1967), p. 35.

NOTE: Figures on the cooperative's average yield during these years are not available.

the cooperative, as Table 6 shows. In two seasons out of four the cooperative surpassed by wide margins the 400,000-ton level the mill had been setting as a target since 1952. Moreover, the mill, whose capacity had been expanded to take care of other suppliers in the region, processed the biggest tonnages in its history. Jenkins must have been very pleased.

The ejido's expenses under Sánchez were very high, however. As cane production increased, so did the ejido's total annual budget. From a final peak under Guerrero of 13 million pesos, it soared further to 25 million pesos for 1959–60.[10] Though most of these funds went to finance the cane harvest, an audit later revealed that over the years at least two million pesos were embezzled by members of Sánchez's administration. Moreover, to at least Jenkins's benefit, Sánchez allowed the interest rate on the mill's loans to climb from less than 8 percent to more than 11 percent.

Despite such costs the ejido's profits under Sánchez were also high. Some of the profits went to construction. Sánchez's major achievement along these lines in Atencingo was a new central office building for the administrators of the cooperative and a huge auditorium for assemblies and movies, all costing about two million pesos. The old office building was then used for maintaining equipment and supervising its use. In addition to his building projects, Sánchez had several— though not enough—wells drilled for irrigation water, and with the aid of government funds, he supported community development projects in various sections of the ejido for school construction, electrification, and road paving. Sánchez also purchased some additional agricultural machinery and tools, though he did not tamper with the mill administration's prerogative to rent its own equipment to the cooperative.[11]

The ejidatarios' incomes generally rose too. In 1959 Sánchez raised most wages by 12.5 percent and created additional high-paying jobs. From seven pesos under Guerrero, the typical laborer's pay for a day of piecework rose to nine pesos. Wages for other jobs rose to twelve and fourteen pesos a day. The weekly salaries for the field captains rose from 75 to 85 pesos, for the mayordomos from 80 to 100 pesos, for the truck and tractor drivers to 140 pesos, and for the field staff supervisors to 200 pesos.[12] Yet, as in the past, the new wage system (which consisted of 31 levels) fostered disputes among the ejidatarios over the better-paying jobs. Moreover, many ejidatarios still refused to accept the lower-paying jobs, at seven to nine pesos a day, with the result that outsiders still had to be hired.[13]

Unlike wages, the ejidatarios' dividends did not increase. They remained for two years at the levels established by Guerrero, and then plummeted as a consequence of the rising costs of construction and wages, and the constant drain of embezzlement: the total dividends distributed after the 1957–58 harvest amounted to some 2.8 million pesos; after the 1958–59 harvest, 2.7 million pesos; and after the 1959–60 harvest, only 2 million pesos.[14] These dividends were distributed in equal shares among the ejidatarios under the very popular policy Sánchez had initiated with some 3 million pesos earned for 1956–57 by the Guerrero regime.[15]

Very little information is available about the produce and income the ejidatarios derived from growing crops other than cane. It is certain that they retained their right, supposedly established under Guerrero, to a half hectare of seasonal land for subsistence agriculture and another half hectare for commercial rice agriculture, farmed either collectively or individually. Apparently profits remained at satisfactory levels during 1957 and 1958, but then declined during 1959 and 1960,* when Sánchez and the Reorganizing Commission tried to reimpose restrictions and collectivization on the cultivation of such crops. Indeed, Sánchez made no determined effort to improve the ejidatarios' incomes by crop diversification, though he did follow policies that enabled him to reap personal profits from the extra crops already being grown. In particular, he helped finance cultivations of melons and tomatoes, the results of which ended up in a Mexico City market stall owned by him and his brothers. Reportedly Jenkins was included in the deals: it has been said that he, and not the National Ejidal Credit Bank, provided Sánchez with the cash for financing these crops.[16]

Overall, then, the Sánchez regime appears to have had a beneficial effect not only on the incomes of Jenkins and Sánchez but also on those of the ejidatarios—at least for two or three years. This upward trend in incomes was accompanied by a considerable internal redistribution of the salaried posts, the better-paying jobs, and the plots for crops other than cane, to the relative advantage of the neo-Jaramillistas. In other words, the general increase in incomes must have been greatly augmented for the neo-Jaramillistas by these additional factors, at the collaborationists' expense. But this significant improvement in their lot during the first three years of the Sánchez regime would not prevent the ambitious neo-Jaramillista leaders from making an issue out of the economic downturn in 1960, and eventually ousting Sánchez.

The Renewal of Instability

During 1957–58, as we have seen, the neo-Jaramillistas made considerable gains within the local patronage system, but they clearly lacked the government support necessary to gain any major reforms. Consequently relative peace and stability prevailed in the Atencingo

---

* The data on this point are quite sparse. Some ejidatarios complained in letters to government officials then about losses or at least failures to make a profit from the rice crop in 1959–60 and from the tomato and melon crops in 1958–59 as well as 1959–60. More than likely, profits were unevenly distributed, with some ejidatarios earning well and others suffering losses.

complex. In 1959 the political and strategic context changed, however. Adolfo López Mateos, a rural reformist, acceded to the presidency, and a new federal regime took command. The new authorities and officials in the Department of Agrarian Affairs and Colonization (DAAC), as the Agrarian Department was now called, the Secretariat of Agriculture (SAG), and the CNC were all more inclined than their predecessors to hear and redress the ejidatarios' grievances. As a result the rebel ejidatarios found themselves in the most hospitable political environment they had experienced since 1952. They accordingly probed for support from the federal government, and soon found it. By the same token peace and stability for the state-controlled regime came to an end.

Sentiments in favor of collective agriculture and conformity to the law ran high in the new federal regime. As a result the initial impact of the federal succession was detrimental to the neo-Jaramillistas' interests, for the Reorganizing Commission ordered Sánchez to collectivize and restrict the cultivation of crops other than cane and to prorate the dividends on the basis of time worked, as the law actually required. When Sánchez moved to put these unpopular measures into effect, vocal opposition to the state-controlled regime arose once again. The neo-Jaramillista officers appealed to Roberto Barrios, the new DAAC chief, to protect the ejidatarios' established rights and privileges despite any illegality.[17] The issue of the dividends was settled rather easily: Barrios sided with the neo-Jaramillistas, whose protests consequently prevailed over the Reorganizing Commission's plans.[18] The equal-shares approach remained in effect. The issue of collectivization for crops other than cane was more problematic. An investigator found that the individualized agriculture was inferior in quality and uneconomical, and that many ejidatarios were illegally renting their plots to other parties. On this basis he recommended that the collective system be retained and improved.[19] But the neo-Jaramillistas continued to protest the irregular intervention of the cooperative management in their affairs, claiming that their rice crops were now unprofitable because of it.[20] In the end Chief Barrios conceded a return to the old individualized system, thus giving the neo-Jaramillistas a victory on that issue also.[21] More important, they had located the first of several allies who would support their broad-based struggle against the state-controlled regime.

Indeed, as soon as the new presidential regime took office, the neo-Jaramillistas began probing for government support on their major reform demands. They first turned to the Secretariat of Industry and Commerce (SIC, formerly the Secretariat of National Economy), demanding the revocation of the 1952 decree and calling for an audit of Sánchez's suspect accounts, an area in which Sánchez was highly vulnerable. They were told, however, that there was little likelihood of a favorable response to their petition.[22] One high official confided that their problem was "very serious because of the big interests that were involved."[23] He agreed to order an audit, but none was actually begun. Moreover, the SIC's Judicial Section now announced that the 1952 decree was legal. Clearly the neo-Jaramillistas had made no headway within the SIC. Still hoping to find legal support for their demands, they took the matter of the 1952 decree to Mexico's attorney general, but he conceded only that it ought to be studied.[24]

Rebuffed but resolute, the neo-Jaramillistas turned to the DAAC for help in late 1959. Barrios, the new chief, was responding favorably on their lesser grievances. Now, in a major petition signed by 1,300 peasants (including women), they asked him to intercede with the president on their behalf, so that major structural changes would be authorized for the Atencingo ejido. Specifically, they wanted the revocation of the 1952 decree; the division of the ejido; parcellation and the end of the collective work system; and the financing of the cane crop by the National Ejidal Credit Bank.[25]

Chief Barrios commissioned Victor Joseph, a middle-level official, to make a thorough investigation of the ejido. In his report Joseph concluded that the ejido's organization and economy were highly deficient. The state governor in fact controlled the cooperative, he wrote, in collaboration with the manager. Little coordination existed between the manager, who did whatever the governor directed, and the elected neo-Jaramillista leaders, who dedicated themselves to rallying the ejidatarios against alleged violations of their rights. Little cooperative spirit was to be found among the ejidatarios; in part the management itself had fostered the lack of cooperation, which had bad repercussions on the ejidatarios' economic well-being. Because of the collective system, moreover, the ejidatarios felt like salaried field laborers, and the complex graded system of work and wage levels only fueled their discontent. Indeed, according to Joseph, the management resembled the paternalistic owner of a private enterprise, and the ejidatarios resembled unionized workers.[26]

To solve these problems, Joseph considered a reorganization "indispensable." Clearly, he wrote, Atencingo had sufficient resources to provide, under proper management, a higher living standard for all the ejidatarios, an adequate supply of sugar cane for the mill, and good profits from all the crops produced. He recommended that a new presidential decree be issued to establish the basis for thorough collectivization and to transfer control from the state governor to the DAAC and the SIC. In his opinion the root problem was how the collective system was managed and not the collective system itself—especially since good agricultural conditions for collectivization existed in Atencingo. Certainly the individual agriculture he had observed there was inferior.[27]

Acting on these recommendations, DAAC officials immediately drafted a decree ordering that the Reorganizing Commission be supplanted by a federal Commission of Control and Vigilance. This new commission would exercise virtually all the powers of the old one, but it would be under the supervision of the DAAC rather than the state governor. The DAAC chief would name the cooperative's manager, and the DAAC representative would act as president of the commission, while the governor would not even be represented. In addition the draft decree specified that all agriculture would be collective, even in the case of corn grown for subsistence.[28]

Plans called for the decree to take effect by the end of 1959, with the signatures of the president, the DAAC chief, and the secretaries of agriculture and of industry and commerce. Such high-level agreement was never reached, however, and the decree was never signed. The reasons are not certain, but clearly the decree's terms jeopardized the interests of various parties in various ways—by increasing federal interference in the governor's domain, by enhancing the DAAC's power relative to that of the SIC, and by deepening the ejidatarios' subjection to collectivism and government control. Even so, the interest shown by Barrios in the Atencingo case, the investigation undertaken by Joseph, and the decree drafted by DAAC officials all demonstrated that the neo-Jaramillistas had found sympathetic allies within the federal bureaucracy. Moreover, the president himself was now becoming involved. Federal support for the Reorganizing Commission was subsiding, and Sánchez and the state governor were now on the defensive. As a result of the neo-Jaramillistas' criticism, Sánchez and the governor were even obliged to write letters to the president and the DAAC chief defending the Reorganizing Commission's record.[29]

Next the neo-Jaramillistas fostered further disintegration in the official chain of command by using their emergent federal-level support to undermine their state-level rulers. They cleverly asked Chief Barrios to appoint a personal representative for the DAAC on the Reorganizing Commission in place of the state's agrarian delegate,[30] who was an ally of the governor. The chief agreed, appointing Armando Padilla Franyutti to the post "to avoid greater abuses by the management."[31] As a result Barrios secured a stronghold at the state level from which to work on the ejidatarios' behalf, whereas the governor lost the complete control he had formerly held over the Reorganizing Commission.

In the months ahead Padilla agreed with the neo-Jaramillistas' view that the ejidal complex needed a major reorganization. He did not agree, however, that Atencingo's problems could be solved by dismantling the collective system, dividing and parceling out the ejido, or diversifying the ejido's crops. Such measures, to his way of thinking, would "automatically shatter the economic unity and liquidate the industry, leaving a considerable number of mill workers laid off without any employment opportunities." Padilla advocated instead a radical plan whereby the federal government would eliminate the state governor's power over ejidal affairs, design a collective work program that "realistically satisfies the ejidal interests," expropriate the mill on behalf of a new cooperative (evidently including the workers), select competent persons to manage the cooperative, and designate federal representatives to supervise the cooperative's activities. Reviving an idea originally put forward by Vicente Lombardo Toledano in 1937 and echoed by José María Suárez Téllez in 1953, Padilla commented that the mill and the railroad system should originally have been included in the ejidal complex to eliminate the friction that had always existed between the mill administration and the agricultural workers. Major precedents existed in the cases of the cooperative societies in the cane growing regions of Zacatepec and El Mante.[32] Essentially Padilla's proposals amounted to a much more radical version of the draft decree that had been rejected in November. As such, they were surely even more impolitic, and apparently they were not seriously considered in attempts to draft an alternative decree that might be acceptable to all parties concerned. After all, not even the ejidatarios had asked for the expropriation of the mill.

Elsewhere in the new presidential regime, meanwhile, the neo-Jaramillista leaders located firm supporters in the new CNC secretary-general, Francisco Hernández y Hernández, and the undersecretary of agriculture, J. Jesús Patiño Navarrete. Both these officials would back the neo-Jaramillistas' demand for full control of the cooperative against the DAAC's recommendation of federal control. Accordingly, they would become the neo-Jaramillistas' closest allies at the federal level, acting as both lobbyists and counselors. Hernández even appointed a special representative, J. Jesús Castro Ruvalcaba, to act as a field adviser in the Atencingo complex itself.

Thus the neo-Jaramillistas were finally gaining a strategic advantage against the state-controlled regime. In addition to the popular support they already commanded, strong government support was materializing from the new presidential regime, and the official chain of command, which extended from the field staff on the ejido up to the president, was clearly breaking apart. The state governor and the cooperative manager were no longer assured of government support above or even within the Reorganizing Commission, and they were about to lose control in the ejido. Most important, beset by a national wave of peasant agitation in the wake of the Cuban Revolution, President López Mateos was poised for a concessionary settlement.

The Technical Tasks

As the prospects for land reform revived, so did the need for completing the neglected technical tasks. Work on them had fallen off since Sánchez had become manager. Neither he nor the new governor, unlike their predecessors, expressed any interest in obtaining an acceptable survey, maps, or the definitive authorization of the ejido. Rather, perhaps like Jenkins himself, they remained satisfied with the indefinite status quo. Certainly such a course avoided issues that might have aroused renewed agitation, and it enabled private property owners like Sánchez's brother to retain control of the ejido's borderlands.

From within the ejido, then, the neo-Jaramillistas were alone in urging the DAAC and the state Agrarian Delegation to finish the maps, which supposedly needed only a little more work.[33] Outside the ejido the CNC, the National Zapatista Front, and even certain middle-level officials within the DAAC[34] supported the neo-Jaramillistas' demand during 1957–58. When Chief Barrios came to office after the presidential succession, high-level DAAC officials vigorously called for the indispensable documentation to be completed.[35] Nevertheless, the responsible parties in the state Agrarian Delegation, as well as in the DAAC's Bureau of Lands and Waters and among the field engineers, persisted into 1960 in their inability to comply. Perhaps new fieldwork had become necessary because of the problematic features of the 1955 survey.

The census had become a less sensitive issue, since most ejidatarios now had their certificates of agrarian rights and since factional conflict had subsided within the ejido. In late 1959, however, Joseph reported as a result of his investigation for the DAAC that the legal figure of 2,320 ejidatarios no longer corresponded to reality: it excluded many fieldworkers who had been in the region a long time but had not been counted in the original census; it included persons who did not exist; and it included persons who were living in different areas, sometimes even in different states, and who appeared only when it was time for dividends to be distributed. "Theoretically there are many ejidatarios," Joseph concluded, "but in fact only an effective rectification of the census could shed light on the reality of who are the true rightful ejidatarios."[36] Though the ejidatarios were apparently reluctant to submit themselves to a new census, their leaders finally agreed to the necessity in the middle of 1960. At least such fieldwork would determine the status of each section of the ejido, thus preparing the way for the prospective division and parcellation.[37]

Meanwhile, the landless villagers began agitating heavily again. Relatively quiescent during 1957 and 1958, they mounted a fresh campaign for land once the new president entered office, and once technical work and land reform again seemed imminent in the still unauthorized Atencingo ejido. Insisting that in effect Jenkins still owned and controlled the land, they once again pressed their claim to it, as they had been doing ever since 1937. In the words of one dramatic plea,

> Each one of us has a few yards of soil to be buried in.... We have no schools, communications, lands, water, houses, food—but we do indeed have bosses, caciques, oppression, suffering, misery, pain, slavery. We are afraid to say this, which is the truth, because others who have tried to speak have been assassinated by the henchmen of Jenkins, the dreadful jackal who has had to drink the blood of our race in order to bathe himself in wealth.... We beg you to tell the head of our nation about the immensity of the land Jenkins has, the many deaths he has caused, the way he has exploited us, the cruelty with which he treats us, the great quantity of arms that are right now pointed to attack us, the danger to our own and our families' lives—only because we ask for what is ours, the land, land of Morelos, lands of Zapata, lands of our great heroes, but not lands of Jenkins. We ask that the great hacienda of Atencingo be distributed among us who deserve it, and thus one more problem of Mexico will be resolved.*

The landless villagers were said to constitute a population of eight thousand peasants, located in more than nineteen villages, including

---

* José Ramales Sánchez et al. to Gen. Augustín Olachea Aviles, secretary of national defense, September 26, 1959, FNDA, p. 267. Curiously, according to a letter written by a DAAC official to the DAAC secretary-general sometime in 1960 (FNDA, p. 162), while DAAC officials were attending to the petition from the landless villagers, they discovered that for some unspecified reason Jenkins had no certificates authorizing legal possession of his private property. Probably the reason was that his property had never been surveyed either.

Atencingo and San Nicolás Tolentino. Now under the leadership of a former Zapatista colonel and a radical mill worker, they reorganized themselves into the United Peasantry of Southern Puebla, affiliated with the Old Agrarian Guard, a newly formed left-wing organization within the CNC that sought to bring dissident elements back into the official fold.[38]

Despite their renewed vigor and organization, the landless villagers were again fended off. The most the DAAC offered was to relocate them in distant regions where the government was creating agricultural colonies; to this end the officials persuaded them to petition for the creation of "new centers of ejidal population."[39] The villagers did not want to migrate, however. They preferred to live, hope, and struggle right where they were—in the Atencingo region. They wanted to form those new centers from what they claimed were Jenkins's holdings. At the very least they wanted rights in the existing ejido, if only the authorities would do new fieldwork to determine whether openings were available.

In sum, during almost three years of the Sánchez administration, virtually no progress was made toward the definitive authorization of the ejido. The responsible parties within the state and federal bureaucracies, at worst obstructing action and at best temporizing, managed to preserve the status quo. Issues that had once seemed on the way to settlement now became progressively unsettled once again. Ironically, just when opportunities for land reform were the best in years, the uncompleted technical tasks again posed an obstacle that would have to be overcome before any division or parcellation of the ejido could occur.

Mobilization and Power

Back in the ejido the neo-Jaramillistas were rallying widespread, enthusiastic popular support for the coming offensive. By now, J. Guadalupe Ramírez Vargas, a veteran opposition leader and the administration council president during 1958–60, had emerged as their top leader. In the middle of 1960 neo-Jaramillista candidates again easily won the elections for the ejidal commissariat and the administration council, the new presidents being two other veterans, Cirilo

Gutiérrez and Carlos Galarza respectively. After Galarza's election Ramírez converted himself into the major popular candidate for manager of the cooperative and became very closely allied with Secretary-General Hernández of the CNC and Undersecretary Patiño of the SAG.

In the succeeding months even the collaborationists jumped on the neo-Jaramillista bandwagon in the campaign for the revocation of the 1952 decree. But the alliance between the two factions was very uneasy. Significantly, whereas the neo-Jaramillistas believed the ejidatarios should elect the new manager in an assembly, the less popular collaborationists wanted the federal government to select and install the most capable ejidatario in the post—the only way the collaborationists could win. Whereas the neo-Jaramillistas stressed parcellation, the collaborationists stressed the division of the ejido as their major reform goal, if only to secure the independence of certain annexes where they still enjoyed majority support.[40] Accordingly, the leaders of the two factions struggled more against each other for power than together for reform.

To complicate the popular pressures on the government authorities, the unrest among the Atencingo ejidatarios fostered unrest in and conflicting demands from other quarters. In general, the neo-Jaramillistas' struggle was having divisive repercussions among peasants and workers throughout the region, as different groups rushed to protect and promote their special interests in land. On the one hand, the mill workers worried that the struggle would lower cane production and threaten the mill's vitality. To protect their livelihood, therefore, they opposed further land reform and offered little sympathy to the neo-Jaramillistas. On the other hand, the landless villagers campaigned vigorously for the ouster of Sánchez and for a radical land reform to their own benefit. They also withheld support from the neo-Jaramillistas, whom they saw as competitors rather than comrades in the struggle for control of the overpopulated region's scarce land resources. At the same time the neo-Jaramillistas received counterbalancing support from the hundreds of their own landless sons and relatives who also lived in the ejido villages, worked in the fields, and hoped for eventual rights as ejidatarios.

In view of the mounting potential for instability, President López Mateos soon decided in favor of a moderate, cooptive solution that would essentially protect the industrial interests while granting power to the ejidatarios. In his first formal move, during August he proposed a decree that would simply revoke the 1952 Alemán decree and return the cooperative to strict regulation by its own constitution and the General Law of Cooperative Societies. His proposal stated at length that the original reasons for the 1952 decree no longer applied, that the ejidal commissariat and the administration council were acting properly, and that further intervention by the federal and state governments was therefore no longer necessary.[41] For unknown reasons this draft decree, like the one earlier offered by the DAAC, never came into effect, though it was scheduled for signing in late August. The president had nevertheless made his move: he was ready to revoke the 1952 decree. Apparently the problem was whether additional provisions should be included, and if so, what those provisions should be. The critical issue was whether to return the cooperative to the ejidatarios or to transfer control to the federal level, as the DAAC draft had proposed. The decision would be an important one in view of the Atencingo ejido's high value as an agricultural-industrial complex.

Until about August the neo-Jaramillistas had carried on their revived struggle by means of combined bureaucratic lobbying and local agitation. Now, however, with power and reform so close, they took more direct action. Sometime in August or September, Sánchez announced the low dividends from the 1959–60 harvest, about 600 pesos apiece. The neo-Jaramillista leaders seized on the issue, claiming fraud, and began to mobilize the ejidatarios for an open confrontation with Sánchez and the Reorganizing Commission. Virtually all the ejidatarios joined the cause, and no sizable group rallied to Sánchez's defense.[42]

During September and October most of the ejidatarios refused to accept their dividends,[43] clamored for an audit of Sánchez's financial records, and flooded high-level federal authorities with petitions and commissions. The ejidatarios' long-standing programmatic and technical objectives were forced on the authorities' attention, with new emphasis on the establishment of local ejidal credit societies in each of the nine proposed ejidos. To dramatize their efforts, the representatives of one important commission sent to the DAAC in the middle of October vowed to remain in Mexico City, "suffering all the deprivations that may be necessary," until their demands were met.[44]

In early November the ejidatarios added forceful tactics to their campaign. Their leaders convened an extraordinary general assembly, obtained a popular mandate for a work stoppage, and notified the president in a telegram of "our irrevocable decision not to deliver cane until our just demands . . . are favorably resolved."[45] The beginning of the 1960–61 cane harvest was just one month away. Then, one morning, Ramírez and other leaders, followed by a clamoring mass of ejidatarios, seized and occupied the cooperative's offices.[46] Clearly Sánchez had completely lost control. Faced by superior political odds, he refused to reappear in Atencingo. Soon afterward he officially "resigned"—or so he later described his action.[47]

In view of the crisis Chief Barrios commissioned the general director of the DAAC's Ejidal Development Section, Rolando W. Delasse, to make a thorough investigation. Delasse concluded that the revocation of the 1952 decree was an urgent matter, for he regarded the decree as the origin of the ejido's problems. Moreover, he advised the DAAC to attend to all the ejidatarios' demands: an audit of the Sánchez administration's accounts; a revision of the census; the approval of the costly mapping survey executed in 1955; the division of the ejido into nine ejidos; the dissolution of the cooperative and the distribution of its goods equitably among the nine proposed ejidos; the parcellation of the nine proposed ejidos into individual plots; the institution of direct contracting between the mill and each individual peasant for his cane crop; and the development of a plan establishing the crop rotations to be allowed in the region. In Delasse's opinion these points were "just and worthy of immediate resolution, for the existing situation is very difficult and dangerous: the spirits of the ejidatarios are aroused, especially with the presence of federal troops there." Thus, in contrast to Padilla, Delasse recommended extravagant concessions to the ejidatarios.[48]

Officials in the DAAC did not entirely agree about what to do, but at least they were resolved that the 1952 decree should be revoked quickly and that the DAAC should play a predominant role in drafting any further reforms. Accordingly they drafted and tendered a second decree for the president's approval. By the draft decree's provisions the DAAC was to receive all the Reorganizing Commission's documents and goods, so that it could take command of any reorganization of the ejidal complex. In addition the DAAC was to be granted authority to audit the cooperative's accounts and investigate whether the cooperative society should be maintained or whether it should be replaced by some other system.[49] Clearly the DAAC was trying to wrest official control of the cooperative from the SIC and to turn the Atencingo complex into a special DAAC enclave. DAAC officials apparently believed that only in this way could they achieve an "integral solution"—a term they frequently used—to Atencingo's problems.[50] Historically their analysis was sound, for the ejido had always been subject to the cooperative, with the result that the interests of the SIC (or previously the Secretariat of National Economy) usually took precedence over those of the DAAC (or previously the Agrarian Department) as far as the Atencingo complex was concerned.

Since the DAAC officials considered a restructuring of authority "indispensable" to ensure a successful harvest and to avoid irreparable economic damage to the ejidatarios and the mill,[51] they submitted their draft decree for immediate signing by the appropriate federal authorities, namely the president, the secretary of industry and commerce, the secretary of agriculture, and the DAAC chief. Aside from the chief, however, these federal authorities did not agree with the provisions, and the draft was never signed. Evidently quite a power struggle was taking place to determine the future links between the Atencingo cooperative and the government. Surely the secretary of industry and commerce would never agree to loss of control over the cooperative society. Moreover, Ramírez and other neo-Jaramillista leaders opposed further government control.

Meanwhile, the DAAC officials seemed ready to tackle another of the ejido's problems—the division of the ejido, a goal they had already supported twice before, in 1946–47 and 1951–52. In November a high-level DAAC official informed the eager president of the neo-Jarami-

llista ejidal commissariat that as soon as the ejidal grant was definitively executed, "orders will be issued to the general director of the
Bureau of Lands and Waters to proceed to undertake the studies for
the division which you solicit."[52] In other words, as soon as the technical work was completed, the ejido could be divided.

Between November and January, however, it was decided that the
results of the 1955 survey were too problematic for easy correction by
lesser DAAC officials or by the state Agrarian Delegation. As a result an engineer was appointed to undertake new fieldwork.[53] With
another census revision also being planned pursuant to the division of
the ejido, the DAAC had thus reverted to the fieldwork stage on the
two most basic, problematic, and politicized technical tasks—the census and the survey. These decisions were justifiable, to be sure, but
they were quite inopportune from the ejidatarios' point of view. The
prospect of further fieldwork was raised at the very moment when it
appeared that DAAC officials were indeed about to allow the division of the ejido. In light of the government's record on the technical
tasks since 1946, starting with fieldwork again was quite likely to
mean that at least months, and perhaps years, might pass before the
tasks were completed, and hence before either division or parcellation
would be possible. Moreover, because of the great number of politically active landless peasants in the region, fieldwork would most
likely be stalled by agrarian agitation. Thus the prospects for an immediate division of the ejido were dim, barring a major effort by the
DAAC chief.

Meanwhile, in November and December, harvest time arrived. The
precious cane stood ripe in the fields. Something definite had to be
done to ease the crisis and get the peasants back to work. Although
the federal authorities still did not entirely agree on what course to
take, they announced a ninety-day interim period, vowing to revoke
the 1952 decree and decide on a joint solution with the president during that time. Either the secretary of industry and commerce or the
secretary of agriculture immediately appointed an interim cooperative
manager, Fernando Cruz Chávez, and the ejidatarios agreeably
started the harvest as the mill administration directed. Fortunately
for Ramírez, the neo-Jaramillista leader, Cruz Chávez selected him

to serve as assistant manager, displacing a collaborationist from the post.[54] Ramírez was now in a choice position to become manager.

The politicking over the ejido's future now proceeded in a quiet way. All parties talked and exchanged viewpoints. The ejidatarios, especially the neo-Jaramillista leaders, were insisting above all that they were capable of managing their own affairs; any new manager, they said, must be "one of our own."[55] At the peak of the discussions Secretary-General Hernández of the CNC and Undersecretary Patiño of the SAG, now close allies of Ramírez, arranged for a personal interview between a commission of ejidatarios, headed by Ramírez, and President López Mateos.[56] The president definitely promised to revoke the 1952 decree, return the cooperative to the ejidatarios, and settle the ejido's agrarian problems. Thus the neo-Jaramillistas would at least win power through their struggle. Many ejidatarios believed that the final resolution would also entail one major agrarian reform, the division of the ejido. Parcellation, though still the preeminent aspiration of the ejidatarios and a live issue among them, appeared most unlikely because of its probable effect on cane production, which the federal government was determined to protect.*

As the ninety-day period was ending, in February 1961, the president and other federal authorities finally arrived at an agreement. A decree was drafted that simply returned the cooperative and the ejido to their original status, on the ground that the conditions necessitating the 1952 decree no longer existed. Essentially, then, the decree merely followed the president's proposal of August 1960. But it also casually directed federal authorities to take any measures for organization and planning in the ejido that seemed "in the best interests of the ejidatarios."[57] No particular measures were specified, however; any further reform, such as the division or parcellation of the ejido would clearly require another presidential decree.

---

* The incident may have no connection to the crisis in Atencingo, but at the height of the crisis in December, curiously enough, the federal government expropriated part of Jenkins's movie theater holdings at a cost of 26 million dollars. Fortunately for Jenkins, however, this sum was sufficient to pay for only the seats, the projection equipment, and long-term leases on the theater buildings. In other words, Jenkins still continued to own the theater buildings involved, for which the government now paid rent through the leases.

Unlike several of its predecessors, this draft decree came into effect. On February 16, 1961, it was signed by President López Mateos; Raúl Salinas Lozano, the secretary of industry and commerce; Julián Rodríguez Adame, the secretary of agriculture; and Roberto Barrios, the DAAC chief. Two days later it became law. Thus, in the classic pattern, the ejidatarios were granted power but no fundamental reforms—not even the division of the ejido, the one reform various DAAC officials had been recommending for years. Only the ejidatarios' minimum demand was met, leaving open the possibility of further struggles for reform.

In early March came the time for the transfer of power—and for the important decision of who would become the new manager of the economically powerful cooperative society. By law the administration council, headed by Carlos Galarza, had the prerogative of naming the cooperative manager. Galarza named Ramírez, a choice that the ejidatario assembly enthusiastically endorsed, especially in the light of Ramírez's long-standing support of parcellation and his background of leadership in the reform struggle. The ejidatarios trusted Ramírez, believing he would indeed bring about the reforms he had promised. Cruz Chávez stepped down from his post but remained on hand until the harvest was completed in June, at the satisfying level of 427,414 tons—ample evidence that the government had managed to maintain a high level of production in spite of the crisis.

Though information on the subject is scarce, the selection of Ramírez was undoubtedly arranged long before the assembly, rather than being left up to the ejidatarios. Official support may have coalesced in Ramírez's favor weeks and even months before. Government authorities were concerned all along that the new manager be capable but controllable to ensure renewed stability in the ejidal complex. As assistant manager under Cruz Chávez and as chief spokesman in the interview with President López Mateos, Ramírez had demonstrated his character and ability. Moreover, he had formed close ties with CNC and SAG officials, who carefully counseled him on his dealings with the government and apparently boosted his candidacy. Thus Ramírez had proved that he could get along with government authorities as well as with the ejidatarios. When he moved into his new position, furthermore, a variety of CNC and SAG advisers moved in as well. In effect the presidential decree transferred power from the state government not only downward to the ejidatarios but also upward to the federal government, by means of discreet, informal cooptation.

Conclusions

From 1957 to 1961—the remaining years of the state-controlled regime in Atencingo—political successions continued to have a major impact on the politics of agrarian struggle. In particular, the combined gubernatorial and managerial successions during 1957–58 had two major consequences. First, the new governor, Fausto Ortega, and the new cooperative manager, Manuel Sánchez Espinosa, following a cooptive strategy of control, conceded to the popular neo-Jaramillistas broad and remunerative participation in the cooperative's patronage system. Second, the successions reintegrated the chain of command that extended upward from the manager to the president. Virtually all the state and federal authorities agreed that no structural reforms should be made. Thus the neo-Jaramillistas achieved gratifying tactical objectives within the local patronage system but lacked the essential government support for achieving their strategic power and reform objectives. As a result their open struggle subsided, and within the ejido stability prevailed to an uncommon degree. Sánchez's cooptive concessions had served to establish his rule.

Then, in 1959, the neo-Jaramillistas' political and strategic position changed as the presidential succession brought a new federal regime to power, one that was more committed both to enforcing the law and to bringing about reform than its predecessor. The neo-Jaramillista leaders soon located sympathetic allies in the DAAC, the CNC, and the SAG. Moreover, the new president himself, Adolfo López Mateos, began to pay attention to the ejido's problems. Thus the ejidatarios could be fairly certain that the 1952 decree would be revoked, and they even had hopes that the ejido might be divided.

Having won impressive government support to match their majority popular support, the neo-Jaramillistas had at last gained the strategic advantage. Seizing the opportunity, they mobilized their masses of followers and precipitated a crisis in order to force the government authorities to intervene in their favor. Whereas in the past the neo-Jaramillistas had relied on such tactics as legalistic appeals, bureaucratic lobbying, and local agitation and propaganda, now they turned to direct action. They seized control of the cooperative offices, forced Sánchez into retirement, and called for a work stoppage that threatened the cane harvest. Given the strategic advantage of support within the government, this tactical combination of bureaucratic lobbying and direct action, intensive but ultimately respectful toward the highest authorities, had worked in the past; now it would work again.

With the ejido's stability and productivity endangered, federal authorities moved to bring the situation under control. Taking advantage of the close ties between the ambitious neo-Jaramillista leader J. Guadalupe Ramírez Vargas and certain CNC and SAG officials, they managed to coopt and calm the neo-Jaramillista leaders. The declaration of a ninety-day grace period and the appointment of an interim cooperative manager gave the ejidatarios a sense of impending victory, persuaded them to return to the fields, and forestalled more damaging direct tactics. A personal interview between a commission of ejidatarios headed by Ramírez and the president undoubtedly secured the ejidatarios' respect for the federal government and prepared them to accept its final decision.

Although they were reconciled to revoking the 1952 decree, the various federal authorities were having considerable trouble reaching agreement on a final compromise solution to the ejido's problems. Indeed, there appeared to be a sharp power struggle among them for control over the valuable ejidal complex. On the one hand DAAC officials sought to wrest control of the cooperative away from the SIC by having local institutional power transferred upward into the DAAC's domain. On the other, SIC officials apparently wanted institutional power transferred back down to the local level, so that they could exercise control on the authority of the General Law of Cooperative Societies.

In the end the president and his fellow authorities decided, in the classic cooptive pattern, to grant the ejidatarios formal institutional power but to postpone agrarian reform. In so doing, they gave way to the ejidatarios enough to defuse the crisis but not enough to jeopardize official economic interests in the sugar industry. Moreover, the federal authorities informally secured control over the cooperative and bypassed the differences between the SIC and the DAAC by having CNC and SAG advisers accompany Ramírez into office. In effect Ramírez became dependent on their support in order to maintain his rule. The complex power that had been centered in the state government was thus transferred not only downward to the ejidatarios but also upward to the federal government.

CHAPTER SEVEN

Peasants Against Peasants, 1961-1969

The fourth phase in the political history of the ejido corresponds to the administration of J. Guadalupe Ramírez Vargas, who became the cooperative society manager in 1961 and was still in command when I left Atencingo in 1969. Its definitive characteristic has been renewed control by the ejidatarios over the cooperative and later the credit society. As a result of early conflicts and Ramírez's eventual failure to keep his campaign promises, the ejidatarios became divided between two leadership factions: a majority ruling faction led by Ramírez and a minority opposition faction led by a coalition of former collaborators with the Guerrero and Sánchez administrations and defectors from the Ramírez administration. Thus there arose a new struggle for power and reform, based on the long-standing reform issues. The struggle has been fierce—sometimes violent—and has routinely involved high-level authorities. During 1968–69 a serious crisis resulted in the administrative independence of two annexes and nearly toppled Ramírez from his powerful position.

The Establishment of the Ramírez Regime

As a result of their long struggle and the new presidential decree, the neo-Jaramillista leaders now controlled the critical top level of the cooperative management, as well as the cooperative administration council and the ejidal commissariat. Once again the Atencingo ejido was to be ruled by the leaders of an ejidatario movement in power.

As before, though, merely to occupy the top positions of authority was not enough for stable and effective rule. Like their predecessors, the neo-Jaramillista leaders accordingly moved swiftly to institutionalize their rule, in particular by consolidating their control over the cooperative's patronage system. Of course, this process was carried out principally according to the wishes of the new manager, Ramírez, who was the foremost leader in the ejidal complex.

Ramírez and his fellow leaders clearly enjoyed the strong government and popular support essential to the formation of a stable regime. At the federal level Francisco Hernández y Hernández, the CNC secretary-general, and J. Jesús Patiño Navarrete, the undersecretary of agriculture, were fully committed to the cooperative's new management. When Ramírez took office, they immediately dispatched representatives who became resident advisers and key spokesmen for the administration in dealings with the government. Furthermore, Ramírez and his fellow leaders had already joined the new CNC-affiliated National Cane Producers' Association. In succeeding years the association rendered valuable services as a lobbyist, thus helping to counterbalance lobbying by the opposition ejidatarios through the older (but now reformed) National Cane Producers' Union, also a CNC affiliate. Finally, Ramírez claimed to have the support of President López Mateos himself. At the state level Governor Ortega was apparently unhappy at having lost control over the ejidal complex, but he grudgingly submitted to federal intervention. Indeed, federal and local control rather than state control would predominate throughout the next nine years.

Aside from official support, Ramírez and his fellow leaders still recognized the independent National Zapatista Front as having been a helpful ally during their years of struggle. That old alliance had outlived its usefulness, however, and by 1962 it completely atrophied. Certainly the new alliance to the official CNC meant that Ramírez no longer needed the Zapatista Front. Moreover, government officials undoubtedly disapproved of any participation by the nongovernment organization in the new ejidatario regime.

At the local level the new manager could expect at least obedience from the ejidatarios, if only because he was now the chief dispenser of jobs and other amenities under the patronage system. But his position as leader of the neo-Jaramillistas and his personal qualities won him genuine allegiance as well. The majority of the ejidatarios prized their new administration as the outcome of their struggle. Moreover, Ramírez was clearly popular in his own right: he had long ago proven his ability as an officer of the cooperative; he had led the struggle against the 1952 decree; and he had promised parcellation and division of the ejido, not to mention higher wages and frequent loans to the ejidatarios. Like many of his fellow leaders, though, he was not one of the founding ejidatarios, or even a true peasant. Born in 1917 in the neighboring state of Oaxaca, he had worked for a while as a carpenter in the mill and then as a field hand, and had not joined the ejido until he was invited to do so by the Jaramillistas in the late 1940's or early 1950's.[1] Yet he certainly looked and acted like a peasant, and one of the poorest at that: many ejidatarios have reported that he wore weathered sandals and torn clothes, never seemed to have any money, and often relied on his friends for meals. Certainly he must have appeared to the ejidatarios as one of their own, not to mention his impressive, even intimidating status as a favorite of the federal government and the president himself.

But if support for the Ramírez regime was strong, it was not unanimous. As Ramírez entrenched himself in office, the other major leadership faction in the ejido, composed of former collaborationists from the Guerrero and Sánchez administrations, began to raise objections. Since the 1961 decree had introduced no major reform aside from delivering the cooperative over to the Ramírez faction, and since the history of antagonism between the two factions eliminated any prospect of cooperation, the former collaborationists were the main losers in the new system. Now they demanded that the federal government retire the interventionist CNC advisers, remove the "technically unprepared" Ramírez management, appoint a new manager, and divide the ejido.[2] Of course, they hoped such measures would help restore them to power.

But by now the former collaborationists had lost their political leverage. Though a capable group, they had never enjoyed significant popular support, relying instead on government support as their source of power. Currently, as we have seen, they controlled a variety of field staff positions and the vigilance councils for both the cooperative and the ejido. They also had majority support in the productive Raboso annex, to be sure; but they had so little support in other sections of the ejido that their total following apparently consisted of no more than some 200 to 250 ejidatarios, a small minority. The former collaborationists evidently had sympathizers within the DAAC and the SIC as well, but they had no aggressive allies, since the presidential decree had stabilized the political situation in favor of Ramírez and his CNC and SAG allies. Lacking effective support, then, the former collaborationists made no progress with their demands for federal intervention against the Ramírez administration. Not until 1962–63, when disillusioned defectors from his own fold formed a coalition with the former collaborationists, would Ramírez encounter serious opposition.

Facing no real challenge in 1961, Ramírez easily consolidated his regime. Most important, in accordance with an assembly mandate that no ejidatario should occupy an appointive post for more than two years, he removed all but a few former collaborationists from the field staff and salaried jobs—sometimes at gunpoint—and then appointed his own partisans in their place.[3] The former collaborationists remained securely at their posts only in the vigilance councils and in the annex of Raboso, where Ramírez lacked sufficient popular support to impose his will, even at gunpoint. To subdue the opposition further, armed Ramirecistas repossessed the cooperative's jeep—again at gunpoint—from the president of the cooperative's vigilance council, who along with his collaborationist friends had been using the vehicle for political activities.[4]

Thus by the end of 1961 the Ramírez regime was entrenched in office with widespread support and a virtual monopoly over the elective and appointive posts in both the ejido and the cooperative. In succeeding years, despite the assembly mandate against long terms in office, essentially the same group of Ramirecistas remained in control.

They simply rotated the posts among themselves, and Ramírez readily won reappointment as manager.

Ramírez's Development Policies

Once in office, dependent on the counsel and good will of the federal government, Ramírez promptly tempered his commitment to agrarian reform, subscribing instead to the official precepts of economic development. Rather than promote crop diversification, the manager performed his prescribed function of supplying the mill with cane. Rather than mobilize the ejidatarios for parcellation, he accepted the authorities' view that parcellation might ruin the ejido's cane agriculture and that in any case it could not be undertaken until the technical tasks were completed and the irrigation supplies improved. Thus Ramírez transformed parcellation—his much publicized ideal—into a long-range aspiration on which he was still resting his appeal in 1969. As for the division of the ejido, he soon repudiated that reform, even though the DAAC appeared ready to concede it. Reversing his earlier stand, Ramírez now charged that division would benefit only the former collaborationists and the mill administration, and that the whole idea was a plot to weaken the cooperative and destroy his regime. By the same token he rejected the proposal to disband the cooperative and found nine separate local ejidal credit societies. Like his government allies Ramírez now contended that the ejidatarios' future depended on maintaining the united ejido, and more important, on developing a powerful centralized administration that could cope with the mill, modernize the ejido's agriculture, and in general provide for the peasants' well-being.

To that end, Ramírez's development policies featured a more advantageous contract with the mill administration, heavy capital investments in mechanization and other improvements, community development projects, and the conversion of the cooperative society into a credit society. First, during 1961–62, Ramírez and his government allies negotiated with the mill administration for a new contract to replace the inoperative one dating from 1956. After a tough fight—involving threats of a strike—Ramírez finally gained his major objectives: a reduction of the exorbitant interest rate on the annual cane financing, and more important, a release from the cooperative's costly obligation to transport cane on the mill's private railroad system.[5]

Immediately after the contractual settlement Ramírez replaced the railroad system with 30 tractors and 160 hauling carts bought for five million pesos from International Harvester. Thus he began an intensive mechanization of the ejido's agriculture that would bring the cooperative a new independence; and thereafter his proudest achievements and chief hopes for autonomous development were embodied in dramatic capital investments. By 1969, according to Ramírez, the cooperative's holdings were worth 35 million pesos, all but a fraction of which had been accumulated by his administration.[6] By then at least 140 more cane carts, 26 trucks, and a dozen bulldozers had been bought. A plant for processing the rice crop for marketing had been constructed at a cost of 4.4 million pesos. A special plot of land for raising cattle on cane bagasse had been bought for 2.2 million pesos. And, to augment the inadequate supply of irrigation water, a number of new wells had been drilled. Such achievements were impressive indeed.[7] Ramírez apparently even aspired to buy the mill and make it an ejidal enterprise, whenever political and economic conditions would permit such a move. In collaboration with government agencies the Ramírez administration also promoted a variety of community development projects, such as introducing electrification, increasing the supply of drinking water, improving roads, building modern schools, and providing medical services in the various ejido villages. Indeed, Ramírez accomplished more in these areas than his predecessors, though in large part because the federal government provided more encouragement and funds than ever before.

Ramírez at first tried to administer his policies through the old cooperative society, subject to the mill-oriented SIC. But for complex financial and political reasons, during 1964–65 he supplanted the cooperative with a local ejidal credit society, organized under the National Ejidal Credit Bank. The financing of the cane harvest remained the prerogative of the mill administration, but the constrictive ties to the SIC were broken. As a result the Ramírez administration gained greater independence from the mill, improved the ejido's capacity for growing crops other than cane, and secured the necessary flexibility and credit standing for making heavy capital investments. Growing progressively as a business operation, during 1967–68 the credit society handled a record 34 million pesos, as compared to 23 million pesos for 1960–61.[8]

In sum, Ramírez sought to develop the Atencingo complex within its existing political context. Rather than strive for the land reforms he had once promised, he essentially continued the policies of staged development established under Guerrero, though instigated by Jaramillo. Unlike Jaramillo, however, Ramírez carefully attuned his policies to suit his political circumstances and maintain his essential government allies. And unlike Guerrero and Sánchez he gave higher priority over the long run to impressive capital investments than to the productivity of the cane fields. It must be said that such policies ultimately did not turn out as Ramírez fancied.

A Politicized Economy

Ramírez did not prove to be particularly adept at managing the ejido's economy. His administration's record on cane production, still its primary economic function, was erratic at best. After a troubled beginning, production and yields rose to record levels during 1963–65, as Table 7 shows. Afterward, though, production began to slip, and yields fell to embarrassingly low levels, particularly in 1965–66 and 1967–68. To make matters worse, costs rose from between 22 and 24 million pesos a year during 1961–66 to between 25 and 28 million pesos a year during 1967–69; though not out of line with general inflationary pressures, these costs were fairly high in view of the low cane yield and the low financial return for those years.[9]

Behind these figures is a complex tale about relationships among the ejidatarios, the Ramírez administration, the government, and the mill, for producing a good harvest is a very complex agricultural-industrial activity. It requires careful planning and organization by the cooperative (or credit) society's staff, and diligent cooperation from the ejidatarios, government officials, the mill administration, and even the mill workers. The whole system of operations is highly vulnerable to disruption by technical, economic, or political problems, and

TABLE 7

Sugar Cane Produced and Processed by the Atencingo Cooperative or Credit Society and Mill, 1960–1968

	Cooperative or credit society			Mill	
Harvest	Total harvested (tons)	Total delivered to mill (tons)	Average yield (tons/ha.)	Total milled from all sources (tons)	Average yield of all sources (tons/ha.)
1960–61	427,414	427,414	ca. 148	572,118	153.7
1961–62	378,359	378,359	ca. 144	481,702	141.6
1962–63	282,819	282,819	—[a]	476,265	163.1
1963–64	431,452	431,452	177.4	623,822	179.2
1964–65	492,957	377,908	138.2	570,522	144.5
1965–66	409,432	348,947	117.8	609,128	131.2
1966–67	473,559	473,559	130.3	—	—
1967–68	427,614	427,614	111.3	—	—

SOURCES: For the cooperative or credit society, local ejidal credit society memorandum, July 12, 1967, MAEM, and Ramírez, annual reports for 1960–68, MACNCI and FNGA; for the mill, Unión Nacional de Productores de Azúcar, *Estadísticas azucareras* (Mexico City, 1967), p. 35.

[a] Dashes signify that information is not available.

disputes between any two parties systematically involve the others. The Ramírez regime suffered considerably from such problems, in a more complicated fashion than its predecessors. The Pérez, Guerrero, and Sánchez regimes had the support of the mill administration and were opposed by most of the ejidatarios. The Jaramillo regime had the support of the ejidatarios and was opposed by the mill administration. The Ramírez regime, however, was sometimes opposed by both the mill administration and a sizable proportion of the ejidatarios. The effects of this combination of internal and external opposition were apparent in poor harvests, rising costs, and later in administrative failings.

From 1961 through 1963 the relationship between the mill and the cooperative was strained considerably, as Ramírez struggled to reduce the mill's contractual supremacy and mechanize the cooperative. Within the government SAG officials were firmly on his side, whereas SIC officials leaned toward protecting the mill's interests. Since the mill administration at first refused to agree to the new contract provisions, Ramírez tried a temporary work stoppage during the 1961–62 harvest. Next the mill administration claimed a temporary breakdown in its machinery. As a result, of course, the harvest was poor, with the cooperative bearing the loss of 60,000 tons of cane left standing in the fields. Both sides agreed that such disturbances were counterproductive. Ramírez then turned to intensive lobbying through his key ally, Undersecretary Patiño of the SAG.[10] By the start of the 1962–63 harvest, the two sides had reached virtual agreement on the new contract provisions, and Ramírez was moving rapidly to mechanize the cooperative's operations.

But the 1962–63 harvest was a disaster. First, the cooperative's new transportation equipment arrived late. Second, the mill workers went on strike for a new contract and for the indemnification of any workers laid off owing to the replacement of the railroad transportation system; of course, the loss of milling time hurt the cooperative as much as it hurt the mill. Third, angry at having lost business for its railroad, the mill administration maneuvered to undermine and even destroy the Ramírez regime. The mill still enjoyed a contractual advantage over the cooperative, which depended on it completely to finance the harvest and buy the harvested cane. For two months the mill administration withheld a credit Ramírez desperately needed to pay the ejidatarios' wages, until Undersecretary Patiño rescued him by countersigning for the loan.[11] Then the mill underwent assorted mechanical breakdowns. Yet, despite the delays, the mill administration would not permit the cooperative to deliver its ripe cane to other mills.[12] Throughout all these difficulties with the harvest, the Ramírez regime was harassed by a renascent opposition struggle, which according to Ramírez had been instigated by the mill's former railroad workers and the mill administration. As a result of these interrelated technical and political disturbances, the cooperative had its worst harvest since 1954, with 160,000 tons of cane left unharvested and a debilitating debt of 2.5 million pesos. The mill escaped production losses, though, by drawing on outside sources that had increased their cane production to take advantage of the Cuban Revolution's impact on the sugar market.[13]

Despite the serious setbacks of 1962–63, the Ramírez regime managed to recover its strength during the next few years. The new contract took effect, and SAG officials obliged the mill administration to adjust to the new production relationship.[14] In 1963, moreover, Jenkins died, an event that may have weakened the mill administration's will and ability to continue battling Ramírez. In 1965 Ramírez improved his political position by having the ejido's affairs moved from the jurisdiction of SIC officials to that of the National Ejidal Credit Bank, then opportunely headed by his former CNC ally, Francisco Hernández y Hernández. Finally, Ramírez ultimately outmaneuvered and demoralized the opposition faction, which became less active after 1965, at least for a time. As a result the cooperative's production relationship with the mill administration stabilized from 1963 until 1967. Thanks in part to good technical advice from SAG advisers, three of the next four harvests were excellent, producing record yields. Moreover, the cooperative's debt to the mill was immediately liquidated, good credit relations were revived, and the new transportation system functioned quite well.

Even so, as a result of further mechanical breakdowns—or what Ramírez called the mill's "inefficiency" and "lack of industrial maturity"—considerable cane was still left unharvested during these otherwise successful seasons.[15] When the problem was foreseen during 1963–64, and compounded by another workers' strike, the mill administration again refused to let the cooperative sell its cane elsewhere. An astonishing figure of 180,000 tons remained unharvested. Ramírez threatened to restrict the ejido's cane agriculture if the mill's service did not improve, and Undersecretary Patiño intervened on his behalf. Accordingly the mill administration let Ramírez sell portions of the two subsequent harvests elsewhere, while the mill's machinery was being repaired.[16]

After 1967 came new agricultural disasters, however. Whereas costs rose, total cane production fell; worse yet, the average yield and the sugar content fell to discreditable levels. Ramírez blamed these failures on dry weather and minor political sabotage in the fields by partisans of the opposition, which was renewing its struggle.[17] Yet the poor harvests were due in large measure to technical deficiencies in the cultivation of new cane stands—deficiencies for which the Ramírez administration was partly responsible. After the 1964 presidential succession Undersecretary Patiño had been succeeded in office, and the dependent Ramírez administration had received less helpful technical advice ever since. Now the results were showing. During 1968–69, moreover, the Ramírez administration would enter a new period of crisis with the mill, as we shall see later.

Left to its own devices, over the years the Ramírez regime demonstrated an erratic ability to perform its primary economic function, cane production. Ramírez's development policies were not paying off, either in greater production or in greater profits. Indeed, the decision to emphasize costly capital investments had contributed little to productivity. Maintaining and operating the agricultural machinery had cost far more than anticipated, with an adverse effect on profit dividends. The other major improvements had not yet begun full operation; any real payoffs from them were still years distant, though their cost was very high in the present. As a result, during 1967–69 the Ramírez administration found itself in a precarious economic situation, deeply in debt and with little prospect of good harvests through 1970. It was these economic difficulties that set the stage for the political crisis of 1968–69.

From this vantage point it becomes clear how deeply politicized the Atencingo ejido's economy had become under Ramírez. At every step economic success or failure virtually depended on government and popular support. Government officials tutored Ramírez in setting development policies. Then his administration won its struggle with the mill administration because it enjoyed majority support among the ejidatarios and firm political support from SAG officials. Without that government support Ramírez might have been defeated, just as Jaramillo was, by rising debts inflicted by the mill administration when its machinery broke down and cane was left unharvested. Instead, with the continued political support of SAG officials, the Ramírez administration even gained permission to sell extra cane to other mills; and with the SAG's excellent technical advice, it managed to produce excellent harvests. Conversely, when SAG support and popular support weakened, the technical and economic performance of the Ramírez administration quickly deteriorated.

It is clear, too, that the Ramírez administration's agricultural failures derived not only from its lack of technical ability but also from the original development decisions, which put insufficient emphasis on directly increasing agricultural productivity. Early investments in new wells for irrigation might have increased productivity dramatically. Some attention could also have been paid to developing the ejido's soil. Yet Ramírez was attracted to impressive capital investments of other kinds, once again as much for political as for economic reasons.

Of course, it was the ejidatarios who paid for Ramírez's costly development policies. Under the Ramírez administration their dividends from cane production fluctuated wildly,[18] rising to record levels after the 1963–64 and 1964–65 harvests, but falling to zero before and afterward:

Harvest	Total dividends	Harvest	Total dividends
1960–61	1.6 million pesos	1964–65	6.2 million pesos
1961–62	2.5	1965–66	2.6
1962–63	0.0	1966–67	2.8
1963–64	4.5	1967–68	0.0

On the average there was little improvement over the record of the Sánchez administration. By popular agreement the dividends were distributed in equal shares, though a regulation was passed, justifiably enough, requiring an ejidatario to work at least 180 days during the harvest cycle in order to qualify for his share.

Mechanization did create some proud new jobs with high salaries. Yet few existing salaries rose, and the basic daily wage for piecework remained at nine pesos, unchanged since 1959. Ramírez had promised to pay fifteen pesos a day, but failed to keep his promise because of costly investments, deficit financing, and unimproved profits. Never before had the common ejidatario gone so many years without a wage increase. Moreover, according to Ramírez's opponents, in the late 1960's Ramírez actually cut back the fieldwork to make money available for other purposes.

For extra income and subsistence purposes, most ejidatarios relied on crops other than cane. They continued to grow corn and beans on their own seasonal plots; and under the Ramírez administration's auspices they grew commercial crops, especially rice and tomatoes, on irrigated plots farmed either collectively or individually. Yet, because Ramírez's policies did not effectively increase diversification, the ejidatarios' incomes from crops other than cane rose little, if at all. As in the past each ejidatario was supposed to be allotted one-half hectare or more of seasonal land plus one-half hectare of irrigated land for individual farming. Under the Sánchez regime Ramírez and his fellow leaders in the opposition had staunchly defended that rule. In 1967, however, over the protests of its own opposition, the Ramírez administration changed the rule so that ejidatarios had a right to only one-half hectare of seasonal land, with additional plots to be made available on an irregular basis at the administration's discretion.[19] This reduction in the amount of land available for crops other than cane enabled Ramírez to extend the precarious cane agriculture and increase production, but it also meant that the ejidatarios' extra incomes from crops other than cane took a sharp plunge.[20]

Overall, then, the average ejidatario's income virtually remained at the same level under Ramírez as under Sánchez, apparently increasing less during 1961–69 than during any comparable period since 1946. The years 1964 and 1965 were relatively profitable, but afterward incomes declined sharply. Within this framework, however, Ramirecistas fared much better economically speaking than the average ejidatario, and members of the opposition fared much worse. As widely reported by his critics, at least, Ramírez relied on a discriminatory patronage system to secure economic and political control, just as Guerrero and Sánchez had done before him. His loyal supporters monopolized the better-paying jobs, collected regular dividends, controlled the better plots for individual farming, and enjoyed ready access to credit and loans. As for his opponents, at best they were from time to time offered the lowest-paying jobs, which they were often too proud to accept; at worst they were offered no work at all, while poor day laborers from Oaxaca and Guerrero were hired in their stead. Then, on the ground that dozens from the opposition faction had not worked the minimum 180 days, Ramírez usually withheld their annual dividends, unless he was forced by agitation to surrender them. Yet he did not see fit to withhold dividends from supporters who had not worked the minimum number of days. Members of the opposition faction were likewise allocated worse plots and less credit than the average ejidatario for individual farming. Clearly they gained nothing from Ramírez's development policies, except for some of the community development projects; indeed, many in the opposition faction claimed they were worse off than ever before, especially those who had held high-paying leadership posts in the past. In essence, the Ramírez regime now treated its political opposition much as the Guerrero regime had treated its opposition, namely Ramírez and his fellow Jaramillistas.

The Emergence of the Opposition

In reaction to Ramírez's policies, it did not take long for the former collaborationists from previous regimes and the disillusioned defectors from the Ramírez regime to form a coalition and mount a new opposition struggle for institutional power and agrarian reform. As their strategic objectives the leaders of the opposition faction campaigned preeminently for the division of the ejido into nine ejidos and the replacement of the central cooperative society with nine local ejidal credit societies, so that each section of the ejido would function independently, according to its own leadership and agricultural capabilities. They customarily demanded parcellation too, but with the understanding that the division of the ejido was to come first. Of course, if these long-standing objectives were reached, the opposition leaders stood to gain institutional power in at least some of the annexes. Crop diversification was still an issue as well. Thanks to the effectiveness of government policies, however, the opposition leaders had adjusted to official economic interests just as Ramírez had, and rarely spoke of diversification measures that might destroy the ejido's cane agriculture. Instead they urged a technical intensification to increase average yield, thereby freeing land for lucrative non-cane crops. Ramírez was taking the same approach, of course, but he was not having success with it.

As their tactical objectives the opposition leaders demanded the completion of the technical tasks as well as an end to the economic discrimination and political repression they suffered. Moreover, they agitated against the alleged financial corruption and agricultural mismanagement within the Ramírez administration. Ultimately they hoped to oust Ramírez, whether by persuading the federal government to intervene or by starting a popular uprising, electoral or otherwise.

In response Ramírez and his fellow leaders made some strong accusations against the leaders of the opposition faction to discredit them in the eyes of the ejidatarios. The opposition leaders were painted as a bunch of collaborationist demagogues whose sole concern was power, not reform. Their charges against the Ramírez administration and their exhortations for structural reform were dismissed as attempts to weaken the popular regime for their own political advantage, so that they might regain their former posts and privileges at the expense of the ejidatarios. If they were truly interested in structural reform and popular welfare, it was argued, then they would have promoted the division and parcellation of the ejido while they were in office, under Guerrero in particular. Instead they had actively opposed the popular Jaramillista demands and collaborated with the state-controlled regime and the mill administration. Even now, according to Ramírez, the opposition struggle was supported and financed by the mill administration and by Sánchez, the mill administration hoping to weaken Ramírez enough to defeat him in the battle over the contract, and Sánchez hoping to prevent Ramírez from pressing fraud charges against his administration. True or not, such accusations were plausible enough for many ejidatarios to believe. Thus Ramírez and his fellow leaders reduced the opposition struggle to the simple terms of power and demagoguery—the same terms in which, ironically enough, their own struggle had formerly been viewed by Guerrero.

If some opposition leaders were immune from such accusations, they still had strikes against them. Most important, the opposition advocated the division of the ejido above all else, favoring parcellation only as a subsequent measure. Yet many ejidatarios did not believe that the opposition leaders would in fact proceed to parcellation once division was achieved. Since parcellation and not division was the prime popular goal, most ejidatarios hesitated to offer the opposition their support. They preferred to take their chances with Ramírez, who was identified as the foremost proponent of parcellation, in the Jaramillista tradition.

Until the middle of 1962 Ramírez encountered opposition only from the small minority of former collaborationists. Too few and too weak to mount an effective struggle, they settled for intensive lobbying in the DAAC and the SIC.[21] Then, during 1962, just as Ramírez was in the thick of his battle with the mill administration over the contract, new challenges to his regime appeared from above, within, and below. Above, government officials who had never warmed to the regime now openly considered opposing it. In particular, DAAC officials acknowledged their willingness to divide the ejido as the former collaborationists demanded, just as soon as the technical tasks were completed.[22] Moreover, both DAAC and SIC officials deplored the financial and technical practices of the Ramírez administration and recommended that its accounts be audited.[23] Apparently the mill-oriented SIC officials also did not want Ramírez to win his battle over the contract.[24] Finally, Francisco Hernández y Hernández, a bulwark of the Ramírez regime, was succeeded as CNC secretary-general by Javier Rojo Gómez, a leading agrarian reformist who would sympathize with the complaints against Ramírez. Thus the official environment became less supportive of Ramírez and more receptive to his opponents.

Within and below, the regime was threatened by a major breach among its supporters. The president of the ejidal commissariat, the veteran neo-Jaramillista Cirilo Gutiérrez, had long advocated the division of the ejido. Now he discovered that in fact Ramírez had forsaken this prime goal. Moreover, Gutiérrez strongly objected to the administration's costly financial policies, and especially to its plan for mechanization. "We know from experience," he wrote, "that the only ones who benefit from multimillion-peso deals are the leaders of the cooperative, while the peasants derive no benefit at all."[25] As a result he turned against Ramírez.

Gutiérrez was not followed by any other top officers of the Ramírez regime. Yet, among the lesser leaders and the mass of ejidatarios who had once followed Ramírez, he was not alone in his opinions. A moderate number, perhaps 150 to 200, joined him. Moreover, the former collaborationists, who numbered perhaps 200 to 250, had been voicing similar doubts for more than a year.[26] No wonder the two groups were in agreement: Gutiérrez lived in Raboso, the one annex the former collaborationists controlled. Now mutual sympathy became alliance. The former collaborationists and the defectors from Ramírez's fold began to band together in a coalition opposition faction with Gutiérrez as their leader. The new faction was numerically quite weak, nevertheless, and many of its members were only halfhearted in their commitment against Ramírez. Moreover, the opposition faction had no resolute government allies, whereas Ramírez was firmly backed by the SAG. Clearly incapable of mounting a decisive struggle for the time being, the opposition leaders simply campaigned for additional popular and government support against Ramírez.

During September the opposition leaders attempted to attract ejidatarios to an informal assembly in Colonia Independencia, now the residential zone of the annex of Teruel, far from Atencingo. As interested ejidatarios arrived, however, Ramírez's field officers for that annex appeared, harassed Gutiérrez with "offensive words," and charged that he had been "sold for the sum of 30,000 pesos" to former manager Manuel Sánchez and his brother, who were still very powerful local businessmen.[27] Finally, the Ramirecista ruffians drew their pistols; thus "Cirilo had to suspend the assembly because these individuals said that it would end in shooting if it was carried on."[28] Afterward the other members of the ejidal commissariat tried to disavow Gutiérrez's presidency and forcibly closed his office in Atencingo.[29]

Undaunted, Gutiérrez rescheduled the assembly for October in the annex of Raboso, the stronghold of the opposition forces. This time he secured formal authorization from the DAAC, and both the DAAC chief and the secretary of industry and commerce commissioned special representatives to attend.[30] With such officials present the anti-Ramírez assembly proceeded unmolested, attended by about five hundred ejidatarios.[31] Thus the opposition leaders concluded their first major attempt at mobilizing for a struggle. Yet widespread support was clearly not materializing. Indeed, during a general assembly for the cooperative society in November, Ramírez tendered his resignation, only to have it rejected by the majority of the ejidatarios present. After all, he was winning his battle with the mill over the contract and was bringing a great deal of impressive machinery to Atencingo.[32]

As evidence of his integrity Ramírez offered to submit his administration's records to an audit.[33] When none was actually undertaken by early 1963, however, Gutiérrez pressed his charges of fraud and financial mismanagement, and convinced SIC officials to commission two inspectors to make preliminary inquiries. On January 23, 1963, the inspectors journeyed from annex to annex with Gutiérrez collecting data, until they arrived at last in Colonia Independencia. Only a few months earlier pistol-waving staff officers there had compelled Gutiérrez to cancel the opposition assembly. Now the armed staff officers and a couple of other pistolero types appeared again, evidently drunk. After an inflammatory exchange, they drew their guns, shot and killed Gutiérrez, stole his portfolio of documents, chased his companions away, and possibly tried to kill them, too.[34] The incident eliminated the major opposition leader, of course, and without him there were no further pretensions about auditing the accounts of the cooperative. As for the two major assassins, the Ramírez administration's lawyer quickly got them out of jail, and apparently they continued serving Ramírez as special pistoleros.[35]

A few months later the terms of the ejidal officers expired, and elections were held. Somehow, apparently by splitting votes and controlling admittance to the assembly auditorium, Ramírez contrived to have his candidates win control of not only the ejidal commissariat but also the vigilance council. Apparently two assemblies were held to secure this result, while hundreds of opposition sympathizers were excluded from the voting.[36] Thus Ramírez survived the months of crisis and emerged with a broader and more integrated regime than before, despite the increase in popular opposition.

The assassination of Cirilo Gutiérrez, damaging as it was to the opposition in the short run, became a seminal event in the development of the opposition struggle. Before the assassination the opposition faction had numbered only some four to five hundred, many of whom were halfhearted at best in their commitment. Lacking the following for a major offensive, the opposition leaders had limited their tactics to bureaucratic lobbying and inflammatory propaganda. In the months after the assassination, though, the faction expanded as perhaps one or two hundred more ejidatarios joined from ejido villages that had yielded few supporters in the past.[37] Moreover, the leadership changed, becoming more collective as old leaders from Raboso were joined by new leaders from other villages. Finally, as local sources generally agree, the assassination awakened a new sense of outrage that invigorated the opposition, enabling its leaders to mobilize for an open struggle.

The Opposition on the March

If the minority opposition faction could not vote Ramírez out of office, how could its leaders win their struggle? Simple bureaucratic lobbying for the piecemeal redress of grievances would do them little good, though they had tried this tactic. For example, with respect to their complaints about job discrimination, in early 1964 Undersecretary Patiño of the SAG did order a thorough investigation. Afterward a few ejidatarios from the opposition faction apparently got their jobs back, at least temporarily. Nevertheless, the affair had little impact: Ramírez was too strong, and job discrimination certainly did not end.[38]

Nor could the opposition leaders rely on using legal proceedings to oust Ramírez. On the major issue of financial mismanagement, they kept demanding a government audit of the Ramírez administration's records, but the SIC officials always managed to postpone action. Furthermore, the opposition could not persuade the authorities to prosecute Ramírez when the SIC audit of the Sánchez administration's records uncovered clear evidence of fraud. That audit was undertaken in 1961, completed in early 1962, and withheld from the public until 1963 or 1964. Then the ejidatarios learned that the fraud involved over two million pesos, and that Ramírez, as former president of the administration council, was directly accountable for some 43,000 pesos out of the total. Undoubtedly Sánchez, Ramírez, and other officers had not kept all the money they had taken. Sánchez had more than likely channeled some money upward to protective government officials; Ramírez had apparently used some to finance his struggle against Sánchez. Now, however, as the current manager, Ramírez was responsible for initiating legal proceedings against Sánchez. Not surprisingly, he neglected to do so. In 1965 the opposition leaders finally filed their own charges, but government officials never made any progress on the case. In fact, they had never favored pressing charges, for reasons one can only guess at.

Ultimately the opposition leaders could hope to win their struggle only by a broad-based offensive that combined agitation and direct action with bureaucratic lobbying and legalistic appeals, and that aimed at major structural reforms as well as short-term objectives such as ousting Ramírez and obtaining the redress of personal grievances. Accordingly, after the assassination of Gutiérrez the opposition leaders began to agitate and lobby heavily for the division of the ejido and the replacement of the cooperative society with independent local ejidal credit societies, while they awaited an opportunity to use more forceful tactics. There was some cause for hope: certain DAAC officials were still prepared to divide the ejido once the technical tasks were completed, and SIC officials were displeased with Ramírez's handling of the cooperative's affairs.

For his part, Ramírez had decided by the middle of 1963 that continued subordination to the SIC, which he now regarded as unsupportive, had become politically and financially undesirable. Not only had SIC officials threatened to audit his accounts, but they had hesitated to provide further credits for his mechanization program unless they, and not Ramírez, were to handle the accounting. Ramírez would not tolerate any such arrangement.[39] Moreover, the cooperative society was not the suitable agency for financing crops other than cane. To surmount these problems Ramírez cleverly proposed to convert the old cooperative society into a single local ejidal credit society, with all the former cooperative's officers and assets intact. If successful, this measure would move his administration from the jurisdiction of the SIC to that of the National Ejidal Credit Bank.

Thus, as a step toward widely different goals, both Ramírez and the opposition leaders demanded that SIC officials dissolve the cooperative society. Unable to take control of the cooperative themselves, the officials agreed, for as one wrote the cooperative had been "functioning with serious problems and irregularities that have impeded its normal performance" over the previous two years.[40] In October SIC officials accordingly held an extraordinary general assembly at which the ejidatarios voted unanimously to liquidate the cooperative society after the forthcoming harvest. With that much settled, the remaining issue was whether to divide the ejido or keep it unified in the future administrative structure to be organized under the National Ejidal Credit Bank.

To force the issue, the eager partisans of the opposition faction dramatically assumed the offensive immediately after the assembly. Between five and six hundred departed to lay their case before the new state governor, Gen. Antonio Nava Castillo, marching ostentatiously along the Pan-American highway toward Puebla, the state capital. The governor disapproved, since the march created embarrassingly bad publicity for him. At dawn the next day, when the banner-waving protestors had traveled about a third of the distance, they were halted and detained by state police. Six top peasant leaders were arrested and taken to Puebla, where they immediately had their interview with the angry governor. After a bitter exchange he promised to attend to their problems, as long as they disbanded the march and returned home. An opportunistic man, he was primarily interested in sparing himself the difficulties caused by the marchers' presence. The leaders were freed, and a few state politicians traveled to the detention scene to offer reassurances. The marchers accepted the turn of events and returned home. In succeeding months, however, the governor broke his promise, evidently choosing to pursue a hands-off policy toward the federally controlled ejido. Thus the march failed to achieve its purpose. Nevertheless, it had demonstrated that the opposition could be mobilized and that the government feared massed public protest.[41]

The opposition leaders almost saw some of their wishes come true at the beginning of 1964. An attempt was made to machine-gun Ramírez to death as he was on the way to his offices one morning in

January. Wounded but still alive, he escaped with his companions in their car, while his assailants fled elsewhere in another car, never to be apprehended. Several top opposition leaders were quickly jailed, but then freed. In fact, the prime suspects were not they but former manager Sánchez, who still feared that Ramírez might press charges against him for fraud, and certain figures in the mill and the state government.[42] Evidence was lacking, however, and Sánchez and the other suspects were powerful people. Typically enough, none of them were formally charged, and the case was never solved.

No further attempts were made on Ramírez's life for the time being, but the shooting did not end. In the succeeding months Ramírez kept more bodyguards at his side, and the opposition leaders complained of a resurgence of pistolerismo in the complex. A few ejidatarios died on both sides. In the most notable case a top opposition leader was arrested after a lesser member of Ramírez's administration council was murdered and one of the pistoleros who had attacked Gutiérrez was wounded.[43] The case has never come to trial, and in 1969 the arrested leader was still languishing in jail, protesting his innocence.

Since Ramírez and most of the opposition leaders remained alive and active, the resort to guns had little effect on the overall struggle. Pistolerismo was only one aspect of the opposition's overriding problems of political repression and economic discrimination, neither of which had been resolved by the end of the 1963–64 harvest. In August 1964 the opposition, now a little larger, took the offensive again. Although the opposition leaders had been rebuffed the previous year by the state governor, they took heart from the sympathetic attitude of CNC, DAAC, and SIC officials, and mobilized another march—this time against the federal regime of President López Mateos, now in his final months of office. About seven hundred strong, the marchers took the road west toward Mexico City. At night, near the Morelos state boundary, state police armed with machine guns tried unsuccessfully to turn them back, but then relented when the morning light revealed the detention scene to public view.[44] In Cuautla the tired marchers boarded buses for the chilly journey across the mountains. Once in Mexico City they were promptly and sympathetically received by Secretary-General Rojo Gómez of the CNC and Chief

Barrios of the DAAC. Notwithstanding the technical tasks, which had never been completed, Barrios vowed that he would order the division of the ejido if the ejidatarios would first secure the final dissolution of the ejidal cooperative society, as a procedural prerequisite. The opposition leaders accordingly went to see Secretary Raúl Salinas Lozano of the SIC. He agreed to the proposal, secured the concurrence of Secretary Julián Rodríguez Adame of the SAG, and ordered that the cooperative society be dissolved. Back at the DAAC offices Chief Barrios in turn signed orders for his subordinates to hold assemblies in Atencingo and the annexes pursuant to the division of the ejido.[45] Though the evidence is not clear, apparently the president himself concurred in this intersecretarial decision.

Jubilant, the marchers returned home, confident that they had won their struggle at last. In the next few months they expectantly campaigned for popular support as the technical work proceeded. Even if ejidatarios in some sections of the ejido would not vote for independence, the opposition partisans were confident that at least Raboso would become independent and then secure its own local ejidal credit society under the National Ejidal Credit Bank.[46]

They were wrong. In the first place, soon after the August march the opposition leaders began to lose what government support they had mustered against Ramírez. Thanks to the presidential succession of 1964, by early 1965 a new federal regime had taken command under Gustavo Díaz Ordaz, a president more interested in order than in reform. Chief Barrios of the DAAC was succeeded by Norberto Aguirre Palancares, who had no personal commitment to the division of the Atencingo ejido. Most important, Ramírez's old CNC benefactor, Francisco Hernández y Hernández, was appointed general manager of the National Ejidal Credit Bank. Thus the official environment no longer favored the opposition leaders. Their only remaining high-level ally was Secretary-General Rojo Gómez of the CNC, and his term was due to expire in the middle of 1965. In the second place, the opposition leaders still commanded only minority support within the ejidal complex as a whole. Apparently they could muster a majority vote only in the annex of Raboso.

In the third place, Ramírez had shored up his defenses. Ever since

1963 he had been quietly proceeding with his own plan to install a single local ejidal credit society in place of the cooperative society. During 1964 he maneuvered to get a credit society registered and put into limited operation for crops other than cane; the credit society functioned alongside the cooperative and under the same administrative officers.[47] At Ramírez's behest officials from the National Ejidal Credit Bank came to Atencingo to sign up ejidatarios for the census required for the formation of the credit society. To secure popular support Ramírez claimed that the establishment of the credit society was a vital step toward parcellation. Indeed, each ejidatario who signed received a number that many believed would entitle them to individual credit directly from the national bank. Such hopes were false, of course, for Ramírez retained full control of the extension of credit to ejidatarios. Yet these false hopes and promises even convinced dozens from the opposition faction to sign, though a hard core of about four hundred refused.[48] Altogether the bank officials gathered 1,528 signatures, representing a clear majority of the authorized ejidatarios, especially since several hundred of them were either dead or living elsewhere. Ramírez and his fellow leaders easily won the election to head the credit society's administration, and bank officials registered the new society during July 1964. Then, for the time being, Ramírez restricted the credit society's activities to rice agriculture, while he quietly waited for the dissolution of the cooperative society.

As a result of these circumstances, the opposition leaders gained nothing from the order Barrios had given authorizing the division of the ejido. Ramírez obtained an amparo, claiming the 1,528 signatures for the local ejidal credit society and an assembly vote as mandates for keeping the ejido intact. Moreover, the DAAC officials refused to allow Raboso alone to detach itself from the ejidal complex; and the uncompleted maps presented another technical obstacle that allowed DAAC officials to temporize. Similarly, the opposition leaders gained nothing from the federal order to dissolve the cooperative society. Of course, they had hoped to replace the cooperative society with several local ejidal credit societies—or at least to gain the independence of Raboso. Instead, much to their surprise, the dissolution order played directly into Ramírez's hands. Now, with the mandate of the 1,528 signatures and the help of Hernández y Hernández in his capacity as general manager of the National Ejidal Credit Bank, Ramírez was permitted by bank officials simply to absorb into the existing credit society all the debits and credits of the old cooperative society. Indeed, the cooperative society's accounts were never liquidated according to official procedure, a departure that spared the Ramírez administration from having its accounts audited by SIC officials. Thus Ramírez emerged entirely unscathed, having navigated what can only be considered an extremely treacherous course. The opposition commonly attributed his success to bribery, a charge that seems plausible enough in the circumstances. In any case, they had lost another battle.

The opposition leaders could not even discredit Ramírez enough to persuade the government to remove him from office, much less charge him with fraud. In April 1965 they sent a major petition to the new president with point-for-point charges against Ramírez. The president accordingly ordered SAG officials to investigate Ramírez's conduct in office. The investigation consisted only of a simple interview, however, and the commissioned investigator declared himself satisfied with Ramírez's verbal refutations and defense.[49] Ramírez was therefore free to stay in command as the manager—or chief delegate, as he was now called—of the expanded credit society.

As of July 1965, then, the cooperative society no longer existed. In its place reigned the Local Ejidal Credit Society of Atencingo and Annexes, with credit from the national bank for crops other than cane, and by special arrangement, credit from the mill for cane. The official leaders and leadership structure remained virtually the same. The major difference was that whereas in the past the popularly elected administration council had named the manager of the cooperative society, now the council's president automatically became the chief delegate of the credit society. In addition the time between general elections was now three rather than two years. Otherwise almost nothing had changed in the administration of the ejidal complex. If anything, the status quo was strengthened, for the bank provided sure support to Ramírez, whereas the SIC had not. Moreover, some four hundred opposition ejidatarios, including most of the opposition leaders, were now legally ineligible to vote or run for office in the new credit society, since they had refused to sign the credit society census. Ramírez had survived the crisis triumphantly, and the opposition had made no economic or political gains at all.

Chagrined at this outcome, some seven hundred opposition partisans mobilized for a third march, this time to confront the new federal regime of President Díaz Ordaz.[50] As usual, the marchers were temporarily obstructed by state police,[51] but they eventually arrived in Mexico City. There things went badly for them. On disembarking from their buses, they went to the DAAC building and started a public demonstration to protest conditions in Atencingo. Soon riot police appeared and dispersed the gathering, which was considered embarrassing to the government. Moreover, the new DAAC chief refused to grant the marchers a special interview. They therefore turned to the CNC, where by now Rojo Gómez had been succeeded as secretary-general by Amador Hernández. Born in Puebla, Hernández had been the state-level CNC leader under Secretary-General Hernández y Hernández, and had actively aided the Ramírez faction during the 1960–61 struggle. His sentiments were still decidedly in favor of Ramírez, if only because Ramírez could allegedly offer far higher bribes than his poor detractors. Refusing to turn against his friend, Hernández accused the opposition leaders of slandering the government.[52] The opposition leaders held their ground, however, threatening to remain in the city until proceedings were initiated to oust Ramírez.[53] Finally, after hours of discussions punctuated with "loud shouting" and "hot-headed phrases,"[54] Hernández relented to the point of proposing that a special commission of CNC and DAAC representatives accompany the marchers back to Atencingo and make an investigation there. The marchers agreed.

A few days later the federal representative, additional state-level officials, and the leaders of the two factions within the ejido met in the Atencingo offices. After arguing for seventeen hours one day and fourteen hours another, the factions reached a nebulous agreement. Ramírez consented to dispense the 1963–64 dividends withheld from dozens of ejidatarios, and the factions agreed to continue their discussions on the questions of job discrimination and of dividing the ejido.[55] In effect, of course, to continue these discussions virtually meant to maintain the status quo. Moreover, on various legal grounds Ramírez managed to continue withholding the ejidatarios' dividends, thereby canceling out his one real concession.

The members of the opposition faction had lost, and they knew it. Ramírez had outmaneuvered and outwitted them at every turn. Their major tactical ventures, the tiring and expensive marches, had failed. During 1963 and 1964, when sympathetic leaders of the CNC, DAAC, and SIC had made some efforts to aid the opposition, there had been hope of ousting Ramírez. During 1965, however, following the presidential succession, Ramírez regained the political advantage of support in government circles. He secured new support from the CNC and the National Ejidal Credit Bank to augment his continuing support from SAG officials. SIC officials had disengaged themselves from involvement in Atencingo. DAAC officials still vowed to divide the ejido as the opposition faction demanded, but only after the survey and maps of the ejido were completed.[56] At the state level a major scandal had caused the president to remove Governor Nava Castillo and name Aarón Merino Fernández interim governor. Merino Fernández and the state's Agrarian Delegation continued to protect the Ramírez regime from the opposition. Ramírez's relations with the mill administration were quite good, and he could still muster or fabricate a majority vote, if only by using his patronage powers or by barring several hundred ejidatarios from the election assembly. Thus the strategic advantage had shifted to Ramírez once again.

Lacking both government and popular support, the demoralized opposition lay low during 1966 and 1967. Aside from some insistent petitions and occasional commissions to government authorities, their campaign languished. As a result these two years were the most secure ones for the Ramírez regime since 1961. The opposition leaders could not even counter the unauthorized reoccupation of the vigilance councils by Ramírez candidates during the 1966 ejidal elections and the 1967 credit society elections.*

---

* The DAAC never recognized these vigilance councils, but it never ordered the Ramirecistas to reconvene the election assembly either. The ejidal commissariat wrote to a DAAC official on December 2, 1966, that to hold another vigilance council election would cause "tremendous agitation" (FNDA, pp. 187–88).

The Technical Tasks and the 1967 Land Invasions

If government officials had properly completed the pending technical tasks during all those years since 1961, then the opposition leaders might have fared better, especially in defending their personal rights as ejidatarios, such as the right to vote, and in progressing toward the division of the ejido. As usual, however, the critical tasks—the survey and mapping, the census, and the definitive authorization of the ejido —remained inextricably politicized. In them the Ramírez regime discovered opportunities to enhance its control over the ejido's land and population, and outside political and economic elites apparently discovered ways to maintain the agrarian status quo. Meanwhile, the opposition partisans and the landless villagers usually bore the brunt of such maneuvers. In 1967, while the opposition as a whole was relatively inactive, certain desperate opposition partisans joined forces with the villagers and tried to strike back at their common enemy, the Ramírez regime.

To be sure, work on a new survey and new maps had begun promptly in early 1961, after Ramírez took office. This time, however, the DAAC officials did not entrust direct control to the state Agrarian Delegation, in whose offices work had bogged down so often in the past. Rather, they specially commissioned one of their own engineers, Domingo López Domínguez, to supervise the fieldwork. In the succeeding months it was López's turn to deal with the confusing boundary disputes with neighboring ejidos and private property owners (including Manuel Sánchez Espinosa and his brother) whose lands had once belonged, directly or indirectly, to Jenkins. It was López's turn to worry about all those outside petitions by landless villagers who claimed rights to the ejidal lands. And it was López's turn to be subjected to the pressures for and against division and parcellation—whether they originated within or without the ejido.

The months turned into years. López completed the basic survey work during 1962, but settling boundary disputes and other sticky problems required protracted legal and bureaucratic dealings involving the DAAC's Bureau of Lands and Waters and the state Agrarian

Delegation. As in the past, officials in these agencies showed little readiness to resolve the sensitive land tenure problems and even less readiness to release the tentative maps. Finished maps seemed no nearer than ever, even though high-level DAAC officials vowed from 1962 on to divide the ejido for the opposition faction and accordingly urged López to complete the work.[57] Thus from 1961 to 1967 the fourth major attempt to survey and map the great ejido proceeded as its predecessors had: officially it was termed informative, but in fact it was inconclusive. As a result the ejido's existing status—and the Ramírez administration—faced no immediate danger from the structural reforms so ardently sought by the opposition.

The census, too, remained embroiled in factional politics, as the Ramirecistas conspired to eliminate their opponents. A major reapportionment of all 2,329 ejidal rights had been scheduled for 1961, but it was postponed until 1965, while Ramírez and his fellow leaders entrenched themselves in office. Then, during 1965, 1966, and 1967, officials of the DAAC and the state Agrarian Delegation, along with the ejidal commissariat, made preliminary field investigations in the various sections of the ejido. Technically, the objective was to collect the names of ejidatarios who were dead or living elsewhere, who illegally rented their individual plots, or who did not fulfill their minimum work requirements. Practically speaking, though, the investigations largely served the ejidal commissariat's political interests. Violations by Ramirecistas were overlooked, whereas numerous members of the opposition faction who were never assigned work, who refused to work as a protest measure, who rented their individual plots while devoting their time to political activity, or who left the ejido temporarily to locate decent work or escape repression were deprived of their rights. Some of the DAAC field inspectors tended to side with the opposition faction,[58] but legally the state Agrarian Delegation controlled these preliminary proceedings. With its collaboration the ejidal commissariat gradually compiled semiofficial documents that challenged the rights of several hundred opposition partisans, thus providing a legalistic justification for depriving them of their voting rights, their jobs, and their dividends. The affected partisans defended themselves by agitating and protesting so adamantly each year that the fieldwork was eventually suspended and no final assembly was ever held to authorize their elimination from the census rolls, though by 1967 the ejidal commissariat and its government allies were almost ready to hold one. In short, the opposition had to fight just to hold its ground, much less gain ground. Like the survey, the census was again proving its worth as a remarkable political device for protecting the ruling elite from its opposition.

Ramírez and his allies in the government also fended off landless villagers who made every effort on the basis of technical issues to obtain rights in or break up the giant, still unauthorized ejido. By now the valley of Matamoros was relatively overpopulated, owing both to natural growth and to immigration from neighboring regions and states. The landless villagers, numbering several thousand, came from petitioning villages and other groups that were between two and three dozen in number. The most active politically were still the displaced former ejidatarios and peons included in the 1938 census, the peasants who had once struggled with Doña Lola against Jenkins, and the sons of these groups—all of whom were still fighting the battles lost in 1937–38. In the late 1930's the villagers had tried land invasion, but that tactic had failed. During the late 1940's and the 1950's, aside from their continued agitation, they had tried bureaucratic lobbying through government-sponsored organizations, such as the National Cane Producers' Union and the Old Agrarian Guard, both CNC affiliates. Owing to skillful temporizing by the government, however, that tactic had failed too. About all that had been accomplished by 1960 was the filing of dozens of applications for "new farming-population centers" to add to the old petitions for ejidal grants and enlargements.

Having gained so little by the official CNC route, the leaders of the landless villagers took a new tack for the 1960's: they turned leftward, affiliating themselves with the new left-wing peasant defense organizations that developed in the wake of the Cuban Revolution. The first of these was the regional Union of Solicitors of Land, Water, and Credit, formed in 1961. In 1963 the union and its local peasant following became part of the national Independent Peasants' Confederation (CCI). When the CCI split in half in 1964, most of the landless villagers—perhaps one thousand—remained aligned with the non-communist branch, the larger of the two. The communist branch attracted few supporters. The General Union of Mexican Workers and Peasants, a socialist organization, also attracted only a small following. According to local CCI leaders, for that matter, very few of the landless villagers were openly affiliated with any of the leftist organizations. Instead they were indirectly affiliated through leaders who chose these organizations as a channel for lobbying.

Basically the villagers could obtain land from the Atencingo complex only if they could gain entry with a census revision, if the survey maps revealed that the ejido embraced more land than acknowledged, or if, prior to its definitive authorization, the ejido was destroyed and redistributed. In 1961 the villagers entertained the idea of a mass land invasion.[59] But Chief Barrios of the DAAC successfully warded off such a move by delegating López to attend to their petitions as his fieldwork progressed.[60] The villagers accordingly decided to await the technical outcome. Meanwhile they also pressured the government to undertake a census revision, so that at least the former ejidatarios and peons included in the 1938 census might be readmitted. Nevertheless, their huge volume of discourse with government agencies brought no results.[61] Much to the villagers' dismay, government officials made little headway toward completing either the maps or the revised census, as previously noted. In effect the technical machinations that were protecting the agrarian status quo from the ejido's opposition faction also worked against the landless villagers.

By 1967 the villagers and their local CCI leaders were growing impatient. Since the lack of progress on the technical tasks dimmed the prospects for political and economic reforms, the leaders of the villagers decided to stage a mass land invasion and appeal for the redistribution of the unauthorized ejido.[62] Of course, they stood the best chance of success if they could first form an alliance with Ramírez's opponents within the ejido and persuade them to invade their own lands.

For years the landless villagers of the CCI had tried to arrange alliances with the opposition within the vast ejido. Fairly regular communications and certain tactical sympathies were shared by the two peasant factions, to the extent that Ramírez often branded his ejidatario opponents as CCI agitators. Yet the opposition partisans had generally feared the implicit competition for their land. Moreover, since they had expected success from their efforts through the CNC and the DAAC, they had been anxious to avoid offending government officials, as any affiliation with the left-wing CCI might have done. During 1964–65 the opposition ejidatarios had thought they were about to win their struggle, with the federal government's assistance. Now, however, their faction was at its lowest ebb, lacking support from the CNC or other government agencies. As a result the demoralized opposition of one annex, San Nicolás Tolentino, decided to take a tactical chance and joined the hundreds of landless villagers already allied with the CCI.[63]

The first invasion took place in April, on the anniversary of Zapata's death, and two more followed in June. All three were failures, the invaders being routed each time by state police. From the crisis the peasants and the CCI leaders gained only new promises from the DAAC chief, the state governor, and a representative of the president that the technical tasks would be completed—officially the only way to end the confusion. Thwarted by police power and arrests, the peasants and the CCI accepted.[64] Thus the technical tasks served once again as invaluable devices for postponing reform. Afterward the demoralized landless villagers returned to a tame routine of bureaucratic lobbying and light agitation, while they patiently waited for results from the government's new promises.[65] For their part, the opposition leaders of San Nicolás Tolentino flatly denied their tactical alliance with CCI members and swore that they remained loyal to the government and the CNC. Meanwhile Ramírez exploited the incident for propaganda advantage.

The Ramírez Regime in Decline

Despite the failure of the land invasions the political and economic strength of the Ramírez regime declined dramatically in the following months, giving the opposition leaders a chance to regain the strategic advantage. First Ramírez lost his major political ally, Secretary-

General Hernández of the CNC, who was fired by higher officials because of his dubious involvement in the nationally embarrassing massacre of copra farmers in the state of Guerrero. When Augusto Gómez Villanueva, a progressive, was named interim secretary-general, both Ramírez and the top opposition leaders immediately rushed to lobby for his support. In response Gómez sent special representatives to make a thorough field investigation of the Atencingo problems, and then proceeded to adopt a neutral stance that in effect constituted a major break for the opposition. In the months ahead the opposition leaders received extensive and sympathetic attention from CNC officials. Moreover, they formed very close ties with the new head of the CNC-affiliated National Cane Producers' Union, and its secretary-general, Armando Medina Alonso, became a major lobbyist on their behalf.

Meanwhile, Ramírez incurred the open hostility of the middle-class townspeople and the dominant faction among the mill workers in Atencingo. The townspeople were angry because he had managed to put unpopular cronies in control of the municipal government and the police department. The mill workers were angry because he had tried to obtain the election of another crony as their secretary-general. One evening in early 1968 a policeman shot and killed a mill worker's son during an argument, and the latent municipal unrest flared into open rebellion. Leaders of the mill workers quickly organized a protest demonstration, and professional agitators from the communist branch of the CCI rushed to the scene.[66] Soon some two thousand mill workers, townspeople, and ejidatarios took to the streets and marched on the offices of the municipal government. All the municipal officials and the entire police department hurriedly fled town. To restore order army soldiers and state police were quickly sent to patrol the vicinity, and the state governor named a personal representative to take temporary command of the municipal government.[67] After several days the crisis was over; nevertheless, its effects endured. In particular, the public outpouring of grievances against Ramírez and his cacique-style rule gave an appreciable boost to the reviving opposition struggle among the ejidatarios. In the following months the dominant faction of mill workers and the small businessmen of

Atencingo gave the ejidatario opposition not only moral support but also financial support for commissions to Mexico City and Puebla.

While the heartened opposition faction was remobilizing and waiting to see what the CNC might accomplish on its behalf, the Ramírez administration was facing serious economic difficulty. Its development policies were not paying off: the cane fields were deteriorating; the 1967–68 harvest was poor, particularly in terms of average yield; the prospects for the next two harvests were also poor; and the financial condition of the credit society was precarious. To offset low cane yields Ramírez tried to make the ejido's cane agriculture even more extensive by infringing on the ejidatarios' established right to grow other crops in addition to cane. As we have seen, in 1967 his administration prepared to limit the ejidatarios to only one-half hectare of seasonal land apiece for individual farming, thus attempting to deprive them of the one-half hectare of irrigated land they had previously been allotted as well. Now, after the 1968–69 harvest, Ramírez ordered the ejidatarios to sow cane in the irrigated areas. Of course, this order would help rescue Ramírez from his production plight, but it also angered a number of the less ardent Ramirecistas, not to mention the opposition.

As a result of his administration's economic difficulties, Ramírez suffered important political reverses on several fronts. In the first place, his relationship with the mill administration deteriorated. After the harvest the mill administrators complained to the federal government about the poor quality of the cane, and responding to lobbying by the ejidatario opposition leaders, they even canceled a credit Ramírez needed for the forthcoming harvest.[68] In the second place, Ramírez lost further government support: in view of the evidence of unsatisfactory agricultural planning, SAG officials paid increasingly sympathetic attention to the complaints of the opposition faction. Third, in reaction to his restrictions on the land available for individual farming, some of his less ardent ejidatario supporters shifted to the opposition. Finally, he was now vulnerable to attack from the opposition on a new and potent issue—the ejido's economy.

Encouraged by so many changes in the political environment, the opposition faction barraged the CNC, the DAAC, the SAG, the state governor, and the president's office with petitions and commissions. Numerous conferences with numerous officials were held in Mexico City, in Puebla, and even in Atencingo. Agreements about how to resolve the crisis were signed by lesser government officials and the leaders of both ejidal factions.[69] For months the opposition seemed on the verge of significant gains. In the end, however, all they gained was the return of their established right to irrigated land as well as seasonally cultivable land for individual farming; and they won that only when violence became imminent. Faced with this threat, federal officials and the state governor intervened on the opposition's behalf, and state police were sent to the fields to prevent tough Ramirecistas from trying to seize the plots in question by force.[70]

Meanwhile, little progress was being made on the more central issues. From his roost in the National Ejidal Credit Bank, General Manager Hernández y Hernández protected his friend Ramírez by refusing to allow the establishment of more than one credit society within the ejido,[71] even though such a practice was not uncommon elsewhere. Moreover, bank officials were making almost no progress on an audit of Ramírez's accounts that supposedly had begun in 1967. Within the confines of the DAAC and the state Agrarian Delegation, officials were abiding by the rule that the survey maps and census had to be completed and approved before any division or parcellation of the ejido could be authorized. Much to the opposition leaders' dismay, in fact, the Agrarian Delegation and the ejidal commissariat were proceeding with their plans to convene a final assembly for the census adjustment soon as a means of eliminating the opposition from the ejido and the credit society. As for the survey, López had indeed submitted maps of the irrigated lands in January 1968, though the opposition ejidatarios were apparently unaware of the fact.[72] Moreover, he was sufficiently advanced in his work to calculate that the real size of the ejido was 11,425 hectares, of which 9,556 were irrigated and 1,780 seasonally cultivable. Historically speaking, these figures represented quite an accomplishment; still they were far from being approved by DAAC authorities and the president, and far from constituting a complete survey in any case. The need to settle the major issues of division and parcellation meanwhile grew more pressing. As López astutely observed, "Letting time pass will only benefit the agitators, who will find magnificently fertile soil for their work."[73]

López was not exaggerating. By September 1968 agitators abounded in the Matamoros valley and throughout Mexico as a result of the national student strike. Moreover, the opposition leaders were once again mobilizing for direct action to compel the government to accede to their major demands. They had grown impatient waiting for federal officials even to convene the annual general assembly for the credit society, at which the dividends would be announced. Finally, officials from the National Ejidal Credit Bank and the DAAC declared that the assembly would be held in a few days, on September 22. But students in Matamoros suddenly began to call for a major demonstration against the government on the same date, hoping to ally themselves with the rebellious peasants in the region. Reacting swiftly, governments officials canceled the Atencingo assembly a day before it was to be held. Army troops in armored cars occupied Matamoros to prevent the student demonstration. Apparently unaware of the cancellation, about a thousand peasants appeared in Atencingo anyway.[74]

The irate opposition leaders saw their opportunity and seized it. Earlier they had considered mobilizing another march against the federal government, but they had abandoned that plan after realizing that government officials, already beset by students threatening to disrupt the Olympics, would not tolerate further unrest in Mexico City. Now, instead, hundreds of hard-core opposition ejidatarios staged a temporary sit-down hunger strike in front of the administrative offices in Atencingo, using portable amplifiers to solicit popular support. After a while they tried to seize control of the office buildings, but army troops ejected them. Apparently the ejidatarios were not quite certain what to do next, when the sympathetic mill workers offered them the use of their basketball pavilion, which was located across from Ramírez's offices. There the opposition, both men and women, reassembled, and there they resolved to remain until the government acceded to all their demands.[75]

Days passed. Many tired and hungry ejidatarios went home at

night, but hundreds returned during the day with members of their families. Large banners proclaimed the cause, and portable amplifiers broadcast the leaders' appeals. Individuals and small groups from the ranks of the Ramirecistas gradually began to join the strike. Mill workers and small businessmen contributed some food and money. A few student agitators visited the scene, but their help was rejected by the opposition leaders, who feared the government's reaction. State police patrolled the area constantly, and army troops were stationed nearby. A hundred or so tough ejidatarios kept guard around the administrative offices, where Ramírez and his cronies were ensconced. And worried representatives of the CNC, the DAAC, the SAG, the National Ejidal Credit Bank, and the state governor came and went in groups, trying to soothe the ejidatarios or to make some minimum deal. Meanwhile, the opposition leaders journeyed in turn to government offices in Mexico City and Puebla to argue for a favorable resolution to the crisis.[76]

The days turned into weeks, but the ejidatarios refused to retreat. Indeed, they still threatened to mobilize a march to see the president in Mexico City. Moreover, every day the minority opposition came closer to becoming the majority faction. Whereas the opposition leaders had previously commanded a majority only in Raboso, they now commanded a majority in Teruel and La Galarza as well, and almost a majority in Atencingo.

The government authorities were not at all eager to alter the structure or even the administration of the ejido. To them the cause of Atencingo's problems was not the structure of the ejido but intense population pressure combined with a demagogic power struggle among leaders who had little intention of introducing the reforms they pretended to advocate for the sake of popular support. If Ramírez did not excel as an administrator, he was still acceptable in their eyes. Sometime in September or October, however, Ramírez suffered an important reversal at the federal level. General Manager Hernández y Hernández of the National Ejidal Credit Bank was fired on the ground of fraud and replaced by a director who adopted a neutral stance between the two ejidal factions. Thus Ramírez suddenly lost his major remaining ally, and the opposition leaders were rid of the man who had blocked the establishment of additional credit societies within the ejidal complex.

Soon thereafter the various government officials involved in the Atencingo case offered to designate part of the ejido especially for the opposition faction and establish a separate credit society there.[77] The opposition leaders refused, demanding complete independence for each of the nine sections of the ejido. Then the government officials returned to the position that any thorough division or parcellation of the ejido had to be postponed until the technical tasks were completed; but with the consent of the mill administration, they offered to establish independent credit societies in each of the three annexes where the opposition commanded a majority, namely Raboso, Teruel, and La Galarza. Those annexes would thus be independent for administrative purposes. The opposition leaders accepted the offer and consented to end their strike on October 16, 24 days after it began. Just before the strike was over, a semiofficial census was taken. It showed that 957 registered ejidatarios were there to be counted as part of the opposition faction, a substantially greater number than the total of 731 who had signed a major petition in August.[78] Quite elated by their victory, the tired ejidatarios went home to rest and prepare for the approaching harvest—and to await official action on the new credit societies.

Official action was not forthcoming, however. Once again the authorities delayed, and the opposition leaders found themselves bogged down in another round of bureaucratic lobbying against Ramírez. At the end of November came harvest time, and the annual general assembly for distributing dividends had not even been convened. On November 24 Ramírez ordered the harvest to begin in Teruel. Immediately the opposition faction called for a work stoppage there, occupying the fields day and night to ensure that no work was done. Though harvesting began on schedule in other sections of the ejido, the work stoppage in Teruel endangered productivity as well as political stability. It lasted 28 days, until December 20, with many ejidatarios even sleeping in the fields while government officials came and went. At last high-level federal and state officials registered the three new credit societies as they had promised and made arrangements for the mill administration to finance the cane agriculture in the three annexes affected. Opposition ejidatarios in Raboso and Teruel thus secured immediate administrative control of their harvest and also received their share of the agricultural machinery.[79] Unfortunately for the opposition faction in La Galarza, a few ejidatarios switched back to Ramírez's side, making any administrative separation impossible for at least another year. The protracted struggle had nevertheless paid off in the form of institutional power and control over the patronage system for the opposition in two annexes.

In the months ahead the annual assembly for distributing dividends still was not convened. Several times it was scheduled and then canceled. As a result two or three hundred irate opposition partisans, both men and women, tried to seize control of the offices in Atencingo very early one morning in the middle of January, when few people were around. As they may have expected, Ramírez happened to appear. They ambushed him and held him hostage for several hours, treating him roughly and threatening to lynch him; they even had the noose around his neck. Meanwhile, Ramirecistas began to congregate outside and prepare for a counterattack. Then the army arrived for the rescue, dislodged the opposition partisans from the buildings, and restored order. State police arrested twenty opposition leaders and jailed them for assault and attempted murder. It became clear, however, that they had only been trying to scare Ramírez into fleeing. Ramírez did go into seclusion for a while, but he certainly did not flee. Charges were not pressed against his assailants, and they were released a few days later.[80]

In late January Ramírez and officials in the DAAC and the state Agrarian Delegation hastened to convene the dreaded assembly for the rectification of the census, based on the prejudicial lists compiled over the years. Since no ejidatario whose rights were being challenged was allowed to enter the assembly auditorium, Ramírez supporters were heavily in the majority. Large contingents of state police and army troops patrolled outside. Inside, officials from the CNC, the DAAC, the SAG, the National Ejidal Credit Bank, and the state government watched while names prepared by the state Agrarian Delegation and the ejidal commissariat were read to the assembly.

By voice vote the claque of ejidatarios generally approved the list.[81] After fifteen continuous sweaty hours the assembly ended, having authorized the elimination from the census rolls of not only 364 deceased ejidatarios but also 102 ejidatarios accused of not working and another 193 accused of absence from the ejido. Of course, virtually all of these 295 ejidatarios were members of the opposition faction, including its top leaders throughout the ejidal complex.[82] Thus by a technical stratagem Ramírez endeavored to dispose of his detractors.

Legally, as neutral CNC officials pointed out, that assembly only initiated the process of depriving ejidatarios of their rights. The accused ejidatarios still had a grace period in which to defend themselves before DAAC officials, and only the president of the Republic himself could finally authorize the removal of their rights. In certain respects, moreover, the general assembly itself may have been illegal. According to the Agrarian Code the accused ejidatarios had the right to attend the assembly and defend themselves, whereas in fact the guards had not let them inside the auditorium. There was also some question whether ejidatarios from one section of the ejido had the right or even had sufficient knowledge to pass judgment on the work habits of ejidatarios from another section. Certainly the judgments would have been markedly different if a separate assembly had been held for each section of the ejido, as the opposition leaders had wished. By means of bureaucratic and legal appeals, then, the accused opposition ejidatarios stood a chance of retaining their rights. In the meantime, nevertheless, Ramírez and his fellow leaders regarded the assembly's actions as virtually definitive—and hence as proper justification for continuing to withhold work, dividends, and voting rights from the accused ejidatarios.[83]

These census rectification proceedings, and the necessity of appealing them, were not the only technical obstacles that distracted and blocked the opposition. Earlier in January DAAC officials had also ordered López to continue his work on mapping the entire Atencingo land system and to expand his operations to include the bordering ejidos. In order to map the Atencingo system properly, it was now becoming necessary to survey and map virtually the entire valley, so complex were the long-standing disputes over land, almost all of them attributable to Jenkins's original machinations.[84] With both the census and the survey again bogged down in the bureaucracy, the Ramírez regime was protected for the time being from further pressures for the division or parcellation of the ejido.

Yet Ramírez was not entirely safe from attack. Though DAAC officials were in effect protecting the ejido's integrity and the Ramírez faction among the ejidatarios, CNC officials urged SAG officials to audit the Ramírez administration's accounts, as demanded by the opposition leaders.[85] In March Ramírez countered this threat by finally convening the long-awaited—and very well guarded—general assembly. At the assembly he announced that there were no annual dividends, publicly criticized the surprised CNC and SAG officials, and submitted the entire conflict to arbitration by the new state governor, the highly respected Rafael Moreno Valle, who had just entered office.[86] The opposition leaders accepted the proposal, and so did the governor. Once again Ramírez had forestalled any possibility of a federal audit or other intervention, for now the center of control and decision making had been shifted away from the federal level and back down to the state level, where it had not been for almost a decade.

In the following months the political struggle finally subsided. Encouraged by new popular support, and to a limited extent, new government support, the opposition leaders had earlier used dramatic tactics to make remarkable gains. For now, however, the conflict had reached a virtual standoff at the local, state, and federal levels; and political alignments were in flux. Accordingly the opposition ejidatarios returned to tactics of intensive lobbying and light agitation, while they probed for new support and waited for fresh opportunities. They were heartened when the new governor declared himself neutral and refused to accept the bribe that opposition partisans widely claim was customarily offered by Ramírez to key officials. Moreover, the 1968–69 cane harvest turned out badly for Ramírez, and quite well for Raboso—though production in Teruel suffered from the work stoppage as well as from prior technical deficiencies. Out of a total of some 393,465 tons of cane harvested by all nine sections of the ejido, Atencingo and the six annexes still under Ramírez produced 343,893 tons (at a low average yield of 112.4 tons per hectare); Raboso produced 49,572 tons; and Teruel produced some 31,000 tons. Under pressure the Ramírez administration did distribute fairly good dividends for this season, but the very high dividends distributed by the new administration in Raboso provided an unflattering contrast. Ejidatarios in Atencingo and the six annexes received slightly more than 1,500 pesos apiece (the total dividends amounted to nearly three million pesos), whereas ejidatarios in Raboso received 3,000 pesos apiece.[87] Indeed, the prospects for future progress by Raboso and Teruel were quite good—a fact that only enhanced the determination of the opposition partisans in the other sections of the ejido. There could be no doubt that their struggle would go on.*

Conclusions

Rather than reveal new characteristics of agrarian struggles, the events described in this chapter have essentially confirmed the characteristics previously identified. Economic and political conditions inside the Atencingo ejido remained highly dependent on outside political events, particularly political successions. In general, when confronted with agrarian unrest, government officials followed a strategy of cooptation and control. They extended support only to those willing to accommodate government interests in economic productivity and political stability. Sometimes they conceded institutional power to restless peasants, but they never conceded structural reform. In crises they augmented cooptation with repression to maintain control.

Within the ejido local rulers followed a similar strategy, rewarding loyal supporters by means of the patronage system and punishing opponents by economic discrimination and political repression. The

---

*I have not returned to Atencingo since 1969. I understand, however, that the struggle I witnessed continued into 1971, resulting finally in the fall of the Ramírez administration and the establishment of independent credit societies in each of the ejido's nine sections. As usual, presidential and other federal successions in 1970 played major roles in these developments. The current agrarian administration in the federal government appears to be the most progressive, responsible, and capable that Mexico has experienced since 1940.

fortunes of Ramírez and his opposition continued to depend on the strategic balance in popular support as well as government support. Agitation and direct actions were the only tactics providing the possibility of a major breakthrough for the opposition, whereas legal and bureaucratic maneuvers were more fruitful for Ramírez. In the long run the opposition leaders were struggling for the structural reforms they had always advocated; in the short run, however, many were willing to settle for administrative power. Most of these observations are by now familiar enough, but three characteristics of the Atencingo ejido's post-1961 history deserve particular notice: the durability of the Ramírez regime; the effectiveness of direct action tactics, especially for the opposition; and the intense internalization of the opposition struggle.

Why was Ramírez able to remain in power so long? Of course, the answer lies in his ability to maintain sufficient levels of government and popular support, combined with his remarkable leadership skills. To maintain government support he diligently accommodated official economic interests and almost always had one or two key federal allies who defended his interests in official circles. Also, financial contributions—not to mention outright bribes—surely played a major role in keeping officials on his side. The strong support of CNC officials during 1961–62 and SAG officials until 1964 enabled Ramírez to entrench himself in office, win his contractual struggle with the mill and hence mechanize the cooperative, and fend off the renascent opposition struggle. His opposition almost succeeded in ousting him with countervailing federal support during 1964, but the presidential succession delivered to Ramírez a strong alliance with officials in the National Ejidal Credit Bank, who saved his administration by transforming it into a single credit society. Soon afterward, Ramírez also acquired strong new allies in the CNC as the result of another succession. With such allies, and with the return of good relations with the mill, the Ramírez regime enjoyed great stability during 1965–67. Then production went into a sudden decline, however, and Ramírez lost his key allies. As a result the opposition revived, seriously endangering his continued rule. In the struggle that ensued, the Ramírez administration lost jurisdiction over two annexes, but it survived the onslaught nonetheless. For one thing, government officials were not eager to discard a peasant leader who had served their interests so well for so long. For another, Ramírez maneuvered adroitly in official circles to postpone any final showdown. Finally, Ramírez did still command majority popular support in most sections of the ejido.

Why so many ejidatarios continued to support Ramírez is not entirely clear—especially in view of his failure to keep his campaign promises or to bring about any significant improvement in the general standard of living. Several possible explanations can be proposed, however. First, though many ejidatarios mistrusted the former collaborationists, Ramírez's image remained fairly favorable in key respects. He continued to be identified as the liberator from state intervention and as the foremost proponent of parcellation, the ultimate popular aspiration. Moreover, many ejidatarios were genuinely proud of his impressive capital investments. Second, Ramírez kept tight control by means of political and economic sanctions. From some ejidatarios he elicited loyalty by means of the patronage system; from others he elicited at least obedience by the threat of economic discrimination and political repression. As we have seen, Ramírez and his fellow leaders even concocted popular support by simply excluding their opponents from election assemblies on assorted legalistic grounds. Further research might show that Ramírez drew his popular support chiefly from the poorest, the least modernized, and the most recently admitted ejidatarios—those who were also the most submissive politically.

With respect to the strategy and tactics of agrarian struggle, dramatic direct action continued to play a vital role. Its essential purpose was to wring major concessions from the government by threatening political stability and economic productivity. Yet such concessions were never ensured without definite preconditions for success. In particular, direct action tactics were most effective in the presence of considerable popular and government support, and when they were combined with respectful bureaucratic lobbying. Examples of successful direct action were the production halts used by Ramírez during his contractual struggle with the mill administration during 1961–62, the second of the three marches undertaken by the opposition partisans in 1964, and the permanent assembly and work stoppage by the opposition in 1968. Examples in which the preconditions were not favorable and the direct actions immediately failed were the opposition's first and last marches in 1963 and 1965 respectively, and the land invasion of 1967. In each of these cases the opposition lacked official support; and in the case of the land invasion, representation by the left-wing CCI was considered too unorthodox to be respectable. The fact that hundreds of peasants were involved in these events was enough to arouse the officials to take repressive measures, but not to make concessions. As a final note, such individual direct action tactics as assassinations and attempted assassinations appeared to have counterproductive effects, ultimately resulting in bad publicity and the loss of support.

In previous periods the agrarian struggle in Atencingo had directly focused on an outside institution—either the mill administration or the state—as the major enemy. After 1961, however, it became highly internalized. More than ever before it pitted peasants against peasants rather than peasants against outside elites. Each ejidal faction commonly accused the other of being a mere pawn of the mill administration or of outside political interests. But such charges were on the whole unjustified, though in some instances tactical expediency dictated alliances with outside political actors. Actually the chronic factionalism was a legacy of the 1952–61 state intervention, when the division of the old Jaramillo leadership into opposing camps had helped the Reorganizing Commission stay in power. Now the animosities created then were still paying off for both the government and the mill administration. For one thing, they ultimately weakened the Ramírez administration in its dealings with the mill administration, which never wanted to face an ejidal government that was powerful enough to gain contractual equality. For another, they inevitably helped forestall the mobilization of any massive peasant struggle that might have forced the government to concede fundamental structural reforms in order to restore political and economic stability.

CHAPTER EIGHT

The Politics of Agrarian Struggle: An Analysis

Perhaps few places in rural Mexico have had such an eventful and often incredible history of political and economic struggle as Atencingo. Some government officials, seeking to preserve the myths of the Mexican Revolution, claim that the Atencingo case is a special one, atypical of Mexican rural conditions and politics. For that matter, many of the Atencingo ejidatarios themselves have accepted this view, if only because government officials have promoted it. Yet others, especially liberals and leftists, claim that Atencingo's history of struggle, though extreme, reveals much about agrarian political processes in Mexico. Indeed, one of Mexico's foremost anthropologists told the author: "You have chosen your case well. The history of Atencingo is the history of Mexico."

Both interpretations seem correct, the more so in combination: the Atencingo case is not representative of Mexican rural conditions in general, yet it brings the politics of agrarian struggle in Mexico sharply into focus. Thus few peasants in Mexico have so many serious problems or demand such fundamental reforms as the Atencingo ejidatarios; few peasants are so politically mobilized; and few peasants have so often resorted to direct action in pressing for reform. At the same time virtually every problem typically encountered in vast ejidal Mexico is to be found in the Atencingo ejido: population pressures, boundary disputes, competition for ejidal rights, the illegal rental of personal plots, the entrenchment of certain leaders in ejidal office, factional power struggles, intrigues with outside political and economic interests, corruption and favoritism, agitation and demagoguery, violence and assassination, to mention only some of the notable ones. Furthermore, the issues of collectivization, parcellation, division, and crop diversification have played fundamental roles not only in the Atencingo case but in the history and ideology of agrarian reform throughout Mexico.

There are additional reasons for regarding Atencingo as a highly revealing case for study. In Mexico the severest agrarian struggles have typically concerned either landholding peasants engaged in commercial agriculture subject to monopoly control by some private or state enterprise, or landless peasants desiring the distribution of sizable tracts monopolized by private individuals or interests. Both groups are represented in the Atencingo region. In the first category are the Atencingo ejidatarios, along with such other groups as demonstrative henequen farmers in restless Yucatan; copra farmers in the violent regions of Guerrero, where political banditry is widespread; exploited woodsmen in Michoacán and Chihuahua, where extremist intellectuals and students twice tried to establish guerrilla fronts; and ixtle and candelilla harvesters of Coahuila, who resorted to hunger marches in 1962. In the second category are the landless and land-hungry villagers of the Atencingo region, along with thousands of other peasants in various parts of Mexico who have disputed and invaded lands monopolized by real estate developers, cattle ranchers, and other agricultural interest groups. Finally, whatever the specific similarities and differences between the peasants of the Atencingo region and those in other parts of Mexico, all Mexican peasants are of course subjected to essentially the same party and government institutions. Accordingly the Atencingo case offers considerable insight into the methods used by the government over the years to contain agrarian unrest while providing the peasants some marginal socioeconomic benefits through infrastructural and community development projects.

Though precise comparative data are unavailable, it thus appears that whatever lessons can be gleaned from the Atencingo case may have fairly broad application to other areas of Mexico. Most important, the case serves to illuminate the political strengths and limitations of organized peasant groups that become engaged in a severe conflict with powerful party-government bureaucracies and economic enterprises in Mexico. To that end this chapter offers a comprehensive analysis of the agrarian struggle in Atencingo: the effects of the strategic context in which the struggle has taken place; the strategies and tactics employed; and the consequences of the struggle.

The Strategic Context

A complete model of the many objective and subjective causes of agrarian unrest and struggle is beyond the scope of this study.* Yet one complex determinative factor stands out in the Atencingo case— the strategic context in which the struggle took place. Essentially a strategic context is determined by the individuals and institutions with interests at stake—what their interests and objectives are, how much power and authority each of them commands, and the patterns of alliance and opposition among them—and by whatever political and legal rules govern the articulation and resolution of conflicts in their society.

The structure of a strategic context sets the opportunities and requirements for an actor to achieve his objectives, and greatly affects the strategies and tactics available to him. Different actors in a system, for example peasants and government officials, may have differ-

---

* Any such model should take into account the politicizing effects of ejidal organization and cane agriculture. Ejidal organization obliges peasants to participate in general assemblies, hold election campaigns, vote on officers and issues, and in general concern themselves with their common problems as ejidatarios. Collective cane agriculture may have an even stronger politicizing effect, for it requires a high degree of organization, leadership, and teamwork that apparently generates a capability for collective political action among the peasants. Certainly throughout history few other types of agriculture have been so closely associated with peasant unrest. Many analyses have attributed this characteristic to the exploitative practices of the sugar producers and the seasonality of employment, but other types of agriculture have been characterized by exploitation and seasonality without being closely associated with peasant unrest. Rather it appears that the critical factor accounting for cane cutters' propensity to rebel is the degree of collective organization and teamwork required by cane agriculture. This explanation is further supported by the example of longshoremen, who have a similar history of unrest and struggle. Like cane cutters, longshoremen may suffer less actual exploitation than other working groups, but they experience a relatively high degree of teamwork that prepares them for collective political action.

ent strategic contexts, whose structure may also change over time. Accordingly, at one time the Atencingo peasants might have powerful allies and a good chance of success through bureaucratic lobbying. At another time they might have powerful allies but also such powerful opposition that only direct action could bring success. At still another time they might have almost no allies at all and hence no hope of success, whatever their tactics. Thus, though not precisely a cause of agrarian struggle, the strategic context certainly conditions and practically determines the form and intensity of agrarian struggle at any given time, even though the general level of discontent might remain fairly constant.

In what sort of strategic context did the Atencingo ejidatarios find themselves? To begin at the simplest level, it is clear that the ejidatarios had very little political or economic power. Rather, they were highly dependent and subordinate partners in the larger political and economic system. Their political and economic conditions were basically imposed from without. The ejidatarios made some decisions, to be sure; but on the major issues, as well as many minor ones, what happened in Atencingo depended decisively on what happened in Mexico City and Puebla. Atencingo was not so much a place where local conditions took their course as it was a regional outcropping of political and economic developments in the elite circles of Mexico City and Puebla. Indeed, this subordination to outside control not only hampered the ejidatarios' attempts to resolve their problems but also contributed to the very generation of those problems.

Powerless as they were, the ejidatarios were also thoroughly and intricately enmeshed in the larger political and economic system: they owned valuable agricultural property; they produced a key commodity that was vital to the nationally important sugar industry; they needed substantial financial and technical assistance; they were organized as ejidatarios and as associates of the cooperative or credit society, rendering them subject to extensive bureaucratic and legal supervision by government agencies; they faced serious problems whose solutions required government action; and their political allegiance to the established government seemed important for electoral reasons. Other factors could be mentioned, but these should suffice to demonstrate that the Atencingo ejidatarios were an integral component of the larger economic and political system at both the state and the national level. Moreover, they were an extremely valuable component. As a result they were the constant targets of manipulation by political and economic elites. The landless villagers, by contrast, played a far less significant role in the larger political and economic system than the ejidatarios, and accordingly their strategic position was quite different.

What was the nature of the system to which the Atencingo ejidatarios were so intricately linked, and in which they struggled? Essentially it was dominated by a set of institutions that embodied political, economic, and legal power: a complex centralized party-government bureaucracy with authority over agrarian affairs; a government-protected monopoly-capitalist enterprise, namely the Atencingo sugar mill; and a set of laws and decrees in effect obligating the ejidatarios to serve the interests of the government and the mill. The outstanding interests at stake were political stability and economic development along certain lines favored by official policy. The bureaucracy, the milling enterprise, and the agrarian laws were designed to promote and protect those interests on behalf of the ruling political and economic elites—while the bureaucracy and the laws also provided an institutional framework within which the ejidatarios might seek a remedy for their grievances.

Conflicts of interest. The ejidatarios were essentially struggling for a liberation based on local institutional power and agrarian reform—two distinct but complementary goals. For the peasant leaders of an agrarian struggle, local institutional power was essential. In the short run it brought them personal power that could be used for personal gain or for the advancement of the group they represented; and it brought their followers such rewards as better jobs and higher incomes. In the long run it was the prerequisite for reform. Confronted with a struggle for both power and reform, government officials typically granted power before they would permit reform; and they paid little attention to the struggle for reform if the struggle for power had not already proved formidable. Thus the struggle for liberation was both a power struggle and a reform struggle—and as such it could pose threats to key elite political and economic interests.

The ejidatarios' agrarian reform goal raised a fundamental economic issue—the inevitable conflict between the official and the popular conception of economic development. In the official conception, of course, protecting the sugar industry was the paramount consideration: not only was the industry a valuable component of the state and national economy, but it was a critical interest of certain political and economic elites. Accordingly the federal government decreed that only cane was to be grown on the lands that specifically served any sugar mill, and that in the cane producing Atencingo ejido, among others, all land tenure and work would be collective rather than individual—the most efficient but also the most restrictive system. In effect, the government officially licensed monopoly capitalism and exploitation, and a complex agrarian bureaucracy was committed to the institutionalization and defense of this system.

Needless to say, the ejidatarios were not in favor of such a system. They preferred an economy and life-style based on a combination of subsistence agriculture and local market capitalism, with each ejidatario personally controlling a distinct plot of land. Cane was simply not the most profitable or the most useful crop they could cultivate. Rice, tomatoes, and melon often brought higher profits at the market, a fact that sometimes prompted major private landowners in the area to produce melon and tomatoes instead of cane; the ejidatarios wanted the right to do the same. Moreover, corn and beans met family subsistence needs and brought an easy profit on the market. Parcellation would satisfy the long-standing desires of the peasantry for personal control over their property and livelihood.

Clearly an open market based on local values would have resulted in an entirely different economy in Atencingo than the one institutionalized by the government in favor of the mill. Of course, populist economic development might also have brought new forms of land fever, new power struggles, and new forms of exploitation. But such concerns seemed remote to the ejidatarios, especially since they were already suffering from such problems under the established system. Thus on the issue of agrarian reform the ejidatarios were ultimately opposed by both the government authorities and the mill administration—though over the years the authorities did relent somewhat in the direction of meeting popular demands for the right to grow crops other than cane, so long as a satisfactory level of cane production was ensured.

The ejidatarios' other major goal, local institutional power over the ejido, also brought them into conflict with the mill administration and the government. According to the laws embodying the democratic principles of the Mexican Revolution, peasants were entitled to control over their local institutions. But for economic reasons the mill administration feared the development of strong, ejidatario-led institutions in the Atencingo complex, and ultimately preferred to bar the peasants from local policy making as much as possible. Indeed, during 1938–46 the mill administration even struggled to ward off federal interference in its domain. Government intervention on the mill's behalf was another matter, however, and during 1952 the mill administration was quick to solicit the government's help in excluding reform-minded ejidatarios from local policy making.

By contrast, the government's economic interests did not strictly determine its politico-institutional policies. Rather it also had primary political interests it expected the ejidatarios' local institutions to serve. In particular, the government was vitally interested in the expansion and security of its powerful bureaucratic and party control over the ejidatarios, their political participation, and their respect for the government—if only for the sake of preserving political stability. These purposes could best be served by granting the ejidatarios some degree of control over their local institutions in exchange for their continued political support. Of course, local institutional power was generally contingent on accommodation to the political and economic interests of the government and the mill administration. Particular ejidatario leaders received official support to hold local office only so long as their doing so in effect confirmed the power of the government and the mill administration over the region. Nonetheless, once they had gained some measure of local power, the ejidatarios—or a faction of them—were in a position to act on their reform goals, if only by taking such relatively moderate steps as instituting limited de facto parcellation and crop diversification, and bargaining for a more favorable contract with the mill administration.

To summarize, the ejidatarios' success in gaining some power and reform hinged largely on their ability to accommodate certain government political interests without jeopardizing the government's economic interests too much. Whereas the mill and most ejidatarios were fundamentally at odds owing to their conflicting economic interests, the government and the ejidatarios at times found in their respective political positions some basis for compromise. The government sided with the mill on economic issues, to be sure, but concessions to the ejidatarios' demands for local institutional power could serve the government's equally strong interest in political stability. For their part, the ejidatarios offered the government their loyalty in exchange for local institutional power, which at times enabled their leaders to wrest a slightly greater share in the region's agricultural wealth from the mill administration. To some degree, then, the ejidatarios were able to achieve reform through power, but they were successful only as long as the changes posed no significant threat to elite interests in political stability and economic productivity.

Institutional structure. The government was not only an interested party to the conflict but together with the legal system provided the institutional framework for resolving that conflict. Thus the structure and responsiveness of the government itself became a critical part of the ejidatarios' strategic context.

Diverse official party and government agencies were involved in the political and economic affairs of the Atencingo ejido: the National Peasants' Confederation, the Agrarian Department, the Secretariat of Agriculture, the Secretariat of Industry and Commerce, the National Ejidal Credit Bank, and the state-level counterparts of these agencies, not to mention the Secretariat of National Defense and various police forces. Such extensive bureaucratic involvement, a direct consequence of Mexico's political and economic development, was designed to take advantage of the valuable agricultural resources in the Atencingo region, while affording some progress for the peasants. In effect it meant that some government control extended into almost every aspect of ejidal affairs. Nonetheless the very structure of the government left the ejidatarios considerable room to maneuver in.

The executive organization was far from monolithic or even strictly hierarchical. Rather, it could be described as a set of parallel hierarchies, one headed by the state governor and several others headed by the federal ministers and presidential appointees, with the president himself presiding over all. Despite a certain harmony of purpose, it is hardly surprising that the various agencies within this complex system sometimes failed to coordinate their efforts, especially when dealing with complicated situations like the peasant opposition struggles in Atencingo. Moreover, limited conflicts of interest and policy within the government were not unusual; in this regard the Agrarian Department was at odds with the Secretariat of Industry and Commerce and the state governor on several occasions. Thus even at relatively high levels of government the effectiveness of tight government control was limited to some extent.

Within individual government agencies, to be sure, the chief official set overall policy and attempted to centralize control, usually through his coterie of personally selected assistants. Nevertheless, the complex structure of the bureaucracy actually gave middle-level officials considerable leeway, as was apparently the case with the Agrarian Department's Bureau of Lands and Waters, which appeared to temporize despite even strong orders to complete maps of the Atencingo complex. Moreover, such state-level agencies as the Agrarian Delegation were responsible not only to the state governor but also—though apparently to a lesser extent—to the federal Agrarian Department. This overlapping of authority evidently afforded the lower-level agencies even greater flexibility, and indeed may have made them more susceptible to outside influence from private sources.

Finally, government control was further qualified by the regularity of political successions in both elective and appointive posts. Although the basic principles of the Mexican Revolution were embodied in laws and decrees that were ultimately respected, government officials did have some choices to make in their handling of specific cases. Thus the personal disposition of a particular high-level official might have great impact on a peasant opposition struggle, especially with respect to a peasant leader's prospects for gaining power.

Certainly this system, in which the Atencingo ejido's affairs were supervised by officials at many levels of government, meant strong government control. To a surprising degree, however, the ejidatarios found opportunity within it to advance their cause, for three main reasons. First, the Atencingo ejidatarios were in a stronger position than most Mexican peasants. The ejido's productivity and political stability were so important to the authorities that their petitions or other political articulations normally bypassed the lowest levels of government and were handled directly by the top level of the state bureaucracy or the middle and top levels of the federal bureaucracy. It was not too difficult for ejidatario opposition leaders to get the personal attention of any official other than the president. Second, the many government agencies involved in ejidal affairs gave ejidatario leaders many alternative channels of access to a top decision maker, whether they sought support themselves or through CNC lobbyists. If they were rebuffed within one agency, then they could probe for support within another. Third, the regularity of political successions meant that an official who was not sympathetic toward the ejidatarios might eventually be replaced by one who was. For this reason political successions were among the major determinants of political change in the Atencingo ejido over the long run. Merely by waiting patiently the leaders of an opposition struggle stood a good chance of eventually gaining a high-level ally within the government. Of course, during 1951–55 and 1965–67 there were virtually no allies to be found, and the opposition struggle was almost hopeless. Yet political successions ultimately altered the strategic context in the ejidatarios' favor by bringing more responsive officials to office.

The structure of the political system thus favored eventual government attention to the ejidatarios' demands and eventual—though limited—government support by particular authorities and officials. At the same time, however, it made prompt and comprehensive government action highly improbable. Even sympathetic officials typically postponed decisions as long as possible while they familiarized themselves with the case and sounded out its political ramifications.

More often than not, they turned the ejidatarios' petitions over to sub-ordinates for thorough investigation. Later, especially in matters of major importance, the sheer complexity of bureaucratic and political coordination made it very difficult for the various state and federal officials to reach a final decision. Of course, major decisions were ulti-mately left to the president, but he never acted without the support or at least acquiescence of the state governor and federal ministers. Ulti-mately the authorities might concede some political change, such as a succession or an administrative reorganization within the ejido, but up to 1969 at least they put up a stiff resistance to structural reforms that might fundamentally affect established economic interests. Major reforms were thus unlikely to be forthcoming except when the ejida-tarios applied very strong pressure indeed.

Such a system put a premium on the demonstration of power as the prerequisite for reform. As a result the Atencingo ejidatarios, or for that matter any peasant group, could not expect mere sympathy on the part of some government official to result in any significant con-cessions. Only by gaining and demonstrating power could they hope to win timely and significant reforms from the government. A show of force had this effect essentially because it potentially threatened key interests of the government or the mill administration, thus cre-ating a public political and economic crisis the government was forced to resolve.

Peasant Strategy and Tactics

Strategy. Given the ejidatarios' relatively weak position within the overall strategic context, what strategies offered them the most hope of success? Three alternative strategies were considered over the years: defiant isolationism, revolutionary struggle, and reformist struggle. Owing to the nature of the strategic context, however, only reform-ist struggle was politically feasible for any length of time or met with any degree of success.

A strategy based on defiant isolationism historically has appealed to discontented peasants with strong parochial identities who blame out-side political and economic interference for their troubles. Often their natural reaction is to try to reject de jure outside control and defiantly

carry out popular de facto policies. In the Atencingo region this strategy failed, however, because both the government and the mill maintained overwhelming capabilities to defend their primary interests
there. Thus on major issues the ejidatarios were unable to ignore the
government's presence or become independent of its control. In the
only instance that contains elements of an isolationist strategy, the
Jaramillo administration defiantly instituted considerable de facto
parcellation and diversification, with politically disastrous results. By
its efforts, moreover, the Jaramillo administration actually created
new ties to the government through the National Ejidal Credit Bank.
In sum, a strategy of defiant isolationism was hopelessly impolitic and
well-nigh impossible to carry out, for the ejidatarios could not afford
to ignore the government.

A strategy of revolutionary struggle was equally unsuitable. Revolutionary conditions have not existed in Mexico for decades, and the
ejidatarios as a group never engaged in revolutionary struggle against
the government, though revolutionary fantasies have not been uncommon. The 1946–47 joint struggle by the workers and ejidatarios
against the mill administration had some revolutionary qualities. Yet
the ejidatarios as well as the workers were in fact closely allied to government agencies, and the popular struggle only enhanced the federal
government's control over the region. The harshest rhetoric ever leveled against the government by the ejidatarios, in the December 1954
propaganda booklet, cloaked a plea for responsiveness, not a demand
for the overthrow of the government. In the late 1960's the ejidatarios
listened to proposals by outsiders who styled themselves revolutionaries or radicals, particularly certain university students and professional agitators. But in general they took interest in such advice only
for temporary tactical purposes, not for framing general strategy.
Whatever their reservations about certain officials and policies, most
ejidatarios deeply respected the government's authority and firmly
believed in the benevolence of the president. Far from wanting to
overthrow the government, they actively sought its support.

This brings us to the third alternative—the strategy of reformist
struggle, in which the ejidatarios worked through the established institutional system for reform rather than trying to ignore or revolu-

tionize it. Given the government's political strength, not to mention its military and police power, reformist struggle was the only practical strategy, and the only one to bring any success. Briefly, the essence of the strategy was to acquire, mobilize, and demonstrate a combination of both popular support and government support. Historically, only by demonstrating both types of support could ejidatario opposition leaders gain the strategic advantage and thus wrest significant concessions from the government. To the contrary of some theories of struggle, indeed, it seems quite clear that popular support alone, though it might succeed in gaining the government's attention, was far from sufficient for winning concessions from the government, especially on major issues. Thus the landless villagers of the Atencingo region could invade ejidal lands by the hundreds or attend rallies by the thousands—only to be suppressed or ignored by government officials. Similarly the 1946–51 Jaramillo regime and the leaders of the sizable opposition during 1955–56 and 1965–67 failed to achieve their major objectives because they lacked government allies to complement their popular support. By contrast, the rebellious ejidatario factions achieved major breakthroughs, as in 1946, 1961, and 1969, when both kinds of support were at peak levels.* Much lower levels of support were sufficient for success on simple tactical issues, such as keeping one's name on the census rolls, but even then help from some government official was often required. Only on one occasion did government officials apparently make concessions very unwillingly owing to the dangerous level of volatile popular support for the opposition leaders: in 1955, soon after Jaramillo's assassination, when the Agrarian Department chief enabled the ejidatario opposition leaders to win the elections for the cooperative society. Yet in fact that concession turned out to be a clever control device the officials used to pacify the opposition.

If popular support and government support were complementary

---

* Although I have no firsthand information on the events of 1971, when independent credit societies were established in each of the ejido's nine sections, it seems clear that this breakthrough followed the pattern of earlier ones. Popular support for the administrative reform had apparently increased, and government support had been enhanced by the presidential succession of 1970, which had brought a reformist federal administration to office, and by the continuation of progressive leadership in the CNC.

factors, they were also largely independent. The demonstration of mounting popular support did not necessarily attract government allies for a cause, though it did attract the government's attention. Depending on the circumstances, then, repression or renewed government control—not government support—might be the response to the growing popularity of an opposition struggle. This point is demonstrated most clearly by the repression of land invasions by the landless villagers in 1938–39 and 1967, as well as by the difficulties of the Jaramillistas when they lacked official allies in the mid-1950's.

The search for government support was thus an integral part of the reformist strategy. The ejidatario leaders' chances of locating government allies at a given time were poor, but there was a high probability that if they were persistent over a period of time they could eventually succeed. As we have seen, if they failed to obtain a favorable response within the state-level hierarchy headed by the governor, then they could probe for support within the federal-level ministries. If they failed to locate allies in one ministry, then they could try another. Ordinarily, they applied pressure on all fronts simultaneously, and often they at least secured some middle-level allies who would try to intervene on their behalf at higher levels. If ultimately they failed to locate high-level support, the ejidatario leaders waited for political successions, which took place at the state and federal levels every few years. The odds were fairly good that a succession would bring them an ally, and thus they always hastened to press their demands and probe for support after any major succession. As we have seen, significant government support—and thus significant developments in the ejidal power struggle, if not the reform struggle—usually came as the result of political successions.

In general, the leaders of an ejidatario opposition struggle enjoyed optimum levels of support when a majority of the politically active ejidatarios (about two-thirds to three-fourths of the total number of ejidatarios) were on their side, and when the CNC secretary-general and at least one high-level official served as their allies. The high-level officials whose support was historically most critical were the Agrarian Department chiefs, the secretaries of agriculture, and the state governors. When the ejidatario opposition leaders secured just one of these as an ally, their chances of gaining the president's sympathy, successfully countering their opponents, and thus securing major concessions were markedly improved.

The CNC played a vital role, even though it had no authority to set policy. It was the CNC, not the Agrarian Department or the federal ministries, that spearheaded the federal authorities' penetration of Jenkins's domain in 1946–47 and provided the critical mediating link between the ejidatarios and the federal government. During 1950–52 criticisms of Jaramillo transmitted through a CNC affiliate, the National Cane Producers' Union, as well as the CNC's own lack of support for Jaramillo, aided the government's emerging campaign against the Jaramillo regime. During 1953–54 sympathy and support from top CNC officials legitimized the Jaramillistas' minority opposition to the state-controlled Guerrero regime. During 1960–61 strong support and careful guidance from the CNC greatly helped the Ramírez faction to wrest control of the cooperative from the Reorganizing Commission, to win easily their power struggle against the collaborationist faction, and to establish a new regime. Ramírez's control over the ejidal complex was most secure when CNC support for him was strongest, as in 1961–62 and 1965–67. By the same token, when CNC attention to the minority opposition within the ejido was strongest, then Ramírez's control was weakest, the ejido's political stability was threatened, and the minority won concessions from the government, as in 1962–65, when Chief Barrios ordered the division of the ejido, and in 1967–69, when independent local ejidal credit societies were established in Raboso and Teruel.

No other organization defending peasant interests had comparable policy effects. During 1955–61 the neo-Jaramillistas relied in part on the moderately leftist National Zapatista Front, which did lobby vigorously on their behalf and certainly provided an alternative channel for gaining the government's attention. Nevertheless, there is no evidence to indicate that sponsorship by the Zapatista Front directly resulted in any major breakthrough for the neo-Jaramillistas. The Front apparently rendered some tactical assistance, but could offer little tactical gain.

Other peasant defense organizations were even less useful and less attractive as sponsors, though individuals and small groups opportunistically flirted with them at times when effective recourse to the CNC was not a possibility. In particular, guidance from the communist CCI was rejected because it would only endanger the ejidatarios' relations with the government. A working relationship with the noncommunist CCI did not come about either, because the landless villagers it represented were generally considered unwelcome competitors for the ejidal lands, and because government officials frowned on the organization.

To summarize, CNC sponsorship was in effect required for major breakthroughs by the leaders of an ejidatario opposition struggle. Without CNC support it was practically impossible to win support at higher levels of government. By contrast, alliance with an anti-government lobby tended to be counterproductive, for the government would not let it win.

Tactics. Given the ejidatarios' preference for the reformist strategy, what tactics were the most suitable and effective for them to use? Broadly speaking, the ejidatarios have resorted to four types of tactics: legal proceedings, bureaucratic lobbying, agitation and propaganda, and direct action. Whatever the tactic, including direct action, their most common and most successful style of dealing with the government has combined firmness with respectfulness. Firmness in presenting their demands earned the government's attention, while their own respectful attitude, especially toward the president and the Republic as such, confirmed the reformist quality of the struggle and thus warranted some government responsiveness.

Two tactics commonly used in reform struggles in other countries were simply not significant in Atencingo: electoral campaigning and political lobbying through elected officials. At the local level winning election to ejidal office depended not so much on campaigning for the office as on successfully waging a power struggle by other tactics. At the state and federal levels peasants could exercise only marginal influence over the selection and election of party candidates. Moreover, elected officials, aside from the president and the governor, rarely became involved in agrarian struggles once they took office. Instead they tended to remain on the fringes as defenders of the politically powerful individuals and institutions to whom they owed their posts and privileges. Civil servants in the bureaucracy were far more likely than elected officials to aid an ejidatario reform movement, for the bureaucracies and the executive offices—not the legislatures or political parties—were the real centers of responsibility and decision.

Of the four tactics specified at the start of this section, legal proceedings were historically the least effective. This was especially evident during the 1952–60 period, when a multitude of juridical pleas by the ousted Jaramillistas obtained no favorable responses in the courts. The three remaining tactics, however, were all extremely valuable.

Bureaucratic lobbying, conducted through some combination of commissions and petitions, was an essential ingredient of all struggles; indeed, it was the standard tactic. Once the decision was made to work through the system no other tactic served so well to inform the government about the ejidatarios' needs and intentions and to probe for political allies. Indeed, the government had institutionalized bureaucratic lobbying as the preferred mode for resolving political disputes. The CNC, a sector of the official political party, constituted little more than a vehicle for bureaucratic lobbying on behalf of the Mexican peasantry. Yet government officials found it all too easy to stall and temporize on their own ground, within the bureaucracy— no doubt one reason why they were so eager to have the ejidatarios take their problems there. Accordingly bureaucratic lobbying alone rarely—perhaps never—served to win concessions from the government. In addition to lobbying the peasants had to resort to tougher tactics, such as agitation and direct action, to elicit a favorable response from high-level officials.

Agitation in conjunction with propaganda was an indispensable tactic for any opposition struggle by peasants, owing to its many uses in acquiring and demonstrating a tactical or strategic advantage. Within the ejido agitation and propaganda served locally to direct attention to the weaknesses in the existing administration, to attract new partisans to the opposition, to test the leadership capabilities of the major ejidal factions, and to demonstrate the opposition's capacity to mobilize. At the state and federal levels they served to publicize the opposition struggle, perhaps to embarrass the government, to gain the attention of government officials, to get official investigators into the fields, to undermine government support for the existing administration, and even to attract government support for the opposition.

Useful as it was, in only one instance did agitation directly win a major concession from the government—in 1957 when Governor Ortega displaced Guerrero as manager. In that instance, however, the concession could be credited less to the ejidatarios' pressures for reform than to the new governor's opportunistic desire to establish personal control over the lucrative cooperative. Nevertheless, given a modicum of popular and government support, agitation did sometimes serve to win concessions on minor issues, especially if it seemed likely to escalate into direct action. Thus after Jaramillo's assassination, agitation coupled with popular support enabled the opposition within the ejido to win the cooperative society elections. Earlier the Jaramillo regime used agitation and propaganda to defend its claim to the lands involved in the enlargement of the ejido. Agitation was also the tactic most often used to defend personal and group interests during fieldwork on the technical tasks. In some cases local agitation and propaganda incurred harsh repressive measures, as evidenced by the assassinations during the Guerrero and Ramírez administrations. Yet the assassinations brought increased popular support for the opposition, thus enhancing the effectiveness of further agitation and propaganda.

The fourth tactic, direct action, also played a major role in the various opposition struggles. Violent confrontation and a work stoppage enabled the ejidatarios to win control of the cooperative in 1946–47. Building seizures, a miniature coup d'état, and a threatened work stoppage helped convince the federal government to return control of the cooperative to the ejidatarios in 1960–61. A dramatic march to Mexico City moved authorities to order the liquidation of the cooperative and the division of the ejido in 1964. And a twenty-day demonstration, combined with a work stoppage in three annexes, won the administrative independence of two annexes in 1968–69.

In each case the direct action tactic forced a major breakthrough. Direct actions enabled the opposition leaders to mobilize popular support, to generate sensational news that embarrassed the government, to provide government supporters with evidence of the urgent need for concessions, to counter the bureaucratic and political influence of their opponents, and to gain the direct attention of top government officials, even the president. Given strategic support, no other tactic served so well to threaten the government's fundamental political and economic interests. Thus, given a strategic advantage, no other tactic served so well to precipitate a crisis and win major concessions from the high-level authorities. Certainly no major breakthroughs were ever achieved by an ejidatario opposition faction without resort to direct action.

Such tactics were fundamentally reformist rather than revolutionary or radical in significance, despite their occasional antigovernment overtones and violent results. They were simply a way of demonstrating power in a system that required the demonstration of power as a precondition for reform. Indeed, in terms of the historical experiences and standards of the region, direct action tactics were just an essential part of the political game, tactics the government was prepared to accept and manage, with the help of its police and army.

Yet direct actions were never in themselves sufficient for success, either on major or on minor issues. The invading landless villagers were repulsed in 1937, 1939, and 1967 without achieving their objectives. The Jaramillo regime cut back its cane production, but failed to win its battle against the mill administration during 1949–51. The ejidatarios who invaded their own annexes in 1949 failed to secure separate ejidos. In 1954 the work stoppage attempted by the Jaramillistas was readily suppressed. And in 1963 the state governor simply rebuffed the ejidatarios who marched toward Puebla to demonstrate their opposition to the Ramírez regime. In each of these cases the peasant opposition forces lacked sufficient government support, or popular support, or both; as a result, they lacked the strategic advantage necessary for the tactic's success. By contrast, when a large popular following and influential government allies already supported a peasant opposition struggle, and when high-level government officials were already preparing some major resolution of the conflict, then direct action tactics served as a final dramatic pressure that forced the government to act.

As a rule, then, the success or failure of a given tactic depended on the strategic context; that is, the tactic was only as effective as the strategic support it actively demonstrated. Thus the leaders of a reformist struggle had the least success with legalistic appeals and only slightly better success with simple bureaucratic lobbying, for such tactics operated within bureaucratic confines where elite interests were best protected and popular support was least significant. By the same token they had more success when, given substantial popular and government support, they supplemented their bureaucratic lobbying with agitation, and still more success when they resorted to direct action, the tactic that most dramatically demonstrated the extent of their support and at the same time forced the government to respond.

Government Strategy and Tactics

Strategy. In general the government relied on a strategy of cooptation and control, though in a crisis it might resort temporarily to a strategy of direct intervention or even repression.* Ultimately the strategy of cooptation and control rested on the government's ability to maintain a united front in defending elite interests, to coopt opposition leaders, and to demobilize popular support for any recalcitrant opposition leaders who could not be coopted. Of course, this strategy ran counter to the opposition's objectives of rallying popular support and locating key allies within the government, while resisting cooptation. It worked basically because, as described earlier, the closely knit ruling elites of Mexico had amassed over time an enormous concentration of power in their central government and party institutions, including the military.

What made the system—and thus the strategy—so durable was, first of all, the remarkable elite integration of the so-called Revolutionary Family of top leaders—and second, the institutionalization of a vast

---

* The original treatment of cooptation and control in Mexico is Bo Anderson and James Cockcroft's "Control and Cooptation in Mexican Politics," *International Journal of Comparative Sociology*, VII (March 1966), 11–28. A definition of cooptation is "the process of absorbing new elements into the leadership or policy-determining strata of an organization as a means of averting threats to its existence or stability"; Philip Selznick, *TVA and the Grassroots* (Berkeley, Calif., 1949), p. 259. The best current discussion of general political practices is contained in Roger D. Hansen, *The Politics of Mexican Development* (Baltimore, 1971).

middle-level bureaucracy whose obedient functionaries were tightly controlled through the patronage powers of the top elites. This bureaucracy was carefully attuned to the protection of elite interests. The middle-level bureaucrats accordingly became the major instruments of cooptation and control in Mexico.

Tactics. In practice the government's strategy as applied to the Atencingo case took the form of several outstanding tactics. First, government officials did everything possible to immerse the peasants deeply in elaborate and time-consuming bureaucratic procedures, thus deflecting their attention away from the major reform goals. Advisers and counselors were appointed by the CNC and other agencies to analyze the ejidatarios' problems and to mediate between the ejidatarios and elite groups. Numerous meetings were held with the ejidatarios, and eventually they were given an audience with a high-level official, if not several high-level officials. Universally respected presidential decrees and other agrarian laws were invoked; and lengthy procedures were outlined for settling and resolving conflicts step by step. Sometimes conflicts of interest and lack of coordination among various government agencies further complicated the process and delayed any final resolution. Meanwhile, promises were routinely made and broken by government officials. The weight of evidence accumulated over the years indicates strongly that the primary purpose of such extensive efforts to bureaucratize the opposition struggles was to allow government officials to temporize as long as possible while they maneuvered to coopt or demobilize the opposition.

Among the most potent and striking devices used by the government as a delaying tactic were the technical tasks—the ejidal census and the survey and mapping of the ejidal lands. Even after thirty years the Agrarian Department and the state Agrarian Delegation still had not completed the tasks: several attempts by various teams of engineers had produced only defective surveys and inaccurate maps; and the ejidal census always needed another revision or updating. Moreover, it appeared that this disorganization might continue indefinitely. From a strictly technical and legal standpoint, indeed, the ejidal grant had never been definitively authorized, for such a step would require an acceptable census and survey.

If Atencingo and annexes had been an arid little ejido with natural boundaries, then the technical tasks might have been completed smoothly. But the ejido was invaluable property, the size of nine large ejidos, and hence the object of bitter internal and external power struggles, routinely involving government officials at all levels, the ejidatarios' covetous neighbors, and of course the ejidatarios themselves. As a result the technical tasks had become inextricably politicized, the deliberate casualties of agitation, intrigue, and bureaucratic manipulation. Land reform was obstructed by the lack of an acceptable survey; ejidal rights and hence local elections were controlled by census revision. Thus the technical tasks remained powerful weapons for middle-level bureaucrats to use in preserving the status quo.

Second, government officials vigorously endeavored to reduce a power-and-reform struggle into a simple local power struggle. They typically considered the major cause of the unrest to be the personal demagogic ambitions of peasant opposition leaders—an interpretation that complemented their strategy of cooptation. Of course, to some extent this interpretation was correct: often peasant leaders would put off acting on reform goals once they were in office, as illustrated especially by the case of Ramírez. Yet it appeared to have a deeper purpose: by treating agrarian unrest as merely the result of local power struggles, government officials avoided any implication that the course of the Mexican Revolution itself was at stake, and that only fundamental reforms could solve the peasants' problems.

Third, government officials—and the mill administration—apparently sought to keep the ejidatarios politically weak by encouraging factionalism among them, or at least by attempting to reap political advantage from the factionalism that developed. Certainly the government and the mill administration during the early 1950's manipulated a coalition of landless villagers and dissident ejidatarios to subvert the Jaramillo administration so that the government could justify intervention. Later the balanced factionalism within the ejido—despite the problems it caused for the government—not only kept the opposition force from overthrowing Ramírez (at least for a time) but also kept Ramírez, as chief delegate of the credit society, from becoming such a regional power that he could make further inroads on the mill's contractual supremacy. It appears that over a period of time the government, much to its benefit, managed to some extent to transform what had once been a peasant struggle against the mill administration and the government into an internal struggle between competing peasant factions.

Finally, given a crisis and the necessity of making some concessions in order to demobilize the ejidatario opposition, the government's standard formula was to grant power but withhold reform. Repeatedly—as in the 1946 Jaramillista succession, the 1955 neo-Jaramillista succession, the 1961 Ramirecista succession, and the 1969 administrative division of the credit society—the government resolved a crisis by enabling opposition leaders to gain administrative control while postponing indefinitely action on any promised parcellation, division, or diversification of the ejido. This tactic not only demobilized what had become a threatening mass opposition but brought the opposition leaders into the institutional network, where the government could most easily coopt them through patronage, bribery, and the like. Moreover, once in office the ejidatario leaders were further restricted by their heavy dependence on government advice for the successful management of the complex ejidal enterprise.

The Consequences of Struggle in Atencingo

Over time, what lasting changes did the ejidatarios achieve? Despite a few dramatic breakthroughs, they made very halting progress toward what generally constituted their ultimate structural reform objectives—the parcellation and division of the ejido, and the diversification of the ejido's agriculture—or toward administrative independence for each of the ejido's nine sections, a slightly less prominent objective. When founded in 1937 the giant ejido was entirely collective; it was dedicated to cane agriculture, except for the rice grown in rotation with cane; and it was centrally administered. After 1946 the ejidatario opposition did secure managerial independence from the mill administration and gained limited rights to grow some crops other than cane on very small private plots, in rotation with the cane and rice. In 1964 the old cooperative society was supplanted by a credit society, but without bringing any real administrative changes. In

1969 two annexes did win administrative independence with the establishment of separate credit societies, though they remained subject to the ejido's charter. After thirty years of opposition struggles, then, the ejido still had not been divided, though some progress had been made toward administrative decentralization; it was still basically collective; and it was still confined largely to cane agriculture.

For the most part, the opposition struggles had served merely to bring about political and administrative successions within the ejido and the cooperative, as control—and economic perquisites—circulated among the leaders of different factions. In addition, with government assistance the ejidatarios did win a more favorable contract with the mill. Moreover, they could point to some general socioeconomic progress in their living standards. Yet historically this progress appears to have been less the consequence of agrarian struggle than of the government's increasing intentions and capabilities to modernize the countryside gradually.

This outcome gives dramatic testimony to the power and stability of the government's system of control. Historically the ejidatarios relied on the most appropriate strategy and tactics open to them, given their strategic position as a relatively powerless group. But that was no guarantee of eventual victory. The ejidatarios achieved some changes, especially in the area of administration. Yet the government, and hence to some degree the mill administration, must on balance be considered the real winner of the agrarian struggle in Atencingo. With its wide range of resources, including in times of crisis the military and police forces, the government was far more powerful than the ejidatarios. In particular, the high degree of elite integration throughout government ranks enabled the highest government authorities to stand firm in their defense of established political and economic interests over the years. As a result the government's strategy of cooptation and control proved highly effective. For decades major structural reforms were deferred and economic stability was preserved in the Atencingo region, even while the overt political allegiance of the ejidatarios was sustained.

Notes

Notes

Dates have been converted to a short form in the Notes: e.g., vii.49 for July 1949, and 23.vii.49 for July 23, 1949. The following abbreviations have been used for archival sources, which are described in the Preface:

FNCCI: "Field Notes on the CCI Archives"
FNDA: "Field Notes on the DAAC Archives"
FNGA: "Field Notes on 1969 General Assemblies"
MACNCI: "Materials from an Archive on a CNC Investigation"
MAEM: "Materials from the Archives of Esteban Martínez"
MAPBAC: "Materials from the Archives of Pedro Bueno and Alfredo Carranza"

Chapter Two

1. Interview with Esteban Martínez, 14.vi.69; interview with Dr. Castro, director of the Puebla Institute of Anthropology and History, iv.69.

2. Interview with Martínez, 14.vi.69.

3. See John Womack, Jr., *Zapata and the Mexican Revolution* (New York, 1968), pp. 346–51.

4. An open secret in Puebla. For some biographical material on Jenkins, see "Meet Mr. Jenkins," *Time*, 26.xii.60, pp. 25–26.

5. The preceding three paragraphs on Jenkins are based chiefly on Efrén Osorio Palacios to Agrarian Dept. chief, 19.vii.37, FNDA, pp. 18–20; and on the interview with Martínez, 14.vi.69. The figure for the total size of Jenkins's holdings appears in several places, including the report of the CNC's secretary of cooperative action, José María Suárez Téllez, to the CNC National Executive Committee, 14.xii.53, MAPBAC. The figure for the size of the cultivable lands comes from a memorandum of Martínez, 25.viii.60, MAEM. Curiously, the size of the former haciendas was put at 90,242 hectares by DAAC chief Roberto Barrios (memo to

DAAC gen. director of new population centers, 28.iii.62, FNDA, p. 322).

6. The preceding three paragraphs are based on Martínez, memo, 25.viii.60, MAEM; and on the interview with Martínez, 14.vi.69. The figures on crop yields were reported by representatives of peasants of the Atencingo complex in their petition for an ejidal grant, 9.ix.37, FNDA, p. 4.

7. Interview with Martínez, 14.vi.69.

8. Confirmed by Osorio Palacios to Agrarian Dept. chief, 19.vii.37, FNDA, pp. 19–20.

9. The section on Dolores Campos de Espinosa is based almost entirely on the biography of her in Manuel Sánchez Espinosa, *Atencingo de Cárdenas a López Mateos, 1937–1963* (Puebla, 1963), pp. 6–19. Information about the CROM and labor agitation came from interviews with Juan Gómez, a former ejidatario, 31.vii.69, and Alberto Sánchez, an ejidatario, 18.vi.69. In addition Osorio Palacios (letter to Agrarian Dept. chief, 19.vii.37, FNDA, p. 20) stated that Doña Lola had sympathizers among the leaders of the workers, but that they went over to Jenkins's side, probably as a result of bribes. The development of the local syndicate is discussed in Chapter 3. No additional information is available about the policies of the ejidal grants made during the mid-1930's.

10. Suárez Téllez, report to CNC National Executive Committee, 14.xii.53, MAPBAC; representatives of peasants of the Atencingo complex, petition for an ejidal grant, 9.ix.37, FNDA, p. 4.

11. Interview with Martínez, 14.vi.69.

12. Osorio Palacios to Agrarian Dept. chief, 19.vii.37, FNDA, p. 20.

13. Sánchez Espinosa, pp. 21–22, 51; *El Sol de Puebla* (the Puebla daily newspaper), 26.vi.37.

14. *El Sol de Puebla,* 7.vii.37.

15. The fullest account is to be found in Sánchez Espinosa, pp. 23–24.

16. "Meet Mr. Jenkins," p. 25.

17. Described in Sánchez Espinosa, pp. 24–26, 48–51.

18. *Ibid.,* pp. 25, 51.

19. Undated letter from Vicente Lombardo Toledano, CTM sec.-gen., and Mariano Padilla, CTM sec. of peasant action, to President Cárdenas, FNDA, pp. 9–10; Gov. Maximino Avila Camacho, provisional approval of Atencingo ejidal grant, 5.x.37, FNDA, p. 8. The latter document appears to reflect accurately the position taken by the governor at the Veracruz meeting with the president. The former document also contains some information about the governor's position. Even though it is undated, I take it to be the letter Lombardo Toledano sent to the president before the Veracruz interview, especially since another document (see note 23

below) contains a verbatim quote from it as part of materials read at the interview, and since Suárez Téllez (report to the CNC National Executive Committee, 14.xii.53, MAPBAC) gives August 23, 1937, as the date of such a letter by Lombardo Toledano.

20. Lombardo Toledano and Padilla to Cárdenas, undated, FNDA, pp. 9–10.

21. Sánchez Espinosa, pp. 48–49; "Meet Mr. Jenkins," p. 25.

22. Summaries of the original petitions are contained in FNDA, pp. 1–3.

23. Representatives of peasants of the Atencingo complex, petition for an ejidal grant, 9.ix.37, FNDA, pp. 4–7.

24. A full description appears in articles 199–263 of the Agrarian Code; see *Código agrario de los Estados Unidos Mexicanos* (Mexico City, 1968).

25. Suárez Téllez, report to CNC National Executive Committee, 14.xii.53, MAPBAC.

26. *Ibid.*

27. The decree appears in "Resolución en el expediente de dotación de ejidos al poblado de Atencingo y Anexas, Estado de Puebla," *Diario Oficial de la Federación* (Mexico City), 21.iv.38.

28. Guillermo Coronel y Aburto, Mixed Agrarian Commission engineer, preliminary report to the president of the Mixed Agrarian Commission, 1.x.37, FNDA, p. 7; Pres. Rosendo de la Peña and members of the Mixed Agrarian Commission, final report and proposal to the governor, 5.x.37, FNDA, pp. 7–8.

29. Interview with Guillermo Covarrubias, ejidatario, 5.vi.69.

30. Interview with Fidel Echeverría, ejidatario, 11.viii.69.

31. The figure 5,000 is cited in an article on a study by the state governor in *El Sol de Puebla*, 19.viii.37. The figure 4,000 was reported by representatives of peasants of the Atencingo complex, petition for an ejidal grant, 9.ix.37, FNDA, p. 6.

32. Pointed out by Coronel y Aburto, report to president of the Mixed Agrarian Commission, 1.x.37, FNDA, p. 7.

33. President de la Peña and members of the Mixed Agrarian Commission, final report and proposal to the governor, 5.x.37, FNDA, p. 8.

34. Unfortunately I have not seen a copy of the original authorization. The short description given here is based on the interview with Gómez, 31.vii.69; on Suárez Téllez, report to CNC National Executive Committee, 14.xii.53, MAPBAC; and on José Antonio Cobos, gen. director of cooperative development, Secretariat of National Economy, and Contran Noble, gen. director of ejidal development, Secretariat of Agriculture, investigative report to superiors, 3.i.52, FNDA, pp. 23–51.

35. Quoted in "Meet Mr. Jenkins," p. 25.

Chapter Three

1. Indicated by an unattributed Agrarian Dept. report, 9.v.39, FNDA, pp. 11–12; and by ejidal commissariat of Chietla to Gov. Maximino Avila Camacho, 1938, as noted in FNDA, p. 86.

2. See p. 63 above.

3. Guillermo Davis, Agrarian Dept. inspector, confidential memo to Agrarian Dept. chief, 17.vi.46, FNDA, p. 84; also indicated by Atencingo ejidal commissariat and cooperative representatives, tele. to Pres. Lázaro Cárdenas, 19.x.38, FNDA, p. 20.

4. Davis, memo to Agrarian Dept. chief, 17.vi.46, FNDA, p. 84. See also Chapter 4 below.

5. Atencingo ejidal commissariat and cooperative representatives, tele. to Cárdenas, 19.x.38, FNDA, p. 20.

6. Avila Camacho to Gabino Vázquez, Agrarian Dept. chief, 26.x.38, FNDA, p. 20.

7. Aarón Merino Fernández, agrarian del., letter, xi.38, FNDA, p. 12.

8. Merino Fernández, letter, 3.v.39, FNDA, pp. 12–13.

9. Merino Fernández, letter, 27.iv.39, FNDA, pp. 13–14.

10. Manuel Sánchez Espinosa, *Atencingo de Cárdenas a López Mateos, 1937–1963* (Puebla, 1963), pp. 15–17.

11. Merino Fernández, letter to his superiors, 3.v.39, FNDA, pp. 12–13.

12. *Ibid.*; Sánchez Espinosa, p. 17.

13. Sánchez Espinosa (p. 14) reprints a letter from President Cárdenas to the regional military commander in Puebla directing him to extend protection to Doña Lola and her associates. See also *ibid.*, pp. 17–18.

14. Interview with Juan Gómez, former ejidatario, 31.vii.69; Sánchez Espinosa, p. 19.

15. Notes on the official denials appear in FNDA, pp. 1–3.

16. In the "Acta de posesión provisional," 20.xii.37, FNDA, p. 11.

17. Notes on "Acta de posesión definitiva de ejido," 18.vi.38, FNCCI.

18. See Chapter 4 below.

19. Merino Fernández to Agrarian Dept. sec.-gen., 2.x.39, FNDA, p. 21; Cliserio Villafuente, Agrarian Dept. sec.-gen., letter, 1940, FNDA, p. 21.

20. Unnamed Agrarian Dept. official, orders to Merino Fernández, 6.i.40, FNDA, p. 21; Alfonso Balderrama, agrarian del., report to his superiors, 14.vii.47, FNDA, pp. 239–40.

21. Confirmed by Guillermo Coronel y Aburto, Mixed Agrarian Commission engineer, report on the provisional ejidal grant, xii.38, FNDA, p. 10.

22. On the ejidal offices see the Agrarian Code (*Código agrario de los Estados Unidos Mexicanos* [Mexico City, 1968]).

23. Interview with Gómez, 31.vii.69.

24. Interview with Guillermo Covarrubias, ejidatario, 5.vi.69; commissioned peasants of Atencingo and annexes, *El caso de los campesinos de Atencingo y Anexas: Carta abierta al Sr. Presidente de la República* (Atencingo, 31.xii.54), p. 6.

25. Interview with Covarrubias, 5.vi.69; ejidal commissariat, cooperative administration council, and manager of the cooperative, letter to Pres. Miguel Alemán Valdés and to the Agrarian Dept. chief, 1.viii.49, FNDA, p. 234.

26. Interview with Covarrubias, 5.vi.69.

27. The practices of Jenkins and Pérez in this regard are common knowledge in the Atencingo region. They were mentioned in particular by Esteban Martínez in an interview, 14.vi.69.

28. Interview with Covarrubias, 5.vi.69.

29. Jaramillo's observations in this section are taken from his letter to Cárdenas, 19.v.39, FNDA, pp. 14–16. Treatments of Jaramillo's life are found in Rubén M. Jaramillo and Froylán C. Manjarrez, *Rubén Jaramillo: Autobiografía y Asesinato* (Mexico City, 1963), and in Carlos Fuentes, "La Muerte de Rubén Jaramillo," *Cuadernos Americanos* (Mexico City), no. 6, 1971, pp. 160–71.

30. Interview with Covarrubias, 5.vi.69.

31. Guillermo Davis, Agrarian Dept. inspector, confidential memo to Agrarian Dept. chief, 17.vi.46, FNDA, p. 81.

32. Interview with Covarrubias, 5.vi.69.

33. Davis, memo to Agrarian Dept. chief, 17.vi.46, FNDA, p. 81.

34. Collective interview with ejidatarios of San Nicolás Tolentino, 12.viii.69.

35. The most specific statement was made by Covarrubias (interview, 5.vi.69). No one informed me that dividends were distributed after the first couple of years, but *El Sol de Puebla* (7.vii.42) reported a total dividend for 1941–42 of 408,600 pesos.

36. Interview with Efraín González, ejidatario, 4.vii.69.

37. Collective interview with ejidatarios of San Nicolás Tolentino, 4.vii.69.

38. The most authoritative statement is Davis's (memo to Agrarian Dept. chief, 17.vi.46, FNDA, p. 82).

39. Collective interview with ejidatarios of San Nicolás Tolentino, 12.viii.69.

40. Interview with Pedro Bueno, ejidatario, 19.v.69.

41. Commissioned peasants of Atencingo and Annexes, *El caso de los campesinos*, p. 4.

42. *Ibid.*, pp. 6–7.

43. Interview with Juan Gómez, former ejidatario, 31.vii.69.
44. Interview with Covarrubias, 5.vi.69.
45. Interview with Sr. Rufino Mejía, former ejidatario, 31.vii.69.
46. Interview with Francisco Aguilar, ejidatario, 28.vii.69.
47. Cipriano L. Reyes, ejidal commissariat pres., and J. Guadalupe Ramírez Vargas, administration council pres., to Roberto Barrios, Agrarian Dept. chief, 10.ix.59, FNDA, p. 290.
48. Interview with Aguilar, 28.vii.69.
49. Interview with Gómez, 31.vii.69.
50. Reported esp. by Esteban Martínez in interview, 14.vi.69.
51. Reported esp. by Covarrubias in interview, 5.vi.69.
52. Interview with Gómez, 31.vii.69.
53. Manuel Sánchez Espinosa, *Atencingo de Cárdenas a López Mateos, 1937–1963* (Puebla, 1963), p. 19.
54. Interview with Covarrubias, 5.vi.69.
55. Interview with Gómez, 31.vii.69.
56. Interview with Covarrubias, 5.vi.69.
57. *Ibid.*
58. Interview with Martínez, 14.vi.69.
59. Interview with Aguilar, 28.vii.69; interview with Gómez, 31.vii.69.
60. Interview with Covarrubias, 5.vi.69.
61. *Ibid.*
62. Luís G. Rodríguez, Agrarian Dept. director, to agrarian del., 5.iv.46, FNDA, p. 22.
63. Agrarian del., tele. to his superiors, 2.v.46, FNDA, p. 89.
64. Language reported by Gabriel Leyva Velásquez, CNC sec.-gen., in a letter to Silvano Barba González, Agrarian Dept. chief, 14.v.46, FNDA, p. 77.
65. *Ibid.*
66. *Ibid.*
67. *Ibid.*
68. Marte R. Gómez, sec. of agriculture, to Agrarian Dept. chief, 22.v.46, FNDA, pp. 79–80.
69. Guillermo Davis, Agrarian Dept. inspector, letter to his superiors, 10.vii.46, FNDA, p. 85.
70. According to William Jenkins, tele. to Pres. Manuel Avila Camacho, 11.ix.46, FNDA, p. 90.
71. "Acta de la asamblea general de ejidatarios de Atencingo y anexas," 4.vi.46, FNDA, p. 87.
72. Davis, memo to Agrarian Dept. chief, 17.vi.46, FNDA, pp. 80, 83; Davis, letter to his superiors, 10.vii.46, FNDA, p. 85. Jaramillo was present at the Colón meeting.

73. Davis, memo to Agrarian Dept. chief, 17.vi.46, FNDA, p. 83.

74. *Ibid.*, pp. 80–81; "Acta de la asamblea general de ejidatarios de Atencingo y anexas," 4.vi.46, FNDA, p. 87.

75. Davis, memo to Agrarian Dept. chief, 17.vi.46, FNDA, p. 83.

76. Manuel Hernández G., Agrarian Dept. official, memo, 17.ii.47, FNDA, p. 92.

77. Davis, memo to Agrarian Dept. chief, 17.vi.46, FNDA, pp. 81–85; Davis, letter to his superiors, 10.vii.46, FNDA, pp. 85–87.

78. Davis, memo to Agrarian Dept. chief, FNDA, p. 81.

79. *Ibid.*, pp. 84–85.

80. Most clearly expressed in an undated statement (probably September 1946) from an unknown Agrarian Department official, FNDA, pp. 89–90.

81. Jenkins, tele. to Pres. Avila Camacho, 11.ix.46, FNDA, pp. 90, 91.

82. Unidentified note in FNDA, p. 90.

83. Agrarian Dept. chief to sec. of national defense, 23.ix.46, FNDA, p. 91.

84. Mentioned in interview with Fidel Echeverría, ejidatario, 11.viii.69. More complete data on this period are available from the DAAC archives.

85. Agrarian Dept. chief to sec. of national defense, 23.ix.46, FNDA, pp. 91–92.

86. Figures from a copy of the original census, FNDA, p. 101.

87. Interview with Guillermo Covarrubias, ejidatario, 5.vi.69. The precise figure appears in the original census, but the notation system used in the census was difficult to interpret with confidence.

88. From a copy of the decree issued in December 1946 by President Alemán, FNDA, p. 189.

89. Interview with Covarrubias, 5.vi.69; interview with Francisco Aguilar, ejidatario, 28.vii.69. See also interview with Luís Espinosa, ejidatario, 31.vii.69.

90. Interview with Covarrubias, 5.vi.69.

91. Maximiliano Sánchez et al., memo to Pres. Miguel Alemán Valdés, 12.ii.47, FNDA, pp. 96–97; Sánchez et al., memo to Alemán, 26.ii.47, FNDA, pp. 97–98.

92. Florentino Figueroa, pres., and others of the cooperative councils, and Guadalupe Sandoval, ejidal commissariat pres., to Alemán, 14.iv.47, FNDA, pp. 38–39.

93. Ejidal commissariat to Agrarian Dept. officials, 19.i.47, FNDA, pp. 100–101.

94. Figueroa et al. and Sandoval to Alemán, 14.iv.47, FNDA, pp. 38–39.

95. Ejidal commissariat to Agrarian Dept. officials, 19.i.47, FNDA, p. 97.

96. José Antonio Cobos, gen. director of cooperative development, Secretariat of National Economy, and Contran Noble, gen. director of ejidal development, Secretariat of Agriculture, investigative report to superiors, 3.i.52, FNDA, p. 24.

97. José María Suárez Téllez, CNC sec. of cooperative action, report to CNC National Executive Committee, 14.xii.53. MAPBAC.

Chapter Four

1. Interview with Guillermo Covarrubias, ejidatario, 5.vi.69.

2. Florentino Figueroa, pres., and others of the cooperative councils, and Guadalupe Sandoval, pres. of ejidal commissariat, to Pres. Miguel Alemán Valdés, 14.iv.47, FNDA, pp. 38–39.

3. For the reactions of Criollo and Jenkins, see *ibid.*; for the Secretariat's maneuver, see a memo probably written by Jaramillo to Pres. Adolfo Ruíz Cortines, 1953, FNDA, p. 57.

4. Maximiliano Sánchez et al. to sec. of national economy, 26.ii.47, FNDA, pp. 98–99.

5. Maximiliano Sánchez et al. to Agrarian Dept. chief, 24.xi.47, FNDA, p. 102. This letter, a copy of which was sent to the CROM headquarters, also contained critical remarks about the new pro-CTM local syndicate in Atencingo. Such statements seem to be further evidence that Sánchez and his followers were part of a larger group coopted by the mill administration.

6. Details on some bloody shoot-outs appear in *El Sol de Puebla*, 23.x.47, 19.xii.47, 23.xii.47.

7. M. Sánchez et al., memos to Alemán, 12.ii.47 (FNDA, pp. 96–97) and 26.ii.47 (FNDA, pp. 97–98); Sánchez et al. to sec. of national economy, 26.ii.47, FNDA, pp. 98–99.

8. Remarked by Agrarian Dept. official Manuel Hernández G. in a memo, 17.ii.47, FNDA, p. 93; CNC sec.-gen. to Agrarian Dept. chief, 17.i.47, FNDA, p. 95.

9. Complaint reported by Agrarian Dept. sec.-gen. in letter to agrarian del., ix.46, FNDA, pp. 37–38.

10. Gen. Cándido Aguilar of the Peasant Affairs Coordinating Commission of the Presidency to Agrarian Dept. chief, 19.iv.47, FNDA, pp. 241–42.

11. Peasant Affairs Coordinating Commission of the Presidency, request to Agrarian Dept., late 1947, FNDA, p. 214.

12. Unattributed note, FNDA, p. 40; José Balderrama, agrarian del., major study on lands in the Matamoros valley, 14.vii.47, FNDA, p. 240.

13. The matter came up in Agrarian Dept. inspector Guillermo Davis's confidential memo to Agrarian Dept. chief, 17.vi.46, FNDA, p. 84.

14. William Jenkins to Agrarian Dept. officials, 1950, FNDA, p. 188.

15. Balderrama, major study on lands in the Matamoros valley, 14.vii.47, FNDA, pp. 239–41; the quotation is from *ibid.*, pp. 240–41.

16. From the original petition for enlargement, 11.x.47, FNDA, p. 76. It was published on December 23, 1947, in the state's official publication, *Periódico Oficial del Estado*, according to notes in FNDA, p. 76.

17. Balderrama to Agrarian Dept. chief, 30.vi.50, FNDA, p. 71.

18. *Ibid.*; also indicated by unattributed notes in FNDA, p. 190.

19. Balderrama to Agrarian Dept. sec.-gen., iii.49, FNDA, p. 110; Balderrama to Mario Sousa, Agrarian Dept. chief, 28.iii.49, FNDA, p. 238.

20. For the explanation given to the ejidal commissariat, see Balderrama's letter to Gregorio Maldonado, ejidal commissariat pres., x.49, FNDA, p. 111. For Jaramillo's request that the maps be made public, see his letter to the Agrarian Dept. sec.-gen., 11.iii.49, FNDA, p. 111. For the CNC's request, see Roberto Barrios Castro, CNC sec.-gen., to Gov. Carlos I. Betancourt, 17.x.49, FNDA, p. 76. And for the requests of officials who wanted to delimit the cane supply zone, see Contran Noble, gen. director of ejidal organization, Agrarian Dept., to Bureau of Lands and Waters, Agrarian Dept., 1948, FNDA, p. 214; and Agrarian Dept. sec.-gen. to agrarian del., vi.49, FNDA, p. 216.

21. Especially clear in Carlos Galarza, ejidal commissariat pres., to Agrarian Dept. chief, 11.x.47, FNDA, p. 55.

22. Gregorio Maldonado, pres., and others of the ejidal commissariat, Jesús Aguilar, pres., and others of the cooperative administration council, and Porfirio Jaramillo, cooperative manager, to Alemán and Agrarian Dept. chief, 1.viii.49, FNDA, pp. 232–37.

23. Census data briefly noted in FNDA, p. 76.

24. Balderrama to Agrarian Dept. officials, 31.viii.49, FNDA, p. 232.

25. "Resolución sobre ampliación de ejido al poblado Atencingo y anexos en Chietla, Puebla," *Diario Oficial de la Federación* (Mexico City), 13.iv.54, p. 3, in MAEM.

26. Balderrama, report to Agrarian Dept. chief, ix.49, FNDA, p. 227. The report also refers to some "minimum plan for this year."

27. Notes on unattributed Agrarian Dept. letter, probably 1950, FNDA, p. 224.

28. Galarza to Agrarian Dept. chief, 25.iv.50, FNDA, p. 55.

29. "Resolución sobre ampliación de ejido," p. 3; Balderrama, memo, 21.iv.50, FNDA, p. 225; Balderrama, report, 30.iv.50, FNDA, p. 226. The running disputes with Tilapa and Chietla, described in previous chapters, were decided in favor of Atencingo.

30. Mixed Agrarian Commission, report on the enlargement for Atencingo and annexes, 15.v.50, FNDA, pp. 190–91.

31. Noted in FNDA, p. 192; Jenkins to Agrarian Dept. officials, 1950, FNDA, p. 189.

32. Unattributed Agrarian Dept. memo, probably from 1950, FNDA, p. 70; Balderrama to Agrarian Dept. chief, 30.vi.50, FNDA, p. 71 (which contains the quote). Similar remarks were made by Balderrama in a letter written sometime in 1950 (FNDA, pp. 243–44).

33. Guadalupe Sandoval, ejidal commissariat pres., to Alemán, 10.ii.47, FNDA, p. 99; see also Noble to Agrarian Dept. sec.-gen., 11.iv.47, FNDA, p. 94.

34. Noble to Agrarian Dept. sec.-gen., 11.iv.47, FNDA, pp. 94–95.

35. Gen. Cándido Aguilar of the Peasant Affairs Coordinating Commission of the Presidency to Agrarian Dept. chief, 19.iv.47, FNDA, p. 242.

36. Interview with Guillermo Covarrubias, ejidatario, 5.vi.69; see also notes on an unclear document from January 1948, FNDA, p. 239.

37. Agrarian Dept. sec.-gen. to gen. director of ejidal organization, iii.49, FNDA, p. 111; ejidal commissariat, complaint to Agrarian Dept., 1949, FNDA, p. 215; Agrarian Dept. sec.-gen., memo, 20.x.50, FNDA, p. 108.

38. Interview with Francisco Aguilar, ejidatario, 28.vii.69.

39. Collective interview with ejidatarios of Raboso, 22.v.69.

40. From interview with Alfredo Carranza, ejidatario, 26.vii.69; this point was also specifically made by Esteban Martínez in an interview, 26.vii.69.

41. Interview with Carranza, 26.vii.69.

42. Interview with Pedro Bueno, ejidatario, 18.iv.69, 19.iv.69.

43. Interview with Benito Ojeda, ejidatario, 4.vii.69.

44. Point made especially in interview with Salvador Vásquez, ejidatario, 23.vii.69. Other sources are interview with Agustín Pineda, 22.v.69, and collective interview with ejidatarios from Raboso, 22.v.69.

45. Guillermo Davis, Agrarian Dept. inspector, confidential memo to Agrarian Dept. chief, 17.vi.46, FNDA, p. 84.

46. Noble to Agrarian Dept. sec.-gen., 11.iv.47, FNDA, pp. 94–95; Noble to Bureau of Lands and Waters, Agrarian Dept., 1948, FNDA, p. 214.

47. Gregorio Maldonado, ejidal commissariat pres., request to Agrarian Dept. officials, 1949, FNDA, p. 215.

48. Agrarian Dept. sec.-gen. to agrarian del., vi.49, FNDA, pp. 215–16. The quotation is from *ibid.*, p. 216.

49. M. Sánchez et al., memo to Alemán, 12.ii.47, FNDA, p. 96; interview with F. Aguilar, 28.vii.69. Bueno stated (interview, 19.v.69) that the special plots assigned for growing crops other than cane were one tarea per ejidatario.

50. José María Suárez Téllez, CNC sec. of cooperative action, report to CNC National Executive Committee, 14.xii.53, MAPBAC.

51. Interview with Covarrubias, 5.vi.69.

52. José Antonio Cobos, gen. director of cooperative development, Secretariat of National Economy, and Contran Noble, gen. director of ejidal development, Secretariat of Agriculture, investigative report to superiors, 3.i.52, FNDA, p. 29.

53. Suárez Téllez, report to CNC National Executive Committee, 14.xii.53, MAPBAC.

54. According to calculations provided in a statement distributed March 30, 1969, by the local ejidal credit society of Atencingo and annexes, FNGA.

55. Gregorio Maldonado, pres., and others of the ejidal commissariat, Jesús Aguilar, pres., and others of the cooperative administration council, and Porfirio Jaramillo, cooperative manager, to Alemán and Agrarian Dept. chief, 1.viii.49, FNDA, p. 235.

56. Suárez Téllez, report to CNC National Executive Committee, 14.xii.53, MAPBAC.

57. "Acta de inscripción de una acta constitutiva de la sociedad local de crédito ejidal de Atencingo y anexos," 8.vi.48, MAPBAC.

58. Cobos and Noble, investigative report to superiors, 3.i.52, FNDA, pp. 24–25, 27.

59. *Ibid.*, p. 29.

60. J. Aguilar, pres., and others of the administration council, and Jaramillo to Gov. Carlos I. Betancourt, 26.viii.49, FNDA, pp. 106–7; Alberto Espinosa and others of the Regional Caneworkers' Circle 83 and of the Local Executive Committee of Chietla to Agrarian Dept. chief Sousa, 16.x.50, FNDA, pp. 105–6.

61. J. Aguilar et al. and Jaramillo to Betancourt, 26.viii.49, FNDA, p. 107.

62. Commissioned peasants of Atencingo and annexes, *El caso de los campesinos de Atencingo y Anexas: Carta abierta al Sr. Presidente de la República* (Atencingo, 31.xii.54), p. 7.

63. Cobos and Noble, investigative report to superiors, 3.i.52, FNDA, p. 27.

64. J. Aguilar et al. and Jaramillo to Betancourt, 26.viii.49, FNDA, pp. 106–7.

65. *Ibid.*, pp. 106–8.

66. Commissioned peasants of Atencingo and annexes, *El caso de los campesinos*, p. 7.

67. Cobos and Noble, investigative report to superiors, 3.i.52, FNDA, p. 26.

68. Figures cited in Manuel Sánchez Espinosa, cooperative manager, to Arcadio Noguera, Agrarian Dept. subchief, 27.xi.59, FNDA, p. 299.

69. Interview with Jesús Ortega and Antonio Garza, ejidatarios, 4.vii.69.

70. Interview with Alfredo Carranza, ejidatario, 26.vii.69.

71. Interview with Covarrubias, 5.vi.69.

72. These points were stated most bluntly by Luís Espinosa, ejidatario (interview, 31.vii.69).

73. Commissioned peasants of Atencingo and annexes, *El caso de los campesinos*, p. 8.

74. This point was made most clearly by Fidel Echeverría, ejidatario (interview, 11.viii.69).

75. That Espinosa collaborated with the mill administration was stated most pointedly by Covarrubias (interview, 5.vi.69).

76. Agrarian Del. Balderrama to Agrarian Dept. chief, 30.vi.50, FNDA, p. 71.

77. For the division proposal see A. Espinosa et al. to Agrarian Dept. chief Sousa, 16.x.50, FNDA, pp. 105–6; for the parcellation proposal see National Cane Producers' Union sec.-gen., tele. to Agrarian Dept. chief, 7.xii.50, FNDA, p. 224.

78. Representatives of the Puebla Peasants' Federation "General Miguel Alemán," memo to Alemán, 1951, FNDA, pp. 224–25.

79. *Ibid.*, p. 225; A. Espinosa et al. to Sousa, 16.x.50, FNDA, p. 106.

80. Unknown Agrarian Dept. official, memo to superiors in the Agrarian Dept., 20.x.50, FNDA, pp. 108–9.

81. Balderrama, report to superiors, 30.vi.50, FNDA, p. 226; see also various petitions to the Agrarian Department for another survey from such places as Pueblo Nuevo de Porfirio Díaz, Viborillas de Hidalgo, Ranchería La Cofradía, and others, all from March 1951 (FNDA, pp. 217–18).

82. Balderrama, letter, 1950, FNDA, pp. 216–17; sec. of Mixed Agrarian Commission to Agrarian Dept. Bureau of Statistics, x.50, FNDA, pp. 218–19; Agrarian Dept. official, informative memo, 1950, FNDA, p. 70. In addition, notes in FNDA (p. 191) indicate that private properties in the area were not surveyed—meaning also that the boundaries with the ejido were not defined.

83. A. Espinosa to Agrarian Dept., vii.51, FNDA, p. 219; Carlos Galarza to Agrarian Dept. chief, 25.iv.50, FNDA, p. 55.

84. Balderrama to Agrarian Dept. chief, 30.vi.50, FNDA, p. 71.

85. Balderrama to Agrarian Dept. Bureau of Lands and Waters, 28.iii.-51, FNDA, p. 104.

86. *Ibid.* See also similar remarks by Balderrama in a letter, 1950, FNDA, pp. 243–44.

87. Galarza to Alemán and Agrarian Dept. chief, 7.v.51, FNDA, pp. 55–56.
88. Cipriano L. Reyes, ejidal commissariat pres., and J. Guadalupe Ramírez Vargas, administration council pres., to Roberto Barrios, Agrarian Dept. chief, 10.ix.59, FNDA, p. 290; M. Sánchez et al. to Agrarian Dept. chief, 24.xi.47, FNDA, p. 102.
89. Manuel Sánchez Espinosa, *Atencingo de Cárdenas a López Mateos, 1937–1963* (Puebla, 1963), pp. 29, 52.
90. The open letter to President Alemán was signed on February 28, 1951, and was published in *Excélsior* (Mexico City daily newspaper), 2.iii.51.
91. Commissioned peasants of Atencingo and annexes, *El caso de los campesinos,* p. 5.
92. *Ibid.,* pp. 8–9.
93. *Ibid.,* p. 8; Sánchez Espinosa, p. 29.
94. Interview with Jesús Ortega and Antonio Garza, ejidatarios, 4.vii.69.
95. Teodoro Sánchez et al., petition to Pres. Adolfo Ruíz Cortines, 27.iv.53, FNDA, p. 59.
96. Interview with Echeverría, 11.viii.69.
97. José Antonio Cobos, gen. director of cooperative development, Secretariat of National Economy, and Contran Noble, gen. director of ejidal development, Secretariat of Agriculture, investigative report to superiors, 3.i.52, FNDA, pp. 23, 27, 36.
98. The summaries of the goals of the three institutions appear in *ibid.,* pp. 30–31.
99. *Ibid.,* esp. pp. 32–33.
100. *Ibid.,* p. 24.
101. *Ibid.,* p. 33.
102. The three major plans are outlined in *ibid.,* pp. 33–35.
103. *Ibid.,* p. 37 (containing a correction added by Noble).
104. *Ibid.,* pp. 35–36.
105. *Ibid.,* p. 37.
106. From a typed copy of the directive (in MAEM), originally published as "Acuerdo que crea una comisión que se encargará de vigilar la administración de los bienes e intereses de la Unidad Ejidal Atencingo y Anexas, en el Estado de Puebla," *Diario Oficial de la Federación,* 15.ii.52.
107. Reyes and Ramírez to Barrios, 21.xii.59, FNDA, p. 291; see also Francisco Coronel, pres., and others of the councils of administration and vigilance, to Gilberto Loyo, sec. of national economy, 6.ii.57, FNDA, p. 143.
108. Agrarian Del. Balderrama, report to superiors, early 1952, FNDA, p. 224.

109. Commissioned peasants of Atencingo and annexes, *El caso de los campesinos*, p. 9.

110. Interview with Guillermo Covarrubias, ejidatario, 11.viii.69.

111. *Ibid.*; interview with Efraín González and Benito Ojeda, ejidatarios, 13.viii.69.

Chapter Five

1. Col. Félix Guerrero, cooperative manager, annual report for 1955–56, 17.xi.56, MAPBAC.

2. Interview with Arturo López, 10.viii.69.

3. "Acuerdo que crea una comisión que se encargará de vigilar la administración de los bienes e intereses de la Unidad Ejidal Atencingo y Anexas, en el Estado de Puebla," *Diario Oficial de la Federación* (Mexico City), 15.ii.52, MAEM.

4. *Ibid.*

5. "Reglamento de la Comisión Reorganizadora de la Sociedad Cooperativa Ejidal de Atencingo y Anexas, F.C.L.," *Diario Oficial de la Federación*, 17.xi.52, pp. 8–9.

6. Interview with Miguel García, 10.vii.69; Manuel Sánchez Espinosa, *Atencingo de Cárdenas a López Mateos, 1937–1963* (Puebla, 1963), p. 29.

7. Indicated by Aguilar's signature on a letter from Agustín Valle Cuenca, ejidal commissariat pres., et al. to Castulo Villaseñor, Agrarian Dept. chief, 1.vii.54, FNDA, p. 42.

8. Interview with Alfredo Carranza, ejidatario, 26.vii.69.

9. Exchanges between the agrarian del. and Villaseñor during March 1953, FNDA, p. 243.

10. Point made especially by María Jiménez, ejidatario's wife, in interview, 18.vi.69.

11. Interview with López, 10.viii.69.

12. This point is clear from a variety of sources; for example, interviews with the ejidatarios Guillermo Covarrubias (5.vi.69), Francisco Aguilar (28.vii.69), and Manuel Fernández (28.vi.69).

13. Interview with López, 10.viii.69.

14. Guerrero, annual report for 1955–56.

15. Interview with Covarrubias, 5.vi.69.

16. Figures for the dividends were compiled from an unattributed undated memo found in the Agrarian Dept. Archives; from Guerrero, annual reports for 1954–55 (31.vii.55, FNDA, pp. 126–27) and 1955–56; and from Gov. Fausto Ortega to Pres. Adolfo López Mateos, 24.xi.59, FNDA, p. 298.

17. Interview with Fidel Echeverría, ejidatario, 11.viii.69.

18. Based on José María Suárez Téllez, CNC sec. of cooperative action,

report to CNC National Executive Committee, 14.xii.53, MAPBAC; Guerrero, annual reports for 1954–55 and 1955–56; and Agrarian Dept. investigator Alvaro Morales Jurado, report to Agrarian Dept. superiors, 16.v.55, FNDA, p. 122.

19. A. Morales, report to superiors, 16.v.55, FNDA, pp. 118, 122.

20. *Ibid.*, p. 117.

21. *Ibid.*, p. 115.

22. Sixto Uribe Maltos, agrarian del., and Agrarian Dept. representative on the Reorganizing Commission to Agrarian Dept. chief, 16.vii.52, FNDA, pp. 103–4; Gov. Rafael Avila Camacho to Uribe, vii.52, FNDA, pp. 221–22; Agrarian Dept. director of agrarian affairs to Uribe, vii.52, FNDA, p. 222; Uribe to Agrarian Dept. chief, 10.iii.53, FNDA, pp. 248–49. See also a letter from Guerrero to the agrarian delegate (x.52, FNDA, p. 69) in which Guerrero requested that a survey be made as soon as possible. The 1947–48 survey was characterized as only "in general terms" realistic by Uribe in a letter to his superiors, viii.52, FNDA, pp. 222–23.

23. Francisco Coronel and J. Guadalupe Ramírez Vargas to Villaseñor, 1.iv.53, FNDA, pp. 102–3; Teodoro Sánchez et al., tele. to Villaseñor, 18.iv.53, FNDA, p. 255.

24. Commissioned peasants of Atencingo and annexes, *El caso de los campesinos de Atencingo y Anexas: Carta abierta al Sr. Presidente de la República* (Atencingo, 31.xii.54), p. 11. For evidence of the Jaramillistas' attitude toward the Agrarian Delegation, see also Coronel and Ramírez to Villaseñor, 1.iv.53, FNDA, p. 103.

25. Stated explicitly in Juan Morales et al. to Pres. Adolfo Ruíz Cortines and the Agrarian Dept. chief, 1.iii.55, FNDA, p. 258; and in Brig. Gen. Calletano López Garcia, pres. of the National Executive Committee of the National Revolutionary Confederation, to Villaseñor, 21.viii.54, FNDA, p. 252.

26. The figure 300 was given by J. Morales in a letter to Villaseñor, 21.vi.53, FNDA, pp. 245–46. For the claim that Espinosa and his followers helped oust Jaramillo, see esp. J. Morales et al. to Ruíz Cortines and Agrarian Dept. chief, 5.viii.54, FNDA, p. 254.

27. For the claim concerning the commission's purpose, see Julio Mora, sec.-gen. of the National Executive Committee of the National Cane Producers' Union, petition to Agrarian Dept. chief, v.53, FNDA, p. 244. For the claim concerning the purpose of the census, see Agrarian Dept. representative on the Reorganizing Commission to Agrarian Dept. chief, 16.vii.52, FNDA, p. 103.

28. J. Morales et al. to Ruíz Cortines and Agrarian Dept. chief, 5.viii.54, FNDA, p. 254.

29. J. Morales to Agrarian Dept. chief, 21.vi.53, FNDA, p. 246.

30. J. Morales et al. to Ruíz Cortines and Agrarian Dept. chief, 5.viii.54, FNDA, p. 254.

31. The basic calculations appear in Alberto Espinosa, sec.-gen. of Regional Caneworkers' Circle 83, to Gov. Rafael Avila Camacho and Agrarian Delegate Uribe, as members of the Reorganizing Commission, 6.iii.52, MAPBAC.

32. "Resolución sobre ampliación de ejido al poblado Atencingo y anexos en Chietla, Puebla," *Diario Oficial de la Federación*, 13.iv.54, pp. 2–4. The number of hectares added to each section of the ejido by the enlargement was as follows: Atencingo, 135 (64 seasonal, 71 brushland); Lagunillas, 890 (all irrigated); Rijo, 546 (95 irrigated, 457 brushland); Colón, 195 (73 seasonal, 119 brushland, 3 urban zone); Jaltepec, 373 (all irrigated); San Nicolás Tolentino, 289 (all irrigated); Raboso, 169 (42 seasonal, 109 brushland, 17 urban zone); La Galarza, 271 (all irrigated); Teruel, 392 (255 irrigated, 129 brushland, 9 urban zone). For figures on the size of the original grant, see p. 26 above.

33. Disputes between Colón and Chietla and between Colón and San Juan Tilapa were settled in favor of Colón, but by an April 1953 presidential decree the annex of San Nicolás Tolentino lost control of a plot to Matzaco, as recorded in FNDA, pp. 247–48.

34. Interview with Gustavo Alarcón, Agrarian Dept. official, 1.vii.69.

35. From a telegram, 1954 or 1955, briefly noted in FNDA, p. 62.

36. For evidence of the Jaramillista activity, see commissioned peasants of Atencingo and annexes, *El caso de los campesinos*, p. 11. Strong support for the Jaramillistas came from José María Suárez Téllez, CNC sec. of cooperative action, report to CNC National Executive Committee, 14.xii.53, MAPBAC.

37. Agrarian Dept. chief to Agrarian Dept. director of agrarian affairs, late 1955, FNDA, pp. 63–64; Revindication Committee, complaint to Agrarian Dept., i.56, FNDA, p. 131.

38. See J. Morales et al. to Ruíz Cortines and Villaseñor, 1.iii.55, FNDA, pp. 257–58; J. Morales et al. to Agrarian Dept., 25.vii.55, FNDA, p. 129.

39. Villaseñor to J. Morales et al., 3.iii.55, FNDA, p. 257.

40. J. Morales et al. to Ruíz Cortines and Villaseñor, 30.i.55, FNDA, pp. 257–58.

41. Juan Godoy Roque, CNC attorney, report to Arturo Luna Lugo, CNC sec.-gen., 26.ii.55, FNDA, pp. 282–84.

42. Villaseñor, letter, vii.55, FNDA, p. 126. According to notes in FNDA (pp. 132, 138), during 1956 Jenkins requested the return of those lands to him, but the Agrarian Department chief said that this could not be done until the maps and the definitive authorization of the ejidal grant were officially drawn up.

43. Guerrero, annual report for 1954–55.

44. Letter from one Agrarian Dept. official to another, vii.57, FNDA, p. 142.

45. Heleodoro Sánchez and Nereo Velázquez to Pres. Miguel Alemán Valdés, 24.iii.52, FNDA, pp. 219–20; Velázquez et al., petition to Alemán, 19.iv.52, FNDA, p. 221; Velázquez and Vicente Sánchez to Ruíz Cortines, 1.ii.54, FNDA, p. 41.

46. Interview with Carranza, 26.vii.69.

47. Most specifically stated in interview with Efraín González and Benito Ojeda, ejidatarios, 13.viii.69.

48. Memo probably written by Porfirio Jaramillo to Ruíz Cortines during 1953, FNDA, p. 58.

49. T. Sánchez et al., petition to Ruíz Cortines, 27.iv.53, FNDA, pp. 58–60.

50. *Ibid.*, as clarified in other notes about the same petition in FNDA, p. 281.

51. Suárez, report to CNC National Executive Committee, 14.xii.53, MAPBAC.

52. This section on Suárez's report is based on *ibid*.

53. Deputy Lorenzo Azúa Torres, CNC sec.-gen., to Ruíz Cortines, 21.xii.53, FNDA, p. 259.

54. Francisco Coronel et al., memo to Ruíz Cortines, 27.iii.54, FNDA, p. 250. See also Velázquez and V. Sánchez to Ruíz Cortines, 1.ii.54, FNDA, p. 41; and Velázquez, memo to Ruíz Cortines, 4.v.54, FNDA, p. 251.

55. Velázquez, memo to Ruíz Cortines, 4.v.54, FNDA, p. 251.

56. *Ibid.*

57. According to a letter sent by a number of ejidatarios to Ruíz Cortines, 13.v.54, FNDA, p. 249.

58. *Ibid.* See also the act from an assembly of commissioned ejidatarios in San Nicolás Tolentino, 13.v.54, FNDA, p. 250.

59. The Revindication Committee is first mentioned in a letter of June 1, 1954, to Ruíz Cortines (FNDA, p. 41).

60. See Agustín Valle Cuenca, ejidal commissariat pres., et al. to Castulo Villaseñor, Agrarian Dept. chief, 1.vii.54, FNDA, p. 42.

61. According to a letter sent by a number of ejidatarios to Ruíz Cortines, 4.v.54, FNDA, p. 249.

62. Interview with Efraín González and Benito Ojeda, ejidatarios, 13.viii.69.

63. The chief's reply is noted in FNDA, p. 42.

64. Collective interview with ejidatarios of San Nicolás Tolentino, 4.vii.69.

65. Valle et al. to Villaseñor, 1.vii.54, FNDA, p. 42.

66. Collective interview with ejidatarios of San Nicolás Tolentino, 4.vii.69.

67. Mentioned in commissioned peasants of Atencingo and annexes, *El caso de los campesinos*, pp. 10–11.

68. Coronel et al., open letter to Gov. Rafael Avila Camacho et al., 11.ix.54, FNDA, p. 340.

69. Arturo Luna Lugo, CNC sec.-gen., to Agrarian Dept. chief, iii.55, FNDA, p. 64.

70. Commissioned peasants of Atencingo and annexes, *El caso de los campesinos*; the quotations appear on pp. 3–4, 5, 11.

71. *Ibid.*, pp. 9, 12.

72. Interview with Covarrubias, 5.vi.69.

73. The names of several other assassinated ejidatarios are given in a memo sent by Coronel et al. to Ruíz Cortines, 6.i.56, FNDA, p. 44.

74. *Ibid.*, p. 45; interview with María Jiménez, ejidatario's wife, 18.vi.69. The quotation is from Felipe Rodríguez and Saturnino Mejía, tele. to Ruíz Cortines, 18.iii.55, FNDA, p. 259.

75. Esp. interview with Efraín González and Benito Ojeda, ejidatarios, 13.viii.69.

76. Juan Godoy Roque, CNC attorney, report to Arturo Luna Lugo, CNC sec.-gen., 26.ii.55, FNDA, pp. 284–85.

77. *Ibid.*

78. National Zapatista Front officials (Maj. Gen. Benigno Abúndez, chairman; Porfirio Palacios, sec.-gen.; and José María Suárez Téllez, sec. of organization) to Ruíz Cortines, iv.55, FNDA, p. 256. See also a letter written by J. Guadalupe Ramírez Vargas and fellow Jaramillistas to Gen. Donato Bravo Izquierdo, the zone military commander, on May 9, 1955 (MAPBAC), in which the Jaramillistas asked the general to intervene with the president on their behalf. General Bravo had evidently sided with the peasants in their 1946 confrontation with the mill administration. See also Rodríguez and Mejía, tele. to Ruíz Cortines, 18.iii.55, FNDA, p. 259.

79. Agrarian Dept. investigator Alvaro Morales Jurado, report to superiors, 16.v.55, FNDA, pp. 111–25.

80. For the quotations about Guerrero see *ibid.*, pp. 114, 115, 117.

81. Interview with López, 10.viii.69.

82. The ejidal commissariat's views are described in A. Morales, report to superiors, 16.v.55, FNDA, p. 124.

83. For the investigator's observations (including the quotation), see *ibid.*, p. 125.

84. Coronel et al., tele. to Ruíz Cortines, 18.vii.55, FNDA, p. 126; in this telegram the neo-Jaramillistas reiterate a petition filed on their behalf by the National Zapatista Front about one week earlier.

85. For the chief's decision see Villaseñor to Coronel et al., 28.vii.55, FNDA, p. 126. For the neo-Jaramillistas' case see Coronel to Ruíz Cortines, 6.i.56, FNDA, p. 44.

86. Coronel to gen. director of the Judicial Section, Secretariat of National Economy, 21.x.55, FNDA, p. 131.

87. Coronel et al. to Ruíz Cortines, 6.i.56, FNDA, p. 44.

88. Godoy to Luna Lugo, 26.ii.55, FNDA, p. 284.

89. Agrarian del., tele. to superiors, 27.iii.56, FNDA, p. 132.

90. Notes on a legal document signed by Valle, FNDA, p. 138; Coronel and Pedro Castro, vigilance council pres., to Agrarian Dept. chief, xi.56, FNDA, p. 133; notes on letter from one Agrarian Dept. official to another, xi.56, FNDA, p. 135.

91. For the collaborationists' charge see notes on legal papers, FNDA, p. 136. That the neo-Jaramillistas were arrested is mentioned in Coronel and Castro to Agrarian Dept. chief, xi.56, FNDA, p. 133.

92. Luna Lugo and CNC sec. of agrarian syndical action to agrarian del., date unknown, FNDA, pp. 135–36. See also José Balderrama, agrarian del., to Agrarian Dept. chief, 30.iv.57, FNDA, p. 139.

93. Head of Judicial Section, Agrarian Dept., memo, ii.57, FNDA, p. 139.

94. Coronel et al., memo to Ruíz Cortines, 6.i.56, FNDA, pp. 43–45; Coronel et al., memo to Gilberto Loyo, sec. of national economy, 6.ii.57, FNDA, pp. 146–50.

95. Cipriano L. Reyes, ejidal commissariat pres., and J. Guadalupe Ramírez Vargas, administration council pres., to Roberto Barrios, Agrarian Dept. chief, 10.ix.59, FNDA, p. 291; Coronel et al., memo to Ruíz Cortines, 6.i.56, FNDA, p. 45.

96. Coronel et al., memo to Ruíz Cortines, 6.i.56, FNDA, p. 45.

97. Sánchez Espinosa, *Atencingo de Cárdenas a López Mateos*, p. 30; interview with Aguilar, 28.vii.69; notes on a number of petitions filed by Feminine Leagues of the various ejido villages during March 1957 and directed to Ruíz Cortines, FNDA, pp. 137–38. Also, indicative of the changing political context, according to a letter by Chief Villaseñor to the Office of the Presidency (iii.57, FNDA, p. 137), the chief planned to consider the revocation of the 1952 decree with the president in their next meeting.

98. Sánchez Espinosa, pp. 30–31.

99. Interview with López, viii.69.

Notes to Pages 145–51

Chapter Six

1. Manuel Sánchez Espinosa, *Atencingo de Cárdenas a López Mateos, 1937–1963* (Puebla, 1963), pp. 32–39, 43–47.
2. Interview with Manuel Fernández, ejidatario, 28.vi.69.
3. One case was described by Enrique Velásquez, ejidatario (interview, 18.vi.69).
4. Cipriano L. Reyes, ejidal commissariat pres., to Roberto Barrios, DAAC chief, vii.59, FNDA, p. 263.
5. Interview with Francisco Aguilar, ejidatario, 28.vii.69.
6. Reyes et al., memo to DAAC gen. director of agrarian ejidal organization, 23.vii.58, FNDA, pp. 156–59.
7. Ramón Absalón Quiroz, sec.-gen. of National Cane Producers' Union, to Agrarian Dept. chief, 7.vi.57, FNDA, p. 140. For some antecedents of this issue see José Balderrama, agrarian del., documents about problems in Lagunillas, 26.i.56, FNDA, pp. 152–54. See also Reyes et al., memo to DAAC gen. director of agrarian ejidal organization, 23.vii.58, FNDA, pp. 156–59; Luís Ramírez de Arellano, sec.-gen. of Confederated Mexican Peasants' League, to Castulo Villaseñor, Agrarian Dept. chief, 29.x.58, FNDA, pp. 155–56; letter from an official of the Confederated Mexican Peasants' League, 30.xii.58, FNDA, p. 176.
8. Unspecified ejidatarios of Atencingo and annexes to DAAC Dept. of Inspection, ii.58, FNDA, pp. 329–30.
9. "Meet Mr. Jenkins," *Time*, 26.xii.60, pp. 25, 26.
10. Sánchez Espinosa, annual reports for 1957–58, 1958–59, and 1959–60, FNDA, pp. 281, 307.
11. Information on the irrigation wells is contained in Arcadio Noguera Vergara, DAAC sec.-gen. of agrarian affairs, to gen. director of hydraulic development, Secretariat of Hydraulic Resources, 11.iii.60, MAEM; and in José Cermeno Mejía, undated report to the Office of Irrigation, Secretariat of Hydraulic Resources, MAEM. On the community development projects see in general Sánchez Espinosa, *Atencingo de Cárdenas a López Mateos*, pp. 34, 40-42. Sánchez mentioned that he had bought agricultural machinery and tools in a letter to Noguera, 27.xi.59, FNDA, p. 299.
12. Sánchez Espinosa, list of wage raises, i.59, FNDA, pp. 307–8.
13. Victor Joseph, DAAC investigator, report to Roberto Barrios, DAAC chief, x.59, FNDA, pp. 295–96.
14. Sánchez Espinosa, annual reports for 1957–58, 1958–59, and 1959–60. See also Sánchez Espinosa to Noguera, 27.xi.58, FNDA, p. 299.
15. Gov. Fausto Ortega to Pres. Adolfo López Mateos, 24.xi.59, FNDA, p. 298.

16. Interview with friends in Izúcar de Matamoros, 28.vii.69; Sánchez Espinosa, *Atencingo de Cárdenas a López Mateos*, pp. 45–47. Renato Flores ("En el umbral de la violencia," *¿Por Qué?* [Mexico City], no. 36 [7.iii.69], p. 23) also claims that the produce was driven to the Mexico City market in trucks owned by the cooperative and that the best melon was exported to the United States, presumably by Sánchez and Jenkins.

17. Reyes to Barrios, undated [1959], FNDA, p. 46; Barrios to DAAC Office of Inspection, vii.59, FNDA, pp. 262–63; Reyes to Barrios, vii.59, FNDA, pp. 263–64.

18. Barrios, letter apparently to the DAAC Office of Inspection, vii.59, FNDA, p. 263.

19. Joseph, report to Barrios, x.59, FNDA, pp. 296–98.

20. Twenty-eight ejidatarios of Atencingo and annexes to Barrios, 4.x.59, FNDA, p. 175; Reyes, J. Guadalupe Ramírez Vargas, administration council pres., et al. to Barrios, 10.ix.59, FNDA, pp. 291–92; Ramírez to Barrios, ii.60, FNDA, pp. 302–3.

21. Barrios to agrarian del., 4.xii.59, FNDA, p. 46; Porfirio Palacios, sec.-gen., National Zapatista Front, et al. to DAAC chief, 7.iv.60, FNDA, pp. 303–4. The latter document makes the claim that the state governor was now refusing to extend credit to the peasants for their individual farming.

22. Reyes and Ramírez to Barrios, 20.xii.59, FNDA, p. 288.

23. Ramírez to Barrios, ii.60, FNDA, p. 303.

24. Reyes and Ramírez to Barrios, 10.xii.59, FNDA, p. 292.

25. *Ibid.*, pp. 292–93; twenty-eight ejidatarios of Atencingo and annexes to Barrios, 4.x.59, FNDA, pp. 175–76.

26. Joseph, report to Barrios, x.59, FNDA, pp. 293, 294.

27. *Ibid.*, pp. 297, 298.

28. Agrarian Dept. draft decree for the dismissal of the Reorganizing Commission, late 1959, FNDA, pp. 300–302.

29. Ortega to López Mateos, 24.xi.59, FNDA, pp. 298–99; Sánchez Espinosa to Noguera, 27.xi.59, FNDA, p. 299.

30. Ramírez to Barrios, ii.60, FNDA, pp. 302–3; Ramírez to Barrios, ii.60, FNDA, p. 303.

31. From hastily recorded notes about actions taken by Chief Barrios in early 1960 (FNDA, p. 302).

32. The quotations and proposals attributed to Padilla in this paragraph are from an unaddressed letter written sometime in 1960 (FNDA, pp. 199–200). That Padilla wrote the letter is indicated by its tone and contents, which are remarkably similar to the tone and contents of two other documents Padilla is known to have written: a memo for Barrios, 2.vi.60, FNDA, p. 194; and a letter to Barrios, vi.60, FNDA, pp. 195–96.

33. Reyes to agrarian del., x.58, FNDA, p. 155; Reyes, complaint to officials in the Agrarian Dept., 6.i.59, FNDA, p. 161.

34. DAAC director of presidential resolutions, memo to DAAC chief, x.59, FNDA, pp. 264–65; Rafael Carranza, DAAC sec.-gen., to DAAC director of agrarian affairs, 4.xi.58, FNDA, p. 159.

35. Vásquez to agrarian del., 6.iii.59, FNDA, p. 160; Vásquez, memo to DAAC chief, x.59, FNDA, pp. 264–65; Barrios to agrarian del., vi.59, FNDA, p. 266.

36. Joseph, report to Barrios, x.59, FNDA, p. 294.

37. Padilla to Barrios, vi.60, FNDA, p. 196; Rolando W. Delasse, DAAC gen. director of ejidal development, investigative report to Barrios, 9.xi.60, FNDA, p. 311.

38. Domingo López Aguilar et al. of the United Peasantry of Southern Puebla, open letter to López Mateos, 15.v.60, FNDA, pp. 304–5.

39. Padilla to Barrios, vi.60, FNDA, p. 196.

40. Francisco Sánchez Criollo, ejidal vigilance council pres., et al. to López Mateos, 18.i.61, FNDA, pp. 316a–17.

41. Draft decree for the sec. of industry and commerce, the SAG, and the Agrarian Dept., 24.viii.60, FNDA, p. 310.

42. Esp. interview with Alfredo Carranza, ejidatario, 26.vii.69.

43. *Ibid.*

44. Cirilio Gutiérrez, ejidal commissariat pres., Carlos Galarza, administration council pres., et al., statements made in meeting of the DAAC Office of Ejidal Development, 18.xi.60, FNDA, pp. 306–7. The meeting in this section was attended by officials from the Office of Complaints attached to the presidency.

45. Joaquín de León et al., message to López Mateos, 3.xi.60, FNDA, p. 312.

46. Interview with Guillermo Covarrubias, ejidatario, 5.vi.69.

47. Sánchez used the term during my interview with him in December 1968.

48. Delasse, investigative report to DAAC chief, 9.xi.60, FNDA, pp. 311–12.

49. Draft decree for the sec. of industry and commerce and the Agrarian Dept. for the dismissal of the Reorganizing Commission, projected for November 1960, FNDA, pp. 308–9.

50. That DAAC officials frequently used "integral solution" is noted in FNDA, p. 269.

51. Draft decree for the sec. of industry and commerce and the Agrarian Dept. for the dismissal of the Reorganizing Commission, projected for November 1960, FNDA, p. 308.

52. Noguera to ejidal commissariat, xi.60, FNDA, p. 321.

53. Inferred from a personal note in FNDA (p. 272) about the appointment of an engineer prior to 1961. See also notes on a petition from members of the ejidal commissariat (18.i.61, FNDA, p. 272) that demanded the completion of the survey as well as the independence of the nine sections of the ejido.

54. Interview with Velásquez, 18.vi.69.

55. For example, interview with Prudencio Beltrán, ejidatario, 1.viii.69.

56. Interview with Carranza, 26.vii.69; interview with Efraín González and Benito Ojeda, ejidatarios, 13.viii.69.

57. Sec. of industry and commerce, "Acuerdo que deja sin efecto el de 29 de enero de 1952 por el que se creó la Comisión Reorganizadora de la Sociedad Cooperativa Ejidal de Atencingo y Anexas, así como el reglamento respectivo," *Diario Oficial de la Federación* (Mexico City), 18.ii.61, pp. 10–11.

Chapter Seven

1. René Franco Salas, "¿Qué hay detrás del escándalo? José Guadalupe Ramírez, el 'monstruo' de Atencingo," *Siempre!* (Mexico City), 1969, pp. 62–63; interview with Enrique Velásquez, ejidatario, 18.vi.69.

2. Francisco Criollo, ejidal vigilance council pres., et al. to Pres. Adolfo López Mateos et al., 15.vi.61, FNDA, pp. 273–76; Ulíses Rodríguez et al., memo to DAAC chief et al., 15.vi.61, FNDA, pp. 317–18; Saturnino Mejía et al. to Gov. Fausto Ortega, 18.vi.61, FNDA, p. 319.

3. Antonio Gallardo et al. to Agusto Gómez Villanueva, CNC sec.-gen., 14.xi.67, MACNCI.

4. Collective interview with ejidatarios of La Galarza, 4.vii.69.

5. J. Guadalupe Ramírez Vargas, cooperative society manager, annual reports for 1960–61 (10.xii.61), 1961–62 (4.xi.62), and 1963–64 (13.ix.64), all in MACNCI.

6. Propaganda distributed during the general assembly, 30.iii.69, FNGA.

7. Ramírez, annual reports for 1963–64, 1964–65 (2.x.65), 1965–66 (11.ix.66), and 1966–67 (10.ix.67), all in MACNCI; for 1967–68 (30.iii.69), and 1968–69 (24.viii.69), both in FNGA. See also René Franco Salas, "Atencingo: Hechos y números" (*Siempre!* 1969, pp. 60–61), though this article contains much false information.

8. Ramírez, annual reports for 1960–61 and 1967–68.

9. Figures taken from Ramírez's annual reports for 1960–62 and 1963–69.

10. Ramírez, annual reports for 1960–62; Rodríguez et al., memo to J. Jesús Patiño Navarrete, SAG undersec., 3.vii.63, MAPBAC.

11. Esp. interview with Pedro Bueno, ejidatario, 19.v.69.

12. Article in *El Nacional* (Mexico City), 14.vi.69; Roberto Barrios, DAAC chief, to Julián Rodríguez Adame, SAG sec., 4.iv.63, FNDA, pp. 176–77.

13. Ramírez, annual report for 1963–64; interview with Fidel Echeverría, ejidatario, 11.viii.69.

14. Miguel Sánchez F., SAG adviser, notice to the cooperative associates, 19.iv.63, MAPBAC.

15. Ramírez, annual reports for 1964–66.

16. Ramírez, annual reports for 1963–67.

17. Ramírez, annual reports for 1967–69.

18. Dividend figures in this paragraph were compiled from Ramírez, annual reports for 1960–62 and 1963–69.

19. Interior work regulations of the ejido and local ejidal credit society of Atencingo and annexes, approved 26.viii.67, MACNCI.

20. Widely reported by partisans of the opposition faction, and apparently confirmed in Ramírez's annual reports for 1960–62 and 1963–69.

21. For an example of the opposition's lobbying in the DAAC, see Cirilo Gutiérrez, ejidal commissariat pres., et al. to DAAC officials, iv.62, FNDA, p. 313.

22. Arcadio Noguera, DAAC sec.-gen., to Domingo López Domínguez, DAAC engineer, 19.v.62, FNDA, p. 314.

23. Head of DAAC Office of Ejidal Agricultural Development to a DAAC official, 2.v.62, FNDA, pp. 168–69; Hugo B. Margain, undersec. of SIC Bureau of Cooperative Development, notice to members of the ejidal cooperative society of Atencingo and annexes, 14.x.63, MAPBAC.

24. Esp. interview with Martín Iglesias, 11.viii.69.

25. Gutiérrez et al. to Barrios, 24.ix.62, FNDA, p. 180.

26. Data on the opposition are quite sparse and confusing. The figures given are based on the general consensus that the size of the opposition then ranged somewhere between 300 and 500 persons, with a predominance of former collaborationists.

27. Gutiérrez et al. to a government official, ix.62, FNDA, p. 178.

28. Inspector Luís Muñoz of Colonia Independencia, document, 18.ix.62, FNDA, p. 182.

29. Gutiérrez et al. to Barrios, 24.ix.62, FNDA, p. 180.

30. Barrios to Victor Joseph, DAAC official, x.62, FNDA, p. 316a.

31. Estimated principally from a photograph of the assemblage, MAPBAC. Before the assembly began Gutiérrez distributed propaganda leaflets (copies in MAPBAC) in which he bitterly attacked the Ramírez administration for its alleged financial corruption and technical mismanagement.

32. Ramírez, annual report for 1961–62; article in *Excélsior* (Mexico City), 12.xi.62.

33. Ramírez, annual report for 1961–62.

34. The most vivid account was that of Alfredo Carranza, ejidatario (interview, 18.vi.69).

35. Esp. interview with Pedro Bueno and other ejidatarios, 19.iv.69. Later pistolero activity by the two main assassins is described in Renato Flores, "El ingenio de Atencingo: En el umbral de la violencia," *¿Por Qué?* (Mexico City), no. 36 (7.iii.69), pp. 20–23. Yet other sources, such as an article in *Excélsior* (2.xii.65), maintain that the two assassins languished in jail, pleading drunkenness and alleging that Ramírez was the intellectual perpetrator of their crime.

36. Javier Rojo Gómez, CNC sec.-gen., memo to Barrios, 22.iv.63, MAPBAC.

37. All sources agree that the faction expanded. The figure given is estimated from reports that the proximate march consisted of 500 to 600 of the opposition partisans, not all of whom went.

38. Patiño to Sánchez F., 19.ii.64, MAPBAC; untitled field investigation document beginning "En las oficinas de la sociedad cooperativa ejidal de Atencingo . . . ," 6.iii.64, MAPBAC; interview with Carranza, viii.69.

39. Interview with Iglesias, 11.viii.69.

40. Margain, notice to members of the ejidal cooperative society of Atencingo and annexes, 14.x.63, MAPBAC.

41. Interview with José Guzmán, ejidatario, 28.vi.69; interview with Pedro Bueno, ejidatario, 19.v.69; interview with Bueno et al., 13.iv.69; collective interview with ejidatarios of La Galarza, 18.vi.69.

42. Barrios to the attorney gen., i.64, FNDA, pp. 170–71; "Ametrallado el coche del máximo líder cañero de Atencingo, Puebla," *Magazine de Policía* (Mexico City), 27.i.64, p. 27.

43. Officers of the ejidal cooperative society, tele. to Pres. Adolfo López Mateos, 20.iv.64, FNDA, pp. 184–85; Cipriano González to the president's wife, Sra. López Mateos, 18.x.64, FNDA, p. 198; Antonio Gallardo to Ciriaco Tista Montiel, sec.-gen. of interior, 25.iv.64, MAPBAC; and Gallardo to Gov. Antonio Nava Castillo, 26.v.64, MAPBAC.

44. Reported in *Excélsior*, 31.viii.64.

45. Accounts of the marches were given by Enrique Velásquez, ejidatario (interview, 18.vi.69); José Guzmán, ejidatario, who estimated the number of marchers at between 800 and 1,000 (interview, 28.vi.69); Carranza (interview, 26.vii.69); Bueno (interview, 19.v.69); and Bueno et al. (interview, 13.iv.69). The number of ejidatarios on the march was put at 684 by an article in *Excélsior,* 30.viii.64. The Mexico City newspapers

Novedades and *El Nacional* also carried major news articles on the marches at the time. The SIC order appears in Raúl Salinas Lozano, SIC sec., directive for the gen. director of cooperative development, 29.viii.64, MAPBAC; the DAAC order is in Barrios to gen. director of agrarian organization, 31.viii.64, MAPBAC.

46. Propaganda leaflet headed "Alerta ejidatarios de Atencingo y anexos," 27.x.64, MAPBAC.

47. Barrios to gen. director of National Ejidal Credit Bank, 9.iv.64, FNDA, p. 171.

48. Widely reported among opposition partisans, for example in collective interview with ejidatarios of San Nicolás Tolentino, 4.vii.69.

49. Enrique Campos Luna, SAG official, investigative report, 1.vi.65, MAPBAC.

50. That there were 700 was reported in an article in *El Día* (Mexico City), 26.xi.65. To verify, see the letter from Gallardo and Francisco Salazar to Rojo (31.vii.65, MAPBAC), which had 761 signers.

51. Interview with Bueno, 19.v.69; interview with Bueno et al., 13.iv.69.

52. Remarks about Hernández taken from interview with Bueno, 19.v.69.

53. *El Día*, 26.xi.65.

54. *El Sol de México* (Mexico City), 26.xi.65.

55. "Acta levantada con motivo de la resolución al problema del ejido de Atencingo y anexos, muni. de Chietla, ex-distrito de Chiautla, Puebla," 2.xii.65, MACNCI.

56. DAAC sec.-gen. of agrarian affairs to a DAAC official, 24.vii.67, FNDA, p. 211.

57. *Ibid.*

58. Comments in Gallardo and Salazar to Rojo, 31.vii.65, MAPBAC; Luís Alcerrica, DAAC gen. director of agrarian affairs, to Heriberto Camacho, DAAC official, 25.vii.66, FNDA, pp. 276–77.

59. In a letter to President López Mateos (30.viii.61, FNDA, pp. 197–98) the local agrarian radical Domingo López Aguilar claimed that retired revolutionary generals were trying to incite the local landless villagers to invade.

60. Barrios to DAAC gen. director of new farming-population centers, 28.iii.62, FNDA, pp. 321–22.

61. Based on all of FNCCI.

62. Alfonso Garzón, CCI sec.-gen., and Humberto Serrano, CCI sec. of proceedings, to Gov. Aarón Merino Fernández, 31.iii.67, FNCCI.

63. Although the opposition leaders of San Nicolás Tolentino adamantly deny any such alliance, their names are signed on the May 23, 1967, request for an amparo for the June invasions, as noted in FNCCI.

64. Esp. Garzón and Serrano to Pres. Gustavo Díaz Ordaz, 13.iv.67, FNDA, pp. 203–4; López A. to Díaz Ordaz, 24.vii.67, FNDA, pp. 335–36; Ramírez, annual report for 1966–67.

65. Based on all of MACNCI. See agreement signed by Agusto Gómez Villanueva, CNC sec.-gen., et al., 10.x.67, MACNCI.

66. *La Prensa* (Mexico City), 3.iv.69; Ramón Danzos Palomino, CCI sec.-gen., "El ejido de Atencingo: Una bomba de tiempo," *La Voz de México* (Mexico City), 26.v.68.

67. The incident received extensive coverage in the newspapers of Mexico City and Puebla from April 2 to April 4, 1969. Only the basic facts are given here.

68. On the cancellation of credit, see Ramírez, annual report for 1967–68.

69. A good example is the agreement signed in Atencingo by the CNC representative, Virgilio Torres García, and others (14.vii.68, MAPBAC).

70. Reported in various versions; for example, in interview with family of Alberto Sánchez, ejidatario, 18.vi.69.

71. Interview with Carranza, viii.69.

72. That the maps were submitted is indicated by notes on a certificate from the head of the DAAC Office of Maps, 4.i.68, FNDA, p. 333. The fact was apparently concealed from the opposition ejidatarios for months, judging from a letter sent by Gallardo to the DAAC chief (3.vii.68, FNDA, pp. 212–13).

73. Domingo López Domínguez, DAAC engineer, to DAAC oficial mayor, 26.ix.68, FNDA, p. 53.

74. The figure was 1,200 according to a letter sent by Salazar and others to Díaz Ordaz (23.ix.68, MAPBAC).

75. Accounts of the attempts to take over the offices abound in *Excélsior*, 24–27.ix.68; in *La Prensa*, 25–28.ix.68; in an open letter to the federal authorities published by Ramírez and his followers in *Novedades*, 28.ix.68; and throughout my retrospective interviews with witnesses.

76. Based not only on retrospective interviews with witnesses but also on personal impressions from two visits to the scene of the strike.

77. Gómez, notice to the peasants of Atencingo, 8.x.68, MACNCI.

78. The figure 957 is recorded in minutes of an assembly in the basketball pavilion in Atencingo, notarized by Judge Ignacio Reyes González of Matamoros, 14.x.68, MAPBAC. The petition signed by 731 was in the form of a letter sent by Francisco Bonilla and others to Juan Gil Preciado, SAG sec., 8.viii.68, MAPBAC.

79. The significant document is the agreement signed in Matamoros by Gómez and others, 20.xii.68, MAPBAC.

80. Numerous accounts appeared in the Mexico City and Puebla daily newspapers during January 17–22, 1968.

81. Based on personal observation.

82. Figures taken from *Excélsior*, 31.i.69 and 2.i.69; and from my field notes on the assembly, 30.i.69, FNGA.

83. On work problems see Heleodoro Sánchez and Conrado Hernández to Arturo Luna Lugo, DAAC counselor, 4.ii.69, FNDA, p. 54; Luís Alcerrica, DAAC gen. director of agrarian affairs, to the state agrarian del., undated [ii.69], FNDA, pp. 54–55; and state agrarian del. to ejidal commissariat pres., 25.ii.69, FNDA, p. 72.

84. Alcerrica to López D., 9.i.69, FNDA, pp. 74–75.

85. *Excélsior*, 24.i.69 and 2.ii.69.

86. *Ibid.*, 31.iii.69; field notes on the assembly, 30.iii.69, FNGA.

87. Sources for the cane production and dividend figures are as follows: for Atencingo and annexes, Ramírez, annual report for 1968–69; for Raboso, Manuel Hernández Bravo, chief del., annual report for 1968–69, 14.viii.69, FNGA; for Teruel, estimate supplied in interview with Carranza, viii.69.

Index

Index